PRAISE FOR BOBBY ORR

"I agree with Bobby Clarke when he said that Bobby Orr was so good there should have been a higher league than the NHL for him to play in…. He was so much better than everyone else, no one was even close."

DON CHERRY, broadcaster and coach of the Boston Bruins from 1974 to 1979

"From the first time I watched Bobby skate I knew he was going to be the kind of player that comes along maybe once in a lifetime. He changed the game of hockey forever."

GORDIE HOWE, four-time Stanley Cup winner with the Detroit Red Wings, six-time Hart Trophy winner, six-time Art Ross Trophy winner

"Bobby reached levels of play on the ice that have been and always will be unattainable by defensemen. For those of us who know him personally, his character is equally unmatched."

DENIS POTVIN, four-time Stanley Cup winner with the New York Islanders, three-time Norris Trophy winner

"There have been many outstanding players in the history of the National Hockey League, and Bobby Orr sits at the top of the class."

JEAN BÉLIVEAU, ten-time Stanley Cup winner with the Montreal Canadiens, winner of the Art Ross, Conn Smythe, and Hart Trophies

"There are stars, superstars, and then there's Bobby Orr."

SERGE SAVARD, NHL Hall of Famer

PENGUIN

ORR

BOBBY ORR played for the Boston Bruins from 1966 to 1976, and then two more years for the Chicago Blackhawks. Among other records and honors he's received, he remains the only defenseman to win the Art Ross Trophy league-scoring title—twice—and he still holds the record for most points and assists at that position. He also won a record eight consecutive Norris Trophies as the NHL's best defenseman, and three consecutive Hart Trophies as the league's MVP, as well as two Conn Smythe Trophies as the Stanley Cup MVP. Orr was the youngest living player to be inducted into the Hockey Hall of Fame, at thirty-one.

ORR

MY STORY

BOBBY ORR

PENGUIN

an imprint of Penguin Canada Books Inc., a Penguin Random House Company

Published by the Penguin Group

Penguin Canada Books Inc., 90 Eglinton Avenue East, Suite 700, Toronto, Ontario, Canada M4P 2Y3

Penguin Group (USA) LLC, 375 Hudson Street, New York, New York 10014, U.S.A.
Penguin Books Ltd, 80 Strand, London WC2R 0RL, England
Penguin Ireland, 25 St Stephen's Green, Dublin 2, Ireland (a division of Penguin Books Ltd)
Penguin Group (Australia), 707 Collins Street, Melbourne, Victoria 3008, Australia
(a division of Pearson Australia Group Pty Ltd)
Penguin Books India Pvt Ltd, 11 Community Centre, Panchsheel Park, New Delhi – 110 017, India
Penguin Group (NZ), 67 Apollo Drive, Rosedale, Auckland 0632, New Zealand (a division of Pearson New Zealand Ltd)
Penguin Books (South Africa) (Pty) Ltd, 24 Sturdee Avenue, Rosebank, Johannesburg 2196, South Africa

Penguin Books Ltd, Registered Offices: 80 Strand, London WC2R 0RL, England

First published in Viking hardcover by Penguin Canada Books Inc., 2013. Simultaneously published in the U.S.A. by Penguin Group (USA) LLC. Published in this edition, 2014.

1 2 3 4 5 6 7 8 9 10

LIBRARY AND ARCHIVES CANADA CATALOGUING IN PUBLICATION

Orr, Bobby, 1948–, author
Orr : my story / Bobby Orr.

Includes index.
Originally published: Toronto, Ontario, Canada : Viking, 2013.
ISBN 978-0-14-318432-4 (pbk.)

1. Orr, Bobby, 1948–. 2. Hockey players—Canada—Biography. I. Title.

GV848.5.O7A3 2014b   796.962092   C2014-903473-3

eBook ISBN 978-0-14-318868-1

American Library of Congress Cataloging in Publication data available

Visit the Penguin Canada website at **www.penguin.ca**

Special and corporate bulk purchase rates available; please see
www.penguin.ca/corporatesales or call 1-800-810-3104.

I dedicate this book to the following people
who have meant so much to me throughout my life:

My wife, Peggy; our two boys, Darren and Brent;
daughters-in-law, Chelsea and Kelley;
grandchildren, Alexis and Braxton;
my mother- and father-in-law, Clara and Bill Wood;
and finally, my parents, Arva and Doug Orr.

Thank you, one and all.

Contents

FOREWORD

The boys needed a coach, so I volunteered. It's the same thing that happens all across our great country every hockey season, and that year would be no different. They were a good bunch of lads, every one of them, and each was special in his own way. But one who would eventually join us was special in a different way.

He was a minor squirt playing up in the full-squirt division, and the first time I set eyes on him, I couldn't help but think how scrawny he was, that a good gust of wind might knock him over. He was polite, very respectful, and seemed to have a smile permanently pasted on his face. He was a good-looking boy who had a brush cut and came from a nice family. By January, he was so dominant within his division that we decided to move him up to the squirt all-stars, and that was where our paths crossed.

I will always remember the first time I saw him skate in a practice. You might think I'm exaggerating, but from that very first moment, I knew he had "it." When he started to move those skates, it was like nothing I had ever seen on a sheet of ice. His skating was effortless, with a beautiful rhythm to it, his stride so smooth he didn't look like he was even trying. He was a little bit bowlegged, actually, and I had him playing right wing. There was no doubt he was special, and I just knew he had a gift never before seen in our game. Time would prove me right.

Those were different days, and not once did I ever have a parent complain to me for any reason. They never sat near the bench during a game, never asked about ice time for their child. During that particular year, the parents created little green-and-white ribbons that had a shamrock on them, and they wore those ribbons the entire season in support of the boys and the team. That youngster with the brush cut had wonderful parents as well: Arva and Doug. Even though it became obvious as the year wore on that their son was the best of the best, they never once asked for any special consideration. No, Doug never played the big-shot father. Those were different days indeed.

The years pass, and a lifetime seems to go by in an instant. I'm told that the young boy is a grandfather now. He has lived a life that should be an example for everyone who achieves greatness of how to be humble and unselfish and how to treat others. It was a joy to be able to coach him for that season and the next year as well, to get to know him as a person as well as player, and it is a great honor to be asked to reminisce about him now.

But in my mind he's still eight years old, his time as a legend is yet to come, and his future success is all out there somewhere in front of him. I'm with him on a cold, distant January day at an outdoor rink in Parry Sound, and I'm watching him skate the length of the ice, completing a drill during one of our practices.

And I can't help but wonder if that boy could play as a defenseman.

Royce Tennant

INTRODUCTION

I was up at 5 A.M. The day, May 10, 2010, was just like any other day. One thing was different, though. It had been a long time since I had experienced game-day butterflies. But there I was, up before dawn, focused on only one thing. As the day wore on, I didn't feel like making conversation. Over the course of that morning, I was surrounded by friends and family. I shook the hands of countless well-wishers—celebrities, fans, other athletes, politicians.

I wish I could have enjoyed every moment. And I hope I managed to return some of the warmth all those people showed me. But the thing is, I was so tense I could hardly make conversation even with old friends.

It was the prospect of stepping up to a podium that was making me anxious. I've had to face some microphones over the years, of course, and speak to crowds. But to say I don't relish stepping onto a podium to talk about myself doesn't go nearly far enough. A lot of people don't enjoy public speaking, and I'm one of them.

I was scheduled to appear outside the TD Garden, beside where the old Boston Garden used to stand. That's where I was forty years earlier to the day. I scored a goal there on May 10, 1970. The photographer who had been sitting on a stool behind the glass at the corner of the ice had left his seat for a few minutes, and Ray Lussier sat down in his place moments before the puck came to me and I tapped it in, moments before I was tripped and flew into the air. Lussier snapped a photo, and he captured a moment that came to stand for so much that Boston Bruins fans, and hockey fans everywhere, hold dear.

Forty years later, I was back in the neighborhood. And so were many of the guys who had been there when the photo was taken. Bucyk, Sanderson, Doak, Hodge, McKenzie, Marcotte, Coach Sinden, and former Bruins general manager Milt Schmidt. Mayor Menino was there, and Bruins president John Wentzell, and team owner Jeremy Jacobs. There were also a couple of good buddies from the Red Sox in attendance, David "Big Papi" Ortiz plus the great knuckleball pitcher Tim Wakefield, and that meant the world to me. My son Darren and daughter-in-law Chelsea came with our granddaughter, Alexis. And, of course, the fans.

I had to speak to them all, because I was in that photograph. The photo had been cast as a statue. And there I was for the unveiling. It was a clear spring day. The cameras were crowded around. The Bruins were in the second round of the playoffs, and the city was buzzing. Everything seemed to be in place.

But the last thing I wanted to do was stand in front of a microphone and talk about myself or relive a moment of glory. I wasn't looking for praise, and I certainly wasn't there to take credit.

If anything, I wanted to explain that the credit for that moment should be shared much more widely.

I suddenly remembered the first time I had ever seen the photograph of that now-famous flying goal. I was in Lynnfield, Massachusetts, at the Colonial Hotel, having breakfast with my dad and his buddies. It was the morning after we had won the Cup, the morning after I scored that goal. May 11, 1970. You can imagine what the mood was like. It's not every day you fulfill a dream, and it's probably more rare to be able to share a moment like that with your father.

I don't really remember what we talked about at breakfast. There would have been some animated conversation, then maybe a period of silence. It takes a while to get used to getting what you've been striving toward for so long. Then someone handed me a copy of the *Boston Record-American*, and there it was, me flying through the air with that look of surprise and joy written all over my face. I didn't think much about it at the time. The goal was only a few hours old. I'm not the kind of guy who will sit in a crowded restaurant looking at pictures of himself. And I had a parade to get ready for. So I didn't look at that photo for long.

But that parade is now a distant memory while the photo has lingered. It has more than lingered, actually. It has become one of the most famous images in the game. Not because it's me—it's a great photo no matter who is flying through the air. And though I hardly glanced at it in 1970, forty-something years later it conjures up that life-changing game like nothing else: the old Boston Garden packed well past capacity, the noise and humidity as we headed into overtime.

The play took only seconds to unfold. And the photo records only one instant of those few seconds. Yet, for me at least, it captures not just that one play, not just that one steamy May afternoon. Everyone on that Bruins team had done a lot of things right to get to overtime. Rick Smith had already had a two-point night. Our top scorers had been doing the work they'd been doing all season and through the first two rounds of the playoffs. Except for me. I hadn't scored yet in the series against St. Louis. It was the rest of the guys who got us to that first minute of overtime. I don't know what others see when they look at that photo, but I don't see just one guy scoring a goal.

The strange thing about the photo—me, arms outstretched, flying through the air as though nothing else matters—is that I was never really big on celebrating goals. I know most guys like to celebrate after scoring, but I always found it disrespectful. It's not the way I played the game. And yet, there I am, in that famous photo, hands in the air. I could try to blame Blues defenseman Noel Picard's wayward stick and argue that he tripped me. But I have to admit it was a jump for joy, trip or no trip.

Perhaps the better representation would have been to capture the moment a few seconds after my leap—when my teammates piled on me and the rest of the Bruins poured over the boards to join in and celebrate that victory. It wasn't really just my goal, and it wasn't just my celebration, either. There was a mob on the ice, guys in Bruins black and gold, but also the coaches and trainers. The Garden was roaring. It wasn't just one happy guy, flying through the air by himself. But for whatever reason, there was always that famous photo, plucking that one moment out of time.

And now there was this statue—I don't know how many pounds of gleaming bronze—telling the same story. It is a beautiful piece of art, don't get me wrong. But I was struck by what the statue *didn't* say. By capturing a single moment, it had to leave out the moments before and after. By depicting a single person, it left out all the people who won the Cup that year, and all the people who helped us win it—and also the fans who shared in that victory. It would have meant a lot less to score that goal in an empty Boston Garden, just as it would have been absurd to be the only person at the unveiling of the statue. These aren't things that happen to anyone alone. Part of what I want to accomplish with this book is to go beyond that moment in time so that the story around that moment can make better sense.

It's strange to be writing about myself, though. Over all the years I was in the spotlight, I very rarely read about myself. There have been books and magazine and newspaper articles, but I never saw the point in reading them. Whether a writer was praising me or burying me never really mattered, since I was generally first in line to criticize myself. There wasn't a whole lot a journalist could say about my game that would come as news to me. If he wanted to mention some blunder I'd made, I could always add a few more examples. If he wanted to describe a particularly good play, I could probably counter that I'd been lucky, or that the play wouldn't have happened if not for a smart move by a teammate at the other end of the ice. And if I made what I thought was a pretty good play, that was, after all, what I was paid to do. I didn't need to read about it. I knew when I'd played poorly, and I knew when I'd played well. The whole team did.

Sometimes you do everything right and the puck bounces the wrong way. Sometimes you play poorly and get lucky. But on the whole, if you play the game right, you'll get the results you are looking for. The guys in the room all knew that. And if on occasion we forgot how to be honest with ourselves, there were leaders with us who would sort us out. The coaching staff was always more than willing to bring us back to reality in a hurry, too. I mean no disrespect to sportswriters by any of this, but no amount of information provided by any writer was going to alter our view of the game.

In any case, I simply did not enjoy reading about myself. So imagine my hesitancy in sitting down to write a book. Tens of thousands of words about myself. What I did. What I thought. That's not my idea of a good time.

The idea of writing a book has been brought up many times over the years, and all kinds of people have come forward with their own unique slant on how I might approach it. They have offered to write the authorized version of my life, but frankly I have never been interested. What many of them actually wanted was some sort of tell-all account that would dig up dirt then shovel it on people I used to know. I don't claim to be a saint, but that is not my cup of tea and never will be. This book has to be better and go deeper than that.

I think that three points need to be made here as you begin reading the pages that follow. First, I am not particularly comfortable talking or writing at length about other people in a negative way, especially in a format like this, which has the potential to be so much more. Call me old-fashioned, but when I was growing up, and especially playing sports, we learned that you don't throw someone under the bus. Mind you, I have no problem sharing the truth when it comes to a particular topic or event, as you are about to see. But telling the truth and piling on are two different things entirely.

Second, much has been written about my personal life and career over the years, and a lot of what has made its way into print was neither provided nor approved by me. Everyone is welcome to their opinion, and I suppose that some people remember things differently. But facts are facts. I am glad to have the opportunity to offer a few opinions of my own.

And third, one thing I always thought many people got wrong about me was the idea that things were a little easier for me than for other players, or that I was somehow different from everyone else. If that were the case, my story probably wouldn't be worth telling. But I am no different from anyone else. What was easy for me was not what I wanted to write about. I decided that if I was going to do this, I would have to write about what was difficult.

If this book were just about nostalgia, or highlights from my career, it would just reinforce a version of the story I never found particularly interesting. The trophies, the scoring titles, the Stanley Cups—that's all in the history books now. But like that famous photo, or the statue outside the TD Garden, they don't tell you much. They don't speak to values or to motivation. They don't explain inspiration, or add asterisks for the people who helped me (or pushed me). They record, in the simplest way, what happened on the ice, not how I got there, or who I met along the way and what I learned from them.

In any case, there's no question I have been lucky beyond belief with respect to the people I'm fortunate enough to have met. I feel it is finally time for me to reflect on and share with you some of those people. Eventually, I came to realize that this book would allow me to share many thoughts and opinions about the game I love so dearly, and that it wouldn't have to center on me alone.

Of course, those were different times. So much that seemed permanent is gone now. The old Garden has disappeared. The *Boston Record-American*, where the photo of "The Goal" first appeared, is no longer in print. Some very close friends from those days are still with me, but others, some of the closest, are now estranged. I could never have anticipated how the world of 1970, the world that was captured in that statue, would change so much.

Childhood itself is different. Looking at that statue, and working on this book, it seems to me that things really were much simpler back then. I know it's a cliché—the older you get, the more it seems things were better in the past. But the fact that it's a cliché doesn't mean it's not true. Things *are* different. Things *do* change. Rules were different back then. The priorities of Twitter and Facebook are different from the values of team sports, or parental authority, or even gangs of neighborhood kids playing shinny on a frozen river. There is no way around it: the world that statue has immortalized is gone.

But some things don't change. The interesting thing about that goal all this time later is not where it was scored or who took the picture. The important thing is not even who scored it. I think that when anyone who is close to the game of hockey looks at that statue, what they see is not a guy who was lucky enough to be in the right place at the right time, or even a particular goal in a particular game. To be honest, I don't think you even have to be a hockey fan to understand what that statute stands for. I'm thrilled to be the guy cast in bronze, but you don't have to know my name to know that the guy flying through the air doesn't really immortalize a single deed or a bygone era. That statue stands for what is consistent, and really, that is what this book is about.

Sitting at that ceremony outside the TD Garden in Boston, I was reminded that back in 1970, May 10 fell on Mother's Day. And I wished that my mother could have been beside me to see that statue. There is no way a kid in his twenties can understand everything his parents have done for him—not the way he will later in life when he's had children of his own. I would have loved to give her another Mother's Day gift to thank her.

I did have someone else to thank, though—my wife, Peggy. I met her not long after that goal was scored, and she has been as solid as that statue ever since. I have always wanted to keep my private life private—that just seems the most decent thing for everyone concerned. Our wedding in the summer of 1973 was about as quiet as a small-town wedding can be. And now that I am writing things down, I realize there is no way to include her in this book in any way that will do her justice. She is not one story among others. She is not just a chapter. Her role in my life can be found on every page. She met me when I felt I was on top of the world, and she was there for me when so much I had counted on in life was taken away from me. When I give thanks for what is constant in life, Peggy is never far from my mind.

I only committed to sitting down to write this book when I was sure I had something worth sharing. Not because I scored a famous goal, or because I won this or that trophy, or because I hold this or that record. Parents have things worth sharing, as do coaches and other mentors. I am a parent, and a grandparent, and it is in that spirit that I think I have a story worth recording and lessons worth passing along.

Being at that statue-unveiling ceremony allowed me to reconnect with many people. Sometimes it was with a handshake and a chat, other times it was only with a glance and a smile. The time went by so quickly, yet some moments forced me to slow down and pause. As I sat on the podium, I caught sight of Kathy Bailey and immediately thought about her late husband and my former teammate, Ace. I remembered the times we played together for the Bruins on this very site. Ace was a passenger on United Airlines

Flight 175 on September 11, 2001. Not all of the memories that day at the unveiling were happy ones.

Sometimes we are reminded that there are things far more important than hockey. But there is probably not much that is more important than the things a life in hockey can teach you. My wish is that this book will hit a chord with you about some of the important things in your own life as you continue along the journey.

That's the reason for this book.

One

PARRY SOUND

It would have been around 7:30 A.M., maybe 7:45 if Mom had let me sleep in. I'd hear her say, "Bobby, it's time to get up," and then the morning would begin. Most days started off the same at the Orr house back then. Dad would be up and at it early, and off to work at the CIL plant. Mom would usually have some breakfast waiting for us, but other times we'd make our own. Then it would be out the door and off to school.

We walked to Victory Elementary, because there was no one to give you a ride, and there wasn't a school bus to pick you up. It was a decent hike whether we went straight up Bowes Street or took a shortcut through the woods. But in wintertime, the snow got pretty deep, so we usually stayed on the sidewalk. I walked that route so many times, I could probably make my way to my old school blindfolded even today. I might as well have been blindfolded then, for all I stopped to look around. I suppose I was like any other kid, never content to be just in one place. I was always on my way to somewhere else.

That meant one of two places. If it wasn't school, it was the water. I was the kind of kid who was always on the move. In a town like Parry Sound, there was always something to keep us busy. In the warm weather, whether it was after school or on the weekend, I never missed a chance to grab my fishing rod and head across the road directly in front of our house, the road that followed the river. There, I could slip down an embankment and in seconds have my line in the water, imagining that some monster fish would be waiting to take the bait. It might have been only for a few minutes, but it always made my day.

While I never hated school, I loved to fish. It's funny what you remember. I don't recall much from my geography classes, but I clearly remember what it was like to be sitting on the shore of the Seguin River, waiting to see what I could pull from the water. I loved it, and that enjoyment has lasted my entire life.

During the long winter months, I would sit at my school desk and that big clock on the classroom wall would take more and more of my attention as the afternoon started to wind down. I couldn't wait to be dismissed so I could get through the front door of that school once all my books had been put away. I understood that soon enough I would have on a pair of skates and all would be well—as long as there was enough daylight to see the puck. The routine of my daily life as a kid was pretty simple. One way or another, it always seemed to lead me in the direction of a body of water, regardless of the time of year. The only question was whether the water would be frozen solid for hockey or open and flowing for fish.

If you want to answer questions about where you have ended up in this world, it is important to understand first where you came from and where you have been. It's kind of like framing a cherished photograph. Where someone is born and raised serves as the border for many of the events and incidents that will play out in any particular picture. The place where it all begins for any of us puts everything else into context.

For me, home was Parry Sound, Ontario, a small town nestled along the shores of Georgian Bay. I suppose Parry Sound was the same kind of small town you would have found all across Canada at that time. By that I mean it was a safe place, generally very quiet, and a great place to be a kid.

Parry Sound is a few hours north of Toronto, far enough north that there is still a lot of bush and water for kids to explore and enjoy, and a lot of space. It had a small-town flavor. When I was growing up, the permanent population might have been around five thousand people during fall, winter, and spring. But come July and August, I'd guess that those numbers swelled maybe ten times over with cottagers and tourists. The nearby lakes and waterways, and the thirty thousand islands that dot the coast of Georgian Bay, have always been irresistible during the summer months.

Still, despite the annual migration of vacationers, it was a tight-knit community where people knew everybody else's children and kept an eye on them. If someone got into trouble, the word spread quickly, and sooner or later a brother or sister, mother or father would know all the details of your problem. As a result, most of us realized early in life that it was best not to get in trouble unless you wanted it to be a topic of conversation around town.

It is no surprise to me that my grandfather Robert Orr chose a place like Parry Sound when he immigrated from Ballymena, Ireland. The community he came to was quaint and small and had many of the characteristics you might find in a tiny Irish town. It was here that he met and married my grandmother Elsie. My father, Doug, was their third child. In 1943, he married my mother, whose maiden name was Arva Steele, and they decided to continue the family tradition by settling down in Parry Sound. My parents would have five children: Patricia, Ronnie, myself (the middle child), Penny, and Doug Jr.

I can vaguely remember living in a house on Tower Hill, and my most vivid memory of that location was the black-and-white television set in the living room. That would have been in the 1950s, so our programming selections were pretty limited. I can still picture all of us sitting on the floor eagerly watching the test pattern until it was time to go to bed. I suppose you could assume from that description that it didn't take a whole lot to entertain the Orr kids.

But my clearest memories of home and family begin with the old house at 24 Great North Road. It was always filled with family and friends, and years later, when I set up my own company, I called it Great North Road in homage to that long-ago place where my life took shape. As you drive into Parry Sound coming down the big hill on Bowes Street, you will find Great North Road on your left, just before the bridge that leads into the center of town. The road twists and turns to follow the Seguin River. Our home was across the street from the water, just a few houses down from the bridge.

The old homestead was no palace, by any means. The floors, for example, weren't quite level. In fact, anything left on the floor would eventually end up on the other side of the room. On one occasion, my older sister, Pat, had to stay home because she was ill, and when I went up to check on her, she had a unique problem. Our mother, deciding to play it safe, had placed an empty pail at the side of Pat's bed, just in case it was needed in a hurry. Because of the pitch of the floor, the pail would slowly slide away from the bed. It meant that poor Pat had to keep dragging herself out from under the covers to go bring it back. (My contribution to her care was to put a heavy book behind the pail to keep it from moving.)

I remember that during the long Northern Ontario winters, the house could get terribly cold. If you wanted to watch anything on the television set for any length of time, you would have to dress as if you were heading outside. (By the time we moved to Great North Road, we had viewing options far more interesting than the test pattern, so keeping warm while we watched was more of a priority.) We had a big living room in that house, yet the only day of the year all of us actually sat down in it was Christmas Day. We just didn't have the money to heat it the rest of the time.

And when I say parts of the house went unheated, I don't mean it was merely cool. I mean it was literally freezing. On the coldest days, frost would accumulate on the light switches. We used to have to flick off little pieces of ice before we could turn on the lights.

Of course, winter would inevitably give way to spring, and in our home that always produced a minor irritation for everyone. The house was built into a ridge of granite, and as the warmer spring temperatures arrived, the melting ice and snow would run down the face of the rock and stream in through the kitchen door. Perhaps Dad just decided it wasn't worth the time to fix the problem. But I remember that water coming through the door year after year.

No, the old place wasn't much to look at. Years later, after I'd started to become pretty well known, I was standing in front of the house when a father dropped by with his son wanting to say hello to me. The little guy looked up at our place, leaned over toward his dad, and whispered something into his ear. But he spoke just loud enough for me to hear him ask, "Does Bobby Orr really live *here*?" It was no palace, to be sure, but it was home, and it was all we needed.

In fact, that house had something to do with the way I learned to play hockey. I was obsessed with the game, just like the kids around me, and I was always looking for ways to get better at it. Firing pucks at your garage door is probably something that young hockey players have always done. But we didn't have a driveway, so I'd open the door and shoot right through. The granite rock face that channeled the spring runoff into our kitchen provided the back wall of the garage—the rock had been left exposed because nobody ever saw a need to build a wall to hide it. Young hockey players tend to leave a trail of destruction in their wake as they perfect their marksmanship, but I can safely say that, despite firing thousands of pucks, I never put a dent in that granite.

I would use weighted pucks that I created by coring out the rubber and adding melted lead. The heavier pucks were far more difficult to shoot. The idea was that if I could handle heavy pucks, the lighter ones would seem easy in comparison once I got on the ice. I had managed to scrounge up a couple of pieces of plywood, and would lean one of them up against the rock cut, and that would be my net. The other one I'd lay on the floor in the doorway of the garage so I had a smooth surface to shoot from. It was almost as good as shooting off a sheet of ice, and the plywood allowed me to really let fly with those weighted disks. The garage had a light, so even with dusk approaching I could still practice. Trust me, I shot a lot of pucks at that makeshift plywood net during those years when I was a youngster.

Our house was located next to a couple of sets of train tracks. The ones just on the other side of the road were so close that at times you'd have thought the trains were passing right through our living room. The other set of tracks was up higher, located on a trestle that ran across the river just down the street from us. With two sets of tracks in the neighborhood, there was usually some kind of train traffic regardless of the time of day. It's funny how you get to a point when the noise of those trains doesn't even register with you. I guess it would be like living at a busy intersection with cars and trucks coming and going all the time. It was all just a part of living at 24 Great North Road.

There was another place where I spent a considerable amount of time while growing up, and it brings back wonderful memories. That was the cottage my Grandma Orr shared with our Aunt Joyce on Five Mile Bay. All of us grandkids would spend endless hours during the summer months at that cottage, fishing and boating and generally having a great time. When you live in a northern climate and have to contend with a lot of cold weather, you learn to appreciate the warm summers. We took advantage of every day we possibly could at Grandma's cottage, and I always enjoyed her company over those many years. It turned out Grandma and I had something in common that I didn't really think about at the time. She would often make reference to the fact that she suffered from considerable knee pain. "Look at these knees of mine," she would say, while trying to rub away the pain. Soon enough, I would learn what that suffering was all about.

As a child growing up, I had a pretty solid group of friends, and we always seemed to travel together, like a pack of wolves. It was just the way you did things back then. Your inner circle of buddies would play sports with you, hang around town with you, and you generally did everything together. My pack consisted of boys like Neil Clairmont, Jimmy Whittaker, and Roddy Bloomfield, among others. It's funny to look back at those days and think about where those friends of mine ended up. Neil would eventually play professional hockey with the Boston Braves in the American Hockey League, the Bruins' farm team. To this day, I remember that his mother would always feed us and how I looked forward to those meals. Jimmy Whittaker was a player as well, and someone I'd meet up with again during my junior career. Roddy Bloomfield went on to play some pro hockey in Binghamton, New York, and eventually landed the job as Paul Newman's double in *Slap Shot*. That's got to make him one of the most-watched hockey players of all time.

We were all linked by the game in one way or another. In the winter months, we could generally be found out on the bay playing hockey, but we would play anywhere we could find some open space. It didn't matter if we ended up on the bay, in a parking lot, on the river, or at the Victory school rink. As long as we could play hockey, we were happy. I'd leave in the morning with my hockey stick in hand and skates slung over my shoulder, and often my parents would say no more than, "Be home by dark." And that's what we would do. We played all day if we could. Sometimes we got so wrapped up in a game we'd forget to eat anything. Sometimes our toes got so cold we could hardly feel them. But we loved to play, and play we did, often until there was no light left at all. I can still remember how excited I used to get with the anticipation of heading out for a game of shinny. The formal game of hockey, as we all know, is played with six players on the ice for each team. But on any given day when I was a youngster, you might have twenty kids show up on the bay. It didn't matter how many came, we always made the numbers work, one way or another. We would appoint two guys as captains, and they would have the job of choosing up teams. If the total number of players was twenty, then it became a game of ten-on-ten, with everybody participating at the same time.

That was the way we learned how to play the game, and you develop your skills pretty quickly in a pitched battle on that scale. After all, if you wanted to spend any amount of time with the puck on your stick, you had to learn how to stickhandle through ten opponents. That's a great environment for kids to develop skills while at the same time having a ton of fun.

If you could hold your own in those scrimmages, then regulation games didn't seem so tough. In real games, you'd only have to get through five opponents, which seemed easy compared to what we were used to. We rarely had any kind of regulation goalie nets back then, so anything you could get your hands on, we would use. A pair of boots, a couple of mounds of snow, or whatever was handy. We always managed to find the materials we needed to enjoy ourselves, wherever and whenever a game broke out.

It wasn't just hockey, either. When winter was over, instead of going to the rink, we'd all head to a ballpark or a school playground and play baseball instead. Baseball provided me with the same kind of rush of excitement I had during the winter months playing hockey. I just loved the time spent with friends in all kinds of sports environments. Those experiences were probably shared by millions of children from coast to coast back then, because, as Canadian kids, that was something you just did.

It's safe to say that everyone loved to win when they played those games, and I was no different, but to me playing hockey and baseball really wasn't just about winning. Don't get me wrong, I'm not saying we shouldn't have competition. Even my harshest critics over the years couldn't complain that I didn't want to win badly enough. I do believe, however, that learning to handle both winning *and* losing is the most important part of competition. Coming to grips with the idea that the outcome doesn't always go your way is a life lesson, not just a lesson in sport. Sometimes we kept score, sometimes we didn't. But our games were primarily about the sheer joy of play, of being able to go outside with your buddies and simply have a good time.

The one indoor rink in town, the Memorial Arena, was always in use and we simply had to wait our turn. More often than not, we just relied on Mother Nature to provide for us, and I must tell you, there is no finer experience for a hockey player than skating on outdoor ice. (And besides, it's possible it was colder inside the Memorial than it was outside on the bay.)

Just ask the professional players who get the chance to participate in the annual Winter Classic game the National Hockey League, first held in 2008. Those events are always eagerly anticipated by the players, while fans are afforded an opportunity to share in the nostalgia of a different time and place. Such events take everyone back to the roots of our game: the sensation of skate blades cutting into crisp outdoor ice, the crunching sound of ice chips flying in tidy arcs. Those are sights and sounds and feelings that are forever lodged deep in my mind. The fresh, cool air against your face followed by the glorious warmth when you got home and rubbed the feeling back into your toes. Those things were all part of the outdoor experience, and I couldn't wait to go back out again and again.

Those memories represent my youth better than just about anything I can recall, such was the pure joy we felt experiencing the game in that setting. I have been able to attend one of the NHL outdoor events at Fenway Park in Boston. You can see the players looking around, wide-eyed and happy to be there. When you witness firsthand how players gaze up in that ballpark to catch a glimpse of Fenway's famous Green Monster, it can't help but bring a smile to your face. In those instances, these highly paid professional athletes are, at least for a moment, back on a pond somewhere and experiencing the game at its absolute best.

We probably all had the dream, back then, that one day our talent would take us to the big time, and there was nothing wrong with dreaming that dream. That's what fuels every game of shinny or back-lot baseball in the world. Of course, as you move along in your hockey career, reality begins to set in for most people. The dream begins to slowly fade away with the understanding that you will probably never be playing under the bright lights. But that's beside the point—that's not what childhood games are about, anyway. The life lessons we learned about competing remained with us even into adulthood. The types of competitions you engage in as an adult might be different from those you participated in when you were a child, but the rules from childhood still apply. What you learn on the frozen bays and ball fields doesn't become less relevant, no matter where you end up.

Those were simpler times and, given many of the headlines of today, probably a safer time for kids as well. I'll grant you, it might be that the memories grow a little bit sweeter with age as we look back on our youth with yearning. But those days as a kid, the times on the bay with my buddies, they truly remain my fondest memories of hockey. For me, those moments in my life represent hockey in its purest form. It was not about fame or fortune, though we all dreamed of both, and it surely wasn't about final scores. It was sport for the sake of sport, and it was about friends.

Parents today might be surprised to discover what kids can do if they are left to their own devices. We certainly learned to figure things out for ourselves. We had to take the initiative, because the odds were that no parent would be available to shovel off the bay or the rink or a stretch of road. If we wanted to play, we had to do the work to make it happen. We also learned how to give as well as take, because we were all in it together, and it was important to interact with everybody in the group even if they weren't your closest friends. If there is no one there to tell you to play nice, you figure out pretty quickly that there really is a code, and kids naturally respect it.

Every once in a while, tempers would flare, but we figured out how to settle those disputes as well—after all, there was no referee to decide the outcome. You would stand up for yourself on some occasions if you had to. One way or another, every kid who laces up a pair of skates in a shinny game learns that backing down almost never helps. But it also doesn't take long to figure out that if you play by the spirit of the rules, there is usually not much trouble. Actually, when I think back to those times, I can't remember any great conflict or fight that ever erupted on the bay. I suppose we were just having too much fun.

Sports in general, and hockey specifically, forced those lessons on us all, and they stuck with us for a lifetime. No coaches to tell you what to do. No parents to tell you how to behave. No referees to tell you what's fair. And no linesmen to break up trouble if someone loses his temper. Yes, that's freedom. But it's also responsibility—we had to figure things out for ourselves or there wouldn't have been those day-long games we loved so much.

Unfortunately, in many respects those long-ago days are a world removed from what we see today. Where streets and parking lots and schoolyards were once filled with children at play, they're often quiet now. Today, far too often I see baseball gloves and hockey sticks being replaced in no small measure by satellite TV and video games. Why wouldn't kids drift in that direction if they aren't getting enough opportunity to play and not having fun when they do?

I'm not trying to tell anyone not to watch TV, but if you've ever spent a long winter afternoon playing shinny with the whole neighborhood, or a summer evening playing softball with anyone who shows up at the diamond, you will know that kids who don't have the chance to organize themselves and solve their own problems and feel the exhilaration of sport for its own sake are missing out on something irreplaceable. In those days, we rarely waited for an adult to organize our social time or sports experiences. We took that upon ourselves. We were the ones who decided which game to play, where to play it, when to assemble, and who would be on whose team.

Without some form of sports, kids lose something. Being a part of a team, official or otherwise, shouldn't be just for the elite players. Those types of experiences should be enjoyed by *every* child.

My first hockey games seem so distant now. So much of modern sports is scripted for our kids, and that's not the way it was when I was young. That is one way that the pure joy of participating may, to my way of thinking, be diminished for some children. Today, we see entire leagues being owned by a single person or company, and elite or travel-level players often have most of the advantages when it comes to ice time, whether that is at practice or game opportunities. Yet most of the kids who want to participate aren't elite at all—by definition, they can't all be elite. Most kids are average. That's what *average* means.

Most kids just want to play a sport for the sake of participating. Those are the ones we should be helping as much as we can, because they make up the vast majority of the players involved. In my time, it wasn't about being an "all-star" as much as it was about being with your pack of friends. When we eventually did take the game from the bay into our minor hockey leagues, we all knew where our loyalty should rest. It was expected that we would participate in our town league first and foremost before we could step on the ice to play for an all-star team in a tournament or other competition, and that was just fine with me.

It brought communities closer, and no one really cared who the top players were. Rather, we cared that we were together. For most of the tournaments we participated in, we would all be billeted with a local family as opposed to staying in a hotel, because that was just too costly. Billeting usually meant we would stay at the home of a player from the host team, and it was always great fun. Besides being more affordable, billeting allowed you to get to know other players from around the region. While there is still some billeting today, it is not as common as when I was a youngster playing in Parry Sound.

For a lot of folks now, if a son or daughter is going to play it can be a financial burden, and that isn't right. I fear that given the costs associated with ice rental, travel, coaching, and equipment, many children aren't able to get involved. That runs directly counter to the culture I grew up in. To this day, I am grateful for the place and era in which I was born and the framework through which I was raised. Parry Sound will always have a special place in my heart, and the memories of my youth will always draw me back there.

There are names and faces from back then that still make me smile. They were people who took the time to make a difference, not only in my life but also in the whole community. When it came to hockey, many of these people had a dramatic impact on me, though at the time I couldn't possibly have understood their significance. It's interesting what you remember from your childhood. While many images start to blur with the passage of time, others remain crystal clear, as if they happened only last week. I can remember my absolute joy when I received my very first pair of new skates. Up to that point, everything had been hand-me-downs or bought secondhand. But when I turned eleven or twelve, just before the new hockey season began, my dad received a very generous gift from a friend of the family, Mr. Gene Fernier. Mr. Fernier decided it was time I had new blades, and he wanted to buy them for me. I can't recall the model of those skates or who made them, but I have sure held on to that moment. What a thrill it was. Even now, I still remember the excitement and the gratitude I felt.

It was an experience I shared with many young boys and girls who got to taste that thrill in their own way. It's one of the wonderful things about sports. Regardless of your skill level or where you end up in the pecking order, everyone involved shares common feelings, common experiences, and the same exhilaration from participating. It doesn't matter if it's on a grand stage like the Stanley Cup finals, a Canada Cup series, or oldtimers' hockey, or in a smaller setting like a kids' recreation league. The simple truth is that hockey binds those who play it in ways that are almost indescribable. The experiences are ones that all of us can identify with, on any number of levels.

Thinking of those skates reminds me that as a young boy I would always try to save a good portion of whatever money I made from doing odd jobs. After all, there were eventually five Orr children, and we couldn't all expect to receive everything we wanted, because the money simply wasn't there. One of my great thrills was walking into a sporting goods store with my savings in my pocket and asking to see a Hespeler Green Flash. It was the only stick I wanted, and to me it was definitely the hottest ticket on the market. It was something I had waited patiently to purchase. The modern equivalent would be when those fancy composite sticks first became available—every player on every team had to have one, regardless of the cost. But there was one big difference between my Green Flash and most modern twigs. While I can't recall what I paid for that stick, I can guarantee you it didn't cost what the modern ones do. And it seems to me it lasted a lot longer as well. (I might as well add that there is something about the feel of a wooden stick in your hands that can never be totally duplicated in carbon fiber.)

I realize I've been celebrating all the things we kids did on our own back then, but the fact is we were surrounded by people who cared about us and helped us along. I thought of them only as "coach" or "sir" or "ma'am." I couldn't have realized then just how important they would be in my development, both on and off the ice. I can't name them all, of course—so many of them come in and out of a kid's life, maybe helping out in small ways, maybe doing bigger things. There must have been many I wasn't even aware of. Neighbors, volunteers, family members—these people are always contributing in ways kids just take for granted. But there are some who do stand out in my mind, and one whose decision would set the table for the rest of my hockey career. His name is Royce Tennant.

The year was 1956, and I was signed up to play that season for a house league squirt team. I was all of eight years of age, and strange as it seems to me now, only ten years later I would be making my debut in the National Hockey League. But that was a long way off in the future and something that an eight-year-old could only dream about. It was Royce Tennant who would give those dreams distinct shape.

That year, Royce found himself appointed head coach for the squirt all-star hockey team, the Parry Sound Shamrocks. The local minor hockey group was in its infancy, and this was perhaps the first true "rep" team ever assembled at that level. As the season progressed, I was given the opportunity just after Christmas to move up from house league to Coach Tennant's Shamrock rep squad. That was my first time representing my hometown, and to say it was exciting would be an understatement. To go on a road trip to play in another town's rink, even if some of those towns weren't too far away, was a huge thrill for an eight-year-old.

Still, my invitation to join the all-star team didn't necessarily mean I was the greatest player Coach had ever seen. The fact was, he had only twelve players on the team and he needed to fill out the roster. Even with me in the lineup, he was still short-staffed. Perhaps my career would have turned out differently if there had been a couple more eligible kids in Parry Sound that winter. Coach Tennant had to look for ways to double-shift some kids to fill out the lines. As a result, he made the decision that the kid with the brush cut would play one shift as a forward then go back and play another shift as a defenseman.

I've been given a lot of credit over the years for being one of the first true rushing defensemen. But the truth is that the credit should be given to the man who coached me when I was in the squirt division, and to the coaches in my life who would follow. I was told years later by my old coach that what sold him on the idea of moving me back was my ability to skate. That may not make a lot of sense to people outside the game—after all, every hockey player can skate. But even at the highest level of the game, we talk about guys who can *skate*.

Some players just have effortless acceleration, a sort of fluidity that helps them maneuver out of trouble or get back into position when it seems impossible. There have been some great players who weren't noted for their skating—some of the greatest ever. And there have been some beautiful skaters whose hands never caught up to their feet. Still, it was a huge compliment to be told I could skate. It's a part of the game that hasn't changed to this day, because skating has been and always will be the main ingredient for any hockey player's success.

Royce decided way back then that I had the skating mobility to move up ice in a hurry and get back to the defensive zone to cover up when the inevitable mistakes occurred. I was supposed to be resting up after a shift on the wing, but I was thinking the same way I did out on Georgian Bay. When I got the puck, I wanted to go.

When you are just an eight-year-old kid, you don't spend a lot of time analyzing different aspects of the game, you simply go out and play. I just knew that as soon as I got my first taste of the game playing defense, I liked it. I was too young to realize that from back of the blue line you could see the play develop in front of you better than if you played as a forward. But I would learn soon enough that as a defenseman the opportunities to get the puck and use my skating skills in open ice were there on every shift. And even at that early age, I got all the freedom from Coach Tennant I needed to rush the puck. He never asked me to stay back—he just let me play to my strengths.

Take a look at any hockey team, especially in my day, and you'll see that a skinny little kid like me didn't exactly fit the mold. It's generally pretty easy to pick out the defensemen on the team even in the warm-up. They're probably the tallest in the group, quite possibly the burliest, and very seldom the most elegant skaters. I was just a little guy by defensemen's standards. When Royce Tennant was my coach, I couldn't have weighed more than sixty pounds, so the chances of me clearing the front of the net were not encouraging. I wasn't out there to punish guys. I wasn't an obvious candidate for defense.

The defenseman's job is to stay back, get between your goalie and any opposing player, and clear them from in front of your own net so your goalie can see the puck. And once you've retrieved the puck, your fundamental job description is to get the puck out via the safest, most efficient route. Anything more creative than that is still thought of as asking for trouble. No one really thought that a defenseman could actually control the puck and *skate* with it instead of just clearing it out of the zone. At the time, the two notable exceptions in the NHL had been Eddie Shore and Doug Harvey, but that was about it for rushing defensemen. In recent years, the smaller, smooth-skating, puck-moving defenseman has become more common. Guys like Paul Coffey, Erik Karlsson, Kris Letang, and others have become an important part of the game. Back then, though, there wasn't much room for defensemen like that.

To his credit, Royce saw that if everything played out the way he envisioned, it would be the opponent who would have to worry about what was going on in front of *their* net. When you think about it, that's a pretty good way to play defense. As long as you've got the puck, your goalie is safe. Royce put me back there and let me play the game the way I enjoyed it, and that meant I didn't become afraid of making mistakes.

That freedom from my coach gave me the confidence to try some things I'd never imagined I would be able to do. Coach

Tennant was allowing me to go back to that pond-hockey idea that calls on players to become creative, a quality far too often lacking in the modern game for my liking. Many coaches today would never let a defenseman try some of the things I was allowed to try, and that is a pity. I often wonder if *any* coach would let me play the game the way I wanted to play it if I were playing today.

Something tells me I might be collecting a lot of slivers on the bench if I were playing minor hockey right now. Many current youth hockey coaches don't want their players to take chances for fear of turnovers. It's as if their mortgage is dependent on winning at the squirt level. Coach Tennant wasn't afraid of his players making mistakes, and believe me, I made my fair share. I made them then, and I made plenty more right through my playing career. But fortunately, the coaches I ran into along the way allowed me to play the game in a wide-open style, and for that I am very grateful.

One of my great memories from that year was a visit our team made to Maple Leaf Gardens. Coach had set it up so we could play an exhibition game in Toronto and then watch a Maple Leafs–Black Hawks game that night at the Gardens. What a thrill for a bunch of kids from Parry Sound. You can imagine us all walking through the Gardens for the very first time, jostled by the crowd, eyes wide open as we looked at the hockey photos hanging on every wall along each hallway. Hockey heroes from the past and present everywhere you looked.

To top it off, we even had a chance to meet some of the big-league players, including the great captain of the Leafs, George Armstrong. He seemed so grown up to us then, but looking back I realize the Leafs legend was just twenty-six at the time. Armstrong and everyone else we met that day treated us so well, and that left a lasting impression on me. You can never underestimate the importance of events like that in a young person's life. Being responsible to the fans is something I have always taken very seriously.

Hopefully, just like George on that day long ago, I have honored that ideal during my time as a professional athlete and even into retirement. You never know how a single interaction with a person might affect their life, so you must constantly try to be at your best. That's not always easy, but that should be the goal for people in the public eye, and especially professional athletes.

Years later, when I was a young teenager, I attended a summer camp that Royce was running in the Parry Sound area called Camp Wee-Gee-Wa. One of the guests he invited to make an appearance that particular year was none other than Gordie Howe, and that was the first time I actually got to meet the man who was one of my heroes growing up. And by the way, Gordie Howe is still one of my heroes to this day. As an added bonus, Royce set it up so I could go out on a little fishing expedition with Number 9, and it was a dreamlike experience catching fish alongside Mr. Hockey. When the day was done, Coach Tennant asked me, "Well, Bobby, did Mr. Howe give you any advice about your hockey career?" to which I replied, "Yes, Coach, he told me that when I get to the National Hockey League, I should look out for just one thing: his elbows!"

I had other very influential coaches playing Parry Sound minor hockey, including men like Tom Maxwell, Bucko McDonald, Anthony Gilchrist, and Roy Bloomfield. These men carried on the tradition that Royce Tennant had begun, in that I was allowed to play the game of hockey the way I felt most comfortable playing it, and that was with the puck on my stick. Trust me, our coaches didn't engage us in any "trap systems" back then. To us, a trap was something outdoorsmen put out to catch beaver and mink and had no place in a hockey game.

I still have trouble imagining the coach of a group of eight- or nine-year-old players actually wasting time teaching systems. The greatest system any coach can pass along is allowing kids to create and refine skills. Systems need to come into play only much later, if ever. My minor hockey coaches never drilled the fun out of the game, but I wonder how many children get out of minor sport for that reason. Of course, we wanted to get better. And those men helped us get better. But whether they were careful not to over-coach, or just sensed when the kids were having fun, they never robbed us of our creativity. I can't remember any of those coaches *ever* telling me to chip the puck off the boards when things got tough in our own end. We were allowed to try things, creative moves that could get us out of jams on the ice (or into them). That kind of coaching would show itself in the way I played as a professional years later. Without that background of guidance from my minor hockey coaches, I doubt I could ever have become the player I did.

It's worth mentioning a bit more about the legendary Wilfred Kennedy "Bucko" McDonald, because he was a particularly intriguing person.

Maybe he was a great coach because he had come to the game very late in life, having tried out for the Leafs as a walk-on during the Depression at the personal invitation of Conn Smythe before going on to become a league all-star and three-time winner of the Stanley Cup. Maybe his skill as a great communicator was the result of all he had learned in twelve years in Ottawa as a member of Parliament for Parry Sound–Muskoka. (I wonder how many kids ever played under a coach who had been both an NHL player and an MP.) He was also still deep in the hockey world, having coached Rochester in the American Hockey League. And at the time I played for him, he was scouting for the Detroit Red Wings.

Bucko McDonald was a giant of a man and quite a character, someone who always seemed to do things on his own terms. He was our head coach over a couple of seasons when I was in bantam, and he would often act as both coach and chauffeur for players if they couldn't get a ride to the rink for a practice or game. On several occasions, I was the recipient of some of those rides in Bucko's old half-ton truck, but he would rarely go straight to the rink. Many times, if we were playing somewhere other than Parry Sound, I'd hear Bucko's truck pull up to the house, where I would be waiting patiently on the porch, and off we would head to a favorite little truck stop. The restaurant was just outside of town, on Highway 69, and we'd land there before the game in order to have a nice pre-game meal. We would both chow down on all types of delicacies: hamburgers, french fries, ice cream sundaes, and other essential food groups as well. That's hardly what you might call a wise pre-game meal by today's standards, but Bucko never thought anything of it. He always said it didn't matter what you had in your stomach when you played as much as it mattered what you had in your heart. I always had a pretty good appetite as a young fellow, so he never heard any complaints from me regarding our menu selections.

Once his team was put together, he was the kind of person who could see all the pieces of the big hockey puzzle, and he had that skill that all successful coaches have of putting everyone into their own special place within the bigger picture. In my case, Bucko allowed me to go with my first instinct on the ice: never get rid of the puck when you can control it. Hold on to it, and let the play open up in front of you. And again, it keeps coming back to those days on outdoor rinks or rivers or bays, where we simply skated and handled the puck for hours on end. That training allowed me to do the things I did as a player, and my coaches in turn allowed those skills to develop.

If you hold on to the puck and keep your head up, more often than not your opportunity will present itself. At the time I didn't understand, but eventually I came to realize that the first two or three strides were key for me. If I got my feet moving quickly, I would often find myself in open ice. With open ice came a sense of calm for me, and at that point the game always seemed to slow down.

It was just a lot easier to make plays when you were in motion, and Bucko helped to reinforce that concept with me. After all, the best play in hockey is still the give and go, and you can't run that play unless at least one player is in motion. Without speed, you are giving away your most decisive advantage, and your opponent is going to tie you up pretty quickly if he knows how to defend. Keeping your speed up also makes it easier to cover any mistakes.

When my feet were moving and the puck was on my stick, most of the choices became mine, and I always liked being in that position. I can't speak for others, but for me those decisions seemed much easier at high speed. It's funny, but for many players I think the rink seems quite small, particularly when the pace picks up. Yet every time I walk into an NHL-sized rink, I am amazed at how big the ice surface appears to be. There's lots of room out there to navigate, regardless of how big the opponents might be. I believe that Bucko and all of my other coaches helped my career by simply allowing me to go with my gut and skate with the puck.

They all helped make me a more confident player, and with more confidence comes the desire to try different and more creative things on the ice. That lesson in building a player's confidence is something all coaches need to learn. It worked back then, and it still works for today's players.

It is important that I say something else here about my minor hockey coaches, completely unrelated to their coaching abilities. In a far broader sense, they were all people who acted like gentlemen as they were leading their teams, and they encouraged players to act appropriately, both on and off the ice. With people like Royce and Tom and Bucko, you had men who came from different walks of life, yet all of them shared one most important philosophy when it came to coaching youth hockey. They wanted it to be fun. What a revolutionary idea that is! There was no barking at us from behind the bench, no ranting at the officials. There was no humiliation piled on the players when things didn't go well on the scoreboard. There was just a whole lot of fun, and I believe that as a result my coaches helped to develop some pretty good citizens in the process.

When I think of the way hockey can bring together a community and teach kids not just how to compete but how to hold themselves to the very highest standards, I think proudly and very fondly of the bantam team I played on in 1962. That team changed my life.

For one thing, I was with guys I had played with for years. It means a lot to play, and to win, with guys who have been there for you. And win we did. That Macklaim Construction team went undefeated through the regular season. As we headed into the playoffs, the whole town was behind us. Home games at the Memorial Arena were packed. And as we went deeper into the playoffs, we could count on crowds of supporters in the stands, both at home and on the road. We completely overwhelmed Midland in our first series, then dispatched Huntsville to win the district. Then we swept Uxbridge. Then Napanee. We beat Milton on the road in the next round, and the Memorial was boisterous when we hosted Milton the next weekend with a chance to win the provincial title.

I mention *expectation* here, because even when our whole town was being swept up in excitement and pride, that team had its own set of expectations. I'm not talking about the expectation that we would always be victorious or bring home trophies. Sure, we competed, and we competed hard, because we wanted to be winners. No, the main expectations for that '62 team revolved around concepts such as saying "please" and "thank you," reacting with dignity in the face of difficulties, respecting officials, and so on. They were expectations that everyone was supposed to meet, including players, coaches, managers, and parents as well. The further that team went, the more powerfully we stuck to the expectations that had got us there.

I'm sure we had our moments when those expectations weren't reached, be it from our play or conduct on the ice, or from the occasional parental meltdown in the stands. We're all human, and we might not have been a perfect group, but our approach to the game was that there were more important things than just winning and losing. I believe a big part of that team's success, indeed the biggest part, can be traced to those expectations. This may sound a bit old-fashioned or even corny to some, but a lot of those boys turned into men who did great things for our community. The lessons of 1962 came from expectations based not on a *playing* perspective but on a *life skills* perspective. I'm very proud to have been a part of that group.

We didn't disappoint the town that afternoon. We beat Milton and won the provincial title with a perfect record. Ahead of us was still the district Little NHL tournament in Gravenhurst, where we faced Huntsville again in the final and won, our perfect record still intact. That set up the season-ending climax of the provincial Little NHL tournament—a three-day event in Cobourg, where we were billeted with local families.

We beat Winona in the first game, dispatched Milton in the second, and faced off against the host team in the final, the championship and our perfect record on the line.

We skated to a decisive 6–0 victory, and when we got back to Parry Sound the next day, we were hailed as heroes. Even the police and fire departments came up to greet us, sirens wailing, as we rolled into town. But I think I speak for all of my teammates when I say we were as proud of the *way* we won as we were of the fact *that* we won.

In 2012, the Bobby Orr Hall of Fame in Parry Sound honored the members of that team with induction into the Hall. Our coaches and managers that year—Roy Bloomfield, Anthony Gilchrist, and Bucko McDonald—as well as my brother Ron, who served as a trainer, will always be remembered for what they did to bring a community together like that, and for the example they set for a bunch of kids who really just wanted to play hockey.

As I met with some of my old teammates at the induction, what struck me was that while some of the hairlines had receded and we had all put on a few pounds, what hadn't changed were the great memories and stories we shared from one of the best times of our lives. And that, it seems to me, is what minor hockey is really about.

I t wouldn't be fair to finish up my remembrances of those early days in Parry Sound without spending some time discussing my sisters and brothers. I'm not sure if my siblings ever really knew how much I appreciated the sacrifices they all had to make in order for me to achieve my goals in hockey.

The way my career unfolded meant that many weekends my dad would be driving me somewhere in the car. That meant that the other four Orr children didn't have their dad at home. It's difficult to gauge how my development as an athlete affected our family as a whole and my siblings individually. I know there were occasions when my brothers were playing in hockey games and someone in the stands shouted out something like, "You'll never be as good as your brother." That wasn't fair to them, especially when they were just kids. But it was all part of the deal, I guess, even if it wasn't very appropriate. As time went on, ours was not your average family environment, so I've no doubt they all paid a price for my benefit, one way or another.

For anyone today who may be taking a path similar to the one I took, I would give this advice. Always remember that those who are closest to you will be affected by your dreams. Somewhere along the way, they will undoubtedly have to sacrifice something in order to help you realize your goals. You may be the "next one," but in the meantime you have family that will have to assist in paying the freight for your success. You should never forget that and always thank your lucky stars you have people in your corner who are prepared to back you.

In my experience, I've come to realize there are very few "self-made men" in this world. While you have to work hard to become successful, the truth is that most who have gone far received a whole lot of backing from friends and family at key moments.

I would love to be able to thank all the people who helped me back then, but that is all but impossible. But there are two people who gave me everything they possibly could, a couple of people who modeled for me the kind of life I would learn to appreciate more and more as I grew up. The person I am today, warts and all, is a direct result of the example provided by my parents, Arva and Doug Orr.

Two

LESSONS FROM
MY PARENTS

Many years after I left Parry Sound, my parents received a visit from the parents of a young player who was about to explode into the hockey world. Eric Lindros was fourteen years old at the time, and his mother and father came calling to ask for some advice. It seems they had determined that my parents deserved some of the credit for the way I turned out, and they wanted to know exactly how the process of raising an NHL-caliber son should work. Specifically, they wanted some insight into how my father had handled my development as a player. What was it he had done to get me to the top?

My father's response was short and sweet: nothing.

I tell this story to underline a point. I really hit the jackpot when it came to parents.

Certainly, Eric Lindros's parents had every right to be concerned about their son, and especially about the impact his life would have on other members of the family. By the time he was selected first overall by the Nordiques, his was one of the most recognizable faces in Canada. In fact, he was probably the most talked-about player in the game even before he stepped on the ice for his first shift in the NHL. It makes perfect sense that parents would worry about how a family, and a young kid like Eric, might navigate the whirlwind surrounding the next big thing. Indeed, that spectacle, and the stakes involved, has only grown since then.

But some things never change. The game hasn't really changed. And hockey fans never really change. You can no doubt appreciate that as my professional hockey career began to unfold, a certain amount of celebrity came as well. That had huge implications, not only for me, but also for the place I called home. By *home* I mean the house specifically, and in a more general sense the entire town. You can also bet that it changed the lives of my parents and siblings as well. For some people who suddenly find themselves the parents of a well-known athlete, the recognition that comes along with it can grow almost unbearable. But that didn't occur in the case of my parents.

My mother and father were wonderful role models who never tried to teach me how to be a hockey player but insisted I learn what it took to be a decent person. It's not easy to see the things parents do for you when you're a kid (and even harder to appreciate the things they *don't* do for you). While you may appreciate your parents when you are growing up, you understand their methods and parenting skills more fully once you have your own family. They were a wonderful couple united by a powerful desire to raise their children with character and substance. But the individual qualities they each brought into their union helped ensure their success as a couple over the course of their fifty-seven-year marriage.

I think that their core values and basic sense of family and community insulated them and their children from a lot of potential trouble. I remember hearing an account of something that happened involving my mother during those years, and it speaks to the type of person she was. My mom worked at various part-time jobs over the years, and one of them was at a coffee shop in Parry Sound. People knew who she was, and in any small town people are going to want to talk hockey. Whenever anyone asked, "How's your son?" she would come right back with, "Which one? We have three."

In every important way around the house, I was just one of the kids. I don't think it ever occurred to my parents that I should be treated differently. My parents made sure everyone in the family had a special place and not just the one who happened to be getting noticed outside the house for playing hockey. Of course, like all brothers and sisters, we were always jockeying for our parents' attention. I don't imagine that sibling rivalry in all of its different forms was unique to the Orr household. For instance, as we got older, my brothers would stick the needle in a little bit by saying things like, "Oh, Bobby must be coming home—Mom's made a lot of food!" We all dished it out and took our fair share of shots as well.

So how did my parents prepare me to be a hockey player? The answer is that they prepared me to be like anyone else. All parents want the same basic things for their children—namely, health and happiness. That's what you should be preparing your kids for. Success comes and goes, but if your children are healthy and happy, nothing else really matters much. As for the success part, I suppose we all measure success differently, and I've no doubt that my parents had their take on what success was all about. What's important, however, is that they never forced their views on me.

They never attempted to dictate how my life should unfold or how I might achieve my own success. They let me decide those things for myself. I can only imagine that Eric's parents must have been a little surprised by my father's one-word response, but the reality is it truthfully reflected what my mom and dad believed was their role in developing the young hockey player in their house.

My parents didn't make long speeches or philosophize. But that didn't mean we didn't know what they thought or what they stood for. The leadership they both demonstrated for me was only made stronger by their saying little or nothing, especially at pivotal points in my development. All of us kids knew what our parents believed in, because they lived it right before our eyes. In my case, they weren't at every hockey game I played in as a youngster, but they didn't have to be in the stands for me to know they were supporting me. There was no pressure on me to win or be the high scorer or the star of the team. Actually, it was quite the opposite. I can't remember my father ever trying to give me any instruction about how to play the game of hockey.

Every kid likes to win—I certainly did. And kids want to please their parents. Those two things together can really raise the stakes for a kid and make a game feel a lot like work. I was probably a pretty serious little guy, but Dad would often tell me to "go out, have some fun, and let's see what happens." When we talked after the game, he didn't offer his assessment of my play or give me tips. And it seems to me that he was always very positive. That is, he played the role of dad, not coach or career counselor. Now there's a perspective I wish more parents would buy into.

Unfortunately, many parents of up-and-coming athletes today try to live their lives through the child's success, and it never works. That was the basis of the message my father shared with the Lindros family.

M y wife often tells people that my mother was a beautiful person and the backbone of the Orr family. And Peggy is absolutely right about that. Of course, Peggy had a particular soft spot for my mother, because Mom always maintained that I wasn't good enough to land someone of Peggy's quality, but that is another story for another time.

My mother was never out front seeking the limelight. She was very humble by nature and remained the glue of our family until the day she passed away. In fact, the very day of my mother's passing, she spent a lot of time with Reverend Marjorie Smith. At the private service we held in my mother's honor, Reverend Smith told us she had been instructed to pass along a wish that Mom had expressed for all of the Orr children. Her message was that we were simply to "all get along." She believed in the importance of family, and that was my mother's focus even at the very end of her life.

Many people have written over the years that at times during interviews and public appearances I have come across as somewhat shy and reserved. Others have gone further and said that I've even seemed almost reclusive. I believe that this part of my personality most certainly comes right from my mom. To this day, I have trouble sleeping the night before I have to make a presentation or speech, whether it's for five people or five hundred, just as it was when I was a player. I have been in the spotlight more than my fair share ever since I was a kid, and I still dread it. That's how my mother was, too. She was the family leader, but she didn't lead from the front lines. She rarely went to my games, because she didn't want the attention that would inevitably follow. The crowds kind of scared her as well, and sometimes it did get pretty crazy. As a result, she may have attended five or six games in total over my entire life in hockey, though she was well aware of how my career was progressing. She chose to be our tower of strength from a distance, where the spotlight was not directly on her.

Our mom was a giver as opposed to a taker. Hers was a life built on service to her family and community, and her example had a tremendous and lasting impact on all of the Orr children. For Mom, actions didn't just speak louder than words—they were more like commands. As our family friend Bill Watters has often said, "With Arva Orr, we could have turned around the saying, 'Do as I say and not as I do' to read, 'Do as I say *and* as I do,' because that is exactly the way she lived her life."

She was one of the most caring people I have ever encountered and always put the needs of others ahead of her own. There was a television series back in the 1960s called *Hazel* about a housekeeper who was always helping the family she served in any way she could. My old childhood buddy Neil Clairmont was the one who started calling Mom "Hazel," because that was exactly the role she chose to fill. She was the type of lady who had a servant's heart and practiced that kind of giving every day. The result was that my buddies always enjoyed being at our house, because they knew that "Hazel" would inevitably have cooked something up and it would be there waiting for them.

Then again, I can't deny that Mom possessed a slightly sterner side as well. She did not allow a lot of shenanigans, and her standards around our home were to be understood and followed. We didn't have much in terms of possessions, but what possessions we did have were to be respected and cared for. Mom expected all us kids to mind our behavior and general attitude around the house, at school, or anywhere else in the community. She was the enforcer of those rules, and God help any of us who decided not to follow them.

My mother left no room for us to question her interpretation of right and wrong. For example, on one cold and rainy afternoon when I was ten, a buddy and I found ourselves in possession of a pack of cigarettes. I'm not going to say we stole them from a corner store, but I can't recall exactly how they came into our possession. At any rate, we decided we would try our hand at smoking while we fished under the bridge that led right into the heart of Parry Sound. Unfortunately for us, someone spotted us from a shop window. Before we'd coughed our way through our first cigarette, Mom had received a phone call and knew exactly where her son was and what he was doing. I suppose I was feeling pretty pleased with myself, but my blood ran cold when I saw her appear under the bridge, marching purposefully right for me. All I could think to do was try to make a run for it, so I dropped my cigarette and bolted for the far side of the bridge. But when she yelled at me to stop, I froze.

I was busted, and if looks could kill, I'd have been a dead man that day. She grabbed me by the arm and led me back across the road to our house. That was not a very pleasant episode, let me tell you, and it was the last cigarette I ever smoked under *that* bridge.

What I'm about to say might not sound like something you would read in a modern parenting book, but Mom's weapon of choice (for lack of a better term) when any of us veered off the straight and narrow was an old broom she kept handy in the kitchen. You could say Mom believed in the maxim, "Speak softly and carry a big stick"—literally! While her bark was always worse than the actual bite of that broom, it served nevertheless to dissuade us from getting on her bad side. We always knew how much she loved us and how kindhearted she was, but at the same time, we knew that she was the boss.

Mom never set out to be a best friend to her children. She wanted us to know what her line in the sand was and the consequences of crossing it. Inevitably, we did indeed develop closeness and a friendship with our mother in our adult lives. But I must tell you that even as an adult, whenever I found myself sitting at home in Parry Sound chatting with my mother, I would often think about that broom.

Then there was the man of the house, my father, Doug, and he was another case altogether. I'm sure Mom sometimes figured she was really raising six kids, not five, because Dad could be a handful. As quiet and unassuming as our mother was, Dad was just the opposite. I guess the old idea that opposites attract must have applied to my parents. But given the course that my life would take in athletics, my dad was the perfect father for someone like me. As my skills in hockey developed, he was my greatest cheerleader and encourager. He never applied the type of pressure on me or any of my siblings you sometimes see in families. They might have been miles apart in personality, but much like my mother, Dad was the kind of person who consistently gave of himself to benefit his family and friends.

As a boy and into his teens, my father had been a fine athlete. In fact, he was once invited to training camp with the Bruins' farm team. He turned them down, though, and enlisted in the Royal Canadian Navy instead. He spent several years on board corvette-class ships in the Battle of the Atlantic, escorting merchant vessels en route to England.

Dad was already married to my mom when he shipped out with the navy, and when he returned from his tour of duty he picked up where he left off, heading back to work and starting a family. The five children came along pretty quickly, and Dad held down different jobs during that time. In fact, to make ends meet, he often worked two or three jobs at once, and as I grew up, that did not escape my attention. At various times, Dad held the following job titles: beer rep for a brewery; taxi driver for a local cab company; employee at CIL, which, by the way, was where they packed dynamite; and bartender at a local establishment (or two).

Like our mother, he modeled a way of living that deeply affected all of his children. But make no mistake, Dad had a wild side. He enjoyed a good time, and I'm sure my mother often thought about taking that broom to him on occasion. Dad was human and had his faults, like we all do, but he demonstrated some great qualities for me growing up. There wasn't anyone in town that I could name who didn't genuinely like Doug Orr.

As far as his parenting skills went, he basically left us to discover things for ourselves. He was always there if you needed a hand or some advice, but he never forced anything on you. One thing that was non-negotiable, though, was the importance of hard work. I knew early on that he was a hard worker, and that attitude rubbed off on me. He always demanded that whenever we did something, we should put as much energy into it as possible. I truly believe that my passion for hockey can be traced to my father's attitude about so many things, and his expectation that I would make an honest effort has stayed with me through all the years. That effort led to success on the ice, and that success in turn fueled my passion. One expectation of all of the kids at our house involved chores and eventually part-time jobs. Believe me when I say that as a young boy growing up in Parry Sound, life wasn't all hockey for me.

My parents insisted that we learn the value of a day's work, and summer employment represented the start of that responsibility. Looking back, I'd have to say that my job as a bellboy was the toughest on me, because I was so small at the time. The Belvedere was a beautiful old hotel that catered to the summer tourists. It was closed during the winter, so getting one of those summer jobs was a real feather in my cap. Of course, there were expectations at such a fine establishment as to how a bellboy should perform his duties, and there were standards to be met. Unfortunately, I had a little trouble meeting some of those standards.

For example, whenever I went outside to help people into the hotel with their suitcases, they felt sorry for me, because I always struggled to carry the heavier pieces of luggage. I was just a little guy without much meat on my bones, so more times than not the guest ended up carrying his own bags into the hotel. On more than one occasion, I could be seen leading them into the lobby of the Belvedere empty-handed. Now, this did not sit well with my boss, Mr. Peoples, and to avoid getting into trouble I would often have to beg customers, sometimes half wrestle with them in the parking lot, to let me carry at least something into the hotel lobby. I would have taken anything, from a hatbox to a woman's purse, just so long as I had something in my hand, because if I wasn't carrying a bag of some description into that lobby, then I knew what was coming next. But those suitcases sure were heavy! I'm still grateful to all the kind souls who tried to help out the little guy who was the bellboy all those years ago.

Before my time at the Belvedere Hotel was over, things actually got worse. As part of my duties, if I happened to pull the morning shift, I had to spend some time in the lobby with one of those huge electric floor-polishers. Those were big, heavy machines. Probably about the same size as I was. It took all my strength to keep the machine spinning the buffing wheel instead of spinning me. Anyone who caught a glimpse of me trying to handle that beast must have thought they were watching a rehearsal for a comedy show.

And I really wasn't looking forward to going back to the Belvedere the following summer, yet I knew I had to. That was Arva's rule. But after my first year's performance, who knows if Mr. Peoples would have given me another shot anyway. As fate would have it, the hotel went up in flames that winter, so that was the first and last summer I spent at the Belvedere. My father used to chuckle about my employment at the hotel and said on more than one occasion that perhaps I despised the job so much I had resorted to burning the place down.

The other tough job I remember was the one summer I tried baling hay for a farmer. The farmer was a friend of my father's, so he agreed to let me have a go as a farmhand. Everyone knows that working on a farm is tough, but I figured I'd keep myself in shape and put some cash in my pocket at the same time. After all, everything was done manually back then, so it couldn't help but be a great workout.

It was a workout alright. That was a very tough way to earn some extra spending money. Let me tell you, I quickly learned to appreciate what it is to be a farmer and the work that goes into keeping a farm running. If I had ever thought about buying a farm some day in my future, those dreams were crushed.

In addition to all that, my illustrious summer employment history included working at my uncle Howard's butcher shop, picking dew worms at night with a flashlight to sell to fishermen, and working as a salesman at Adam's Menswear. When I got older, I also worked at the Haliburton Hockey Haven, which was run by Wren Blair, Jim Gregory, and Bob Davidson. (That's right, the first time I attended hockey school I was there as an instructor, not a student.) I also did part-time custodial work at my elementary school. I would go in during the Christmas and Easter holidays to scrub and wax the floors. There was an old furnace there that needed cleaning as well, and since I was the only person small enough, it was my job to crawl inside and clean it. It was a dirty job, but someone had to do it.

None of those jobs I took on as a young boy was glamorous by any means, and they weren't always fun. You didn't wake up every day looking forward to the polishing machine or bales of hay that awaited, but you went, because that was expected of you. The bigger purpose of those jobs was to build character, and that is why my parents wanted us working.

I believe experiences like that can benefit any young person. Those positions helped teach me the meaning of hard work and the value of money, lessons that everyone needs to learn.

My father also loved a good joke—especially if he was telling it. Once, when she was a kid, my sister Penny came up with some kind of dance routine, and she decided that our father would have to sit down and watch. It was during Oktoberfest, and I can only guess that Dad might have been out celebrating the occasion a little bit. To this day, I can still hear his laughter as Penny put on her show, and the more he laughed, the more she performed.

Dad enjoyed life to the fullest. Our times together fishing were always filled with practical jokes and storytelling, with laughter as a constant. I can still hear "Yakety Sax," a popular tune of the day, blaring out from a cassette player Dad brought with us on a fishing trip on the Moon River. He'd be in another boat with one of his buddies, and you always knew where they were, because they kept playing that song over and over. That song, and the laughter that went with it, still rings in my ears.

Dad supplied me with one last laugh in the days just after he passed away. I was going through some of his things when I came across a rubber stamp of my signature. It solved a bit of a mystery for me.

Years before, I had told my father that he was going to have to cut back on autograph requests, because I was having trouble keeping up. He would drop a puck to open a tournament in town, and of course people would soon discover he was my father. The next thing you knew, I would be swamped with another list of autograph requests from him. I told him, "Dad, just because someone says hello to you doesn't mean you owe them an autographed picture!"

Sure enough, I noticed almost immediately that he wasn't asking for as many photos as before. I was relieved, but I was curious to know what had happened. As I looked at that stamp, it all made perfect sense to me, and I had to laugh. Undoubtedly, there are a few autographed Orr photos hanging on bedroom walls out there that came from my dad's "printing press." I wonder who my dad convinced to make that stamp up anyway. That's one mystery I'll probably never solve. Let's just say that my father could be slowed down, but he could never be totally stopped once he put his mind to something.

As I look back at the impact my parents had in my life, I realize now that I was taught fundamental concepts that revolved around a central theme of respect. Simple things like holding a door open, speaking politely, or taking your hat off indoors, especially at the dinner table. Those basic ways of treating people with respect became habits for us, and I'm happy that my parents insisted on them. It wasn't as though they would sit us down and formally instruct us in manners. They didn't need to lecture us—there was an unspoken understanding about what was expected of us when we lived under their roof. And they modeled the behavior we were to follow. Some athletes act as if everyone is there only to serve them, and it maddens me beyond description. Mom and Dad wouldn't have allowed that kind of attitude from any of the Orr children. There would have been consequences.

In their later years, and long after I had made my mark as a professional hockey player, Mom and Dad could often be found sitting out on the front porch of their home in Parry Sound when they had good weather. By this time, they were living at a new place on Gibson Street, and I can assure you that the floors in their new home were completely level. People would sometimes drive up, introduce themselves as hockey fans, and ask if they could see some of the hardware my parents had collected from my playing career. Sure enough, they would be invited into the house to take a look at the trophies they had come to see. Episodes like that perhaps best reflect what my parents were all about. After the Bobby Orr Hall of Fame was created in Parry Sound in 2003, you could find Dad there providing tours for schoolchildren or welcoming a busload of seniors. Often I would call to chat with him, only to have him cut me off. "I have to go," he'd say. "I'm off to Victory Elementary School to talk to the kids." If I were to ask him what he was going to talk about, he'd say, "Don't know yet." And he'd be gone. I always got a kick out of him visiting that school, because not only did I attend Victory as a young boy, but so did he. Those types of volunteer activities were a big part of their lives.

Was theirs a perfect marriage? We all know there is no such thing. Ours was a family that had its fair share of problems, just like any family, but we found our way through, in no small measure because of who our parents were and what they stood for.

As an aspiring athlete, you don't know how your life in sports will turn out, and you can only hope that all the practice and preparation will pay off. When I turned fourteen, I would begin my hockey career in earnest as a member of the Oshawa Generals, and this much I know to be true: my mom and dad had prepared me well for what was to come.

Three

OSHAWA

My hockey story is not unlike that of many kids who dream of playing in the National Hockey League, though I suppose my journey started a little bit earlier than most.

One of the hardest parts of becoming a hockey player is leaving home. Think of yourself as a fifteen- or sixteen-year-old packing a suitcase and heading off to a strange city. You end up billeted in the home of a complete stranger, attending a school you've never heard of. The group of friends, the pack of wolves, you've grown up with suddenly vanishes. The safety net of friends you've come to depend on is replaced by strange faces in the hallways of your new high school.

You're playing for a new hockey team, in a huge, unfamiliar rink, being cheered or booed by people you don't know. You're traveling from town to town. You've got bigger, older guys needling you night after night, trying to get you to drop your gloves, trying to see what you're made of. Being plucked from one place and dropped somewhere else is going to be difficult for anyone, let alone a young teenager.

Or, if you have children of your own, think of it from a parent's perspective. Think of giving up a son at such a young age in order for him to pursue his goals somewhere else. That boy of yours, still just a baby in your eyes, is snatched from you and taken in by someone else. That is exactly the scenario my parents had to face, and countless other parents are confronted with the same situation at the end of every summer. I know very well just how difficult it can be for parents to see their kids go, because I was in the room when my mother wrestled with the decision over whether to let me go off to play junior hockey.

In a sense, the most remarkable thing about my rookie season in Oshawa was that it happened at all that year. I was only fourteen and hadn't yet left elementary school, but that was a minor speed bump compared to the fact that my mother was against it. I wanted nothing more than her permission right then, and I knew from experience that cajoling and negotiating were all but useless once she'd made up her mind. So, while she was deliberating, the question of where I would play hockey in the fall of 1962 was entirely in her hands.

I hardly dared speak while my future was being discussed. But my father made my case with his usual persuasiveness, as did another gentleman who played a very important role in my career: Wren Blair.

B ack when I was playing minor hockey, there was no such thing as the NHL Entry Draft. Until 1963, NHL teams could control players' rights, even at a very young age. (In fact, the first draft was for sixteen-year-old players, and two of the six teams in the league, Detroit and Chicago, didn't bother picking in the fourth and final round, as most sixteen-year-olds' rights were already wrapped up.) Teams wanted to lock up the playing rights to any player who might possibly cut it five or six years down the road, and the terms needed to retain those rights were definitely in the team's favor. Teams could ask players to sign what was called an A Form, which committed the kid to trying out with the club; a B Form, which gave the team the right to sign the player without actually committing to him; or a C Form, which completely assigned the player's rights to the team. Once you had signed one of these, you lost any negotiating leverage you might have had with the team. But then, players didn't really negotiate in those days anyway. After all, there were a whole bunch of prospective players but only six teams in the league, so supply exceeded demand. Kids who dreamed of suiting up in the NHL were often all too happy to commit to a team that showed interest in them.

All the teams had "bird dogs" in minor hockey rinks across the country, appraising young talent and guaranteeing a steady supply of it. And without a draft to ensure that talent was distributed evenly across the league, there was a real advantage to getting to young players first. That's one of the reasons the Canadiens were so consistently represented by the very best French-Canadian players. They had the best scouts in the rinks of Quebec—and they had a steady stream of young Québécois players who would give just about anything to sign a C Form with the team they grew up worshipping.

The Toronto Maple Leafs had all the glamorous appeal of the Canadiens back then. Every kid in Ontario grew up idolizing the Leafs (as I did), so the Leafs could count on a reliable supply of starry-eyed young men, and an equally steady supply of tips from minor hockey rinks in far-flung towns. Parry Sound was no different.

In 1960, I had the opportunity to play at Maple Leaf Gardens as a peewee. Mr. Anthony Gilchrist was our coach. He also happened to be an old friend of the legendary George "Punch" Imlach, the general manager and coach of the Leafs. As a friend, and as a Leafs fan, my coach wrote to Imlach to suggest that Toronto tie up my rights and make sure I would be wearing the blue and white when the time came. Here is that letter in its entirety:

March 28, 1960

Mr. George Imlach,
General Manager,
Toronto Maple Leafs,
Maple Leaf Gardens, TORONTO, Ontario

Dear Punch,

First of all I wish to thank you and your staff for the kind-ness extended to the Parry Sound Pee Wee team on their visit to Maple Leaf Gardens. It was greatly appreciated by myself and by the men who accompanied the boys. Many thanks to Anderson for the photos. Mr. Kerluck has secured one for all the boys.

I wish to pass along a bit of information which I feel sure may be of great value to your organization in the future.

You will no doubt remember a fair-haired crew-cut lad who was in the group. You sized him up and made a remark that he was a hockey player. Well, he sure has the earmarks of a combination of Howe and Harvey. His name is Bobby Orr, aged 12 years, and he plays defence on the Pee Wee all-stars for the town team. I paid very close attention to this boy while we had the various teams in Huntsville this last weekend in the Muskoka–Parry Sound District Play-offs in the Little N.H.L. His team is in the Minor Hockey Play-offs now, and they play in Parry Sound on Saturday, April 2. It might pay to have one of your men look him over in Barrie, place him on your list now before Hap Emms sees him, or I feel sure it will be too late.

That was really a good game last night (Sunday). I was pulling for Kelly all the way. I noticed you raising your hat as you left after the game. Best of luck in the rest of the games!

I hope the above may be of some use to you. Our regards to yourself and your family.

Sincerely Yours,
A.A. Gilchrist

Imlach never did write back, though my coach did receive a letter from the Leafs' chief scout, R.E. Davidson. Davidson quite reasonably pointed out that a boy barely twelve years old was a little young to be put on a "protected" list and said that he would keep my name on file. He ended by saying, "I hope that someday Bob Orr will be playing for the Maple Leafs."

In fairness to the Leafs, those Toronto teams of the '60s were Stanley Cup–winning powerhouses. They wouldn't have been spending much time thinking about developing twelve-year-olds.

Still, we lived just up the road from Toronto, and I'd been a Leafs fan from my earliest memories. And yes, Grandpa Orr was a diehard Leafs backer who would have given his right arm to see me wear the blue-and-white uniform that he cherished so much. I have often wondered what I would have looked like in a Toronto Maple Leafs sweater if things had turned out differently. But to be honest, when I was twelve I wasn't sitting by the phone, waiting for a call from the Leafs, or any team for that matter. In fact, the thought would never have crossed my mind. I just wanted to play.

S pringtime in Canada means playoffs, always the best time of the year. In early spring of 1961, I was a twelve-year-old player just a few days away from turning thirteen, and I was starting to get some attention from junior and professional scouts. At that stage in my development, I had no idea who was watching me or what they thought of me as a player. I would hear the odd comment that there was a scout from this or that team watching us, but I never paid much attention to the talk.

Looking back now, it is interesting to realize just how very small the hockey world is. For example, one of those scouts who saw me in action that spring was a gentleman by the name of Scotty Bowman. Scotty is arguably the greatest coach in the history of the National Hockey League and someone whose teams I would play against often in my career. Back then, though, he was an amateur scout for the Montreal Canadiens—a team he would go on to lead to multiple Stanley Cup championships.

Scotty saw me play at a bantam playoff game in Gananoque on a Saturday afternoon that spring, and it was the first he'd ever heard or seen of me. As he told me years later, he was there with a friend that day to scout a couple of players on the Gananoque squad. As he tells the story, at about the five-minute mark of the first period, his buddy leaned over to him as they sat in the stands and said, "Scotty, I don't know what you're thinking, but I keep finding myself looking at that little Number 2 from Parry Sound." Number 2 was what I had on the back of my sweater at the time.

Scotty would eventually make something of a courtesy visit to my family in Parry Sound, but an offer from the Canadiens never materialized. They were at the top of the hockey mountain and no doubt had even bigger fish to fry than the Leafs when it came to recruiting players. My understanding from Scotty is that he sent in a report to the man who was running the Habs, Ken Reardon, and Reardon responded by saying something like, "We don't sign babies to contracts in this organization." Those might not have been his exact words, but that was the message. And who could blame him? But my chances of ever wearing a Habs jersey basically never got off the ground.

I didn't know it at the time, but there were also members of the Boston Bruins organization who happened to be in the area to watch some junior games and scout potential NHL prospects. In fact, the entire front-office staff of the Bruins showed up in Gananoque. Like the Canadiens, the Boston scouts had been told to pay attention to those two lads from the home team. But apparently, like Scotty, some of the Boston group seemed to prefer my style of play instead. Wren Blair was one of those guys.

Within a few days after that game, Wren was sitting in the Orr family kitchen. At the time, he was working for the Bruins as a scout while also managing and coaching the Kingston Frontenacs in the old Eastern Professional Hockey League. Like many coaches and managers I played for throughout my career, Wren told me later that as he watched me play during that game in Gananoque it was my skating that caught his eye. Scouts will tell you that any prospect has to show at least one elite-level skill. The idea is that if you have at least the one skill, then the other parts will hopefully round into shape and develop over time. If you have to be identified as possessing one outstanding skill, I suppose being known as a solid skater is what any hockey player would wish for.

Both Wren and Scotty noticed my skating in that game and believed it allowed me to control the tempo of play when I had the puck on my stick. That part of my game would not change over time. I wish I could tell you some secret drills or training technique that made me an effective skater. The reality is that skating was something that just seemed to come very naturally to me.

I don't mean I didn't put in my time and work very hard at becoming an effective skater, because I did. But if I said I was constantly trying to modify this aspect or that part of my skating, I'd be lying. Changing speed, transitioning from backward to forward skating, making tight turns, these were all things I learned on the bay. That point is worth repeating. When you're playing ten-on-ten, you just naturally learn how to pivot and change pace to find that one spot of open ice.

The basics of my skating, and certainly the rhythm of my skating, seem to have been there from a very early age. I've heard many theories over the years about what makes an effective skater, and I really can't say why some players seem to be better than others. One fellow once told me that because I was bowlegged, turning my skates inward within the width of my shoulders, I had a biomechanical advantage. Other people theorized that being bowlegged might make a player more susceptible to injuries. You can decide which of those two theories, if either, is more realistic, but there is one thing I know for certain. When Wren and Scotty saw me in action, they couldn't have been too impressed with either my size or strength.

Whatever it was the Bruins liked about me, Wren was given the green light by Weston Adams, the owner of the team. And while the Leafs and the Canadiens could afford to focus on bigger things, the Bruins had no such luxury. They were building for the future.

Wren came to Parry Sound to visit with us many times over the next year. Though there was no question of signing any official documents, he got to know my parents pretty well. It was probably no easy matter to get my mother to trust him, but he managed to convince her eventually that he was of good character.

One thing he and the Bruins did to show their goodwill was to sponsor Parry Sound minor hockey for three years, from 1961 to 1964, to the tune of a thousand dollars a year. You might think that three grand doesn't sound like a lot, but back then it was good money for a minor hockey group to get its hands on. That cash represented what would have been the receipts from a lot of bake sales for our local minor hockey association.

Because Wren was traveling a lot as part of his coaching duties, he managed to drop by pretty regularly. On one occasion, as his team was on its way to play in Sudbury, he actually made the bus driver take a detour into Parry Sound just so he could say hello. When Wren finally caught up with me, he found me cleaning floors at the school. Here I was, being courted by the Boston Bruins, and at the same time holding down a part-time job as a janitor. I guess I liked having that spending money.

I've often wondered what the guys on the Kingston team must have thought about the bus having to pull up and wait in Parry Sound. Kind of comical when you think about it—a bunch of pros on their way to play a game and their coach makes them wait while he says hello to a thirteen-year-old kid—but that is exactly what happened. He was a recruiter, and it was typical of Wren. It demonstrates how much he believed in me, and how hard he worked to ensure that I would eventually sign with his Bruins.

He was like a dog with a bone, and no one was going to horn in on his prospect. For a year and a half, those visits never stopped, and we got to know and trust Wren. And the more we thought about the Bruins, the better the idea appealed. If I'd signed with a perennial champion, I would have taken my place at the bottom of a crowded depth chart, and it could have taken me years to claim a spot as a regular on the blue line. The opportunity to get significant playing time would be questionable for any upcoming rookie. But the Bruins were at the opposite end of the spectrum. They were often a last-place team and needed help to get better. We all felt that Boston was the place to go, and in hindsight I can't argue with that decision. And let's not forget—Wren Blair was very persistent.

Eventually, in March of 1962, I hit the magic age of fourteen, an important birthday for prospective players in those days. A player had to be eighteen to sign a C Form, but parents could sign on his behalf once he was fourteen. Signing that deal would mean I was locked up with the Bruins for the duration of my career, at the option of the team, of course. That may sound unfair, particularly by today's standards, when high draft picks sometimes seem to be able to dictate terms to teams. But back then, that's just the way it was. The junior teams were affiliated with the NHL franchises, and scholarships to American universities were not the rival to junior hockey they are today. There was no way around signing a C Form, and in any case, we were happy to do it. After all, it meant being one step closer to the big league.

That summer, Wren came calling once more, and he had an offer. He wanted me to attend a junior camp in Niagara Falls, Ontario, and that was fine with Mom, Dad, and me. It was a weekend in late August that would be attended by both the Oshawa Generals and the Niagara Falls Flyers of the Ontario Hockey Association. Both teams were owned by the Boston Bruins, so the big club could watch a lot of their prospects in one location during the course of the weekend. It was the first step in moving me on to a signed contract with the Bruins.

That camp had a ton of great players who I would see again later in my career, some as teammates and some as opponents. People like Derek Sanderson, Wayne Cashman, Doug Favell, Gilles Marotte, and Bernie Parent were all there. You mention names like those, and you can't help but think that a team with all of that talent would have been pretty tough to play against. It was a big step up from bantam.

I can distinctly remember going into that camp at a weight of 125 pounds soaking wet, and at one point I was asked, along with everyone else, to step on a scale for our weigh-in. When they announced my weight, I could hear chuckles in the background. I guess they thought I was a little small for a defenseman. But I was in my element, and my size, or lack of size, didn't matter in my mind. Was I nervous at that first camp? Yes. Did I know how I would stack up against the competition? No. But I was where I wanted to be, and that was at a rink playing hockey.

I survived my initial test against that caliber of players, and after the camp concluded, Wren came to Parry Sound yet again. It was Labor Day weekend, 1962, and this time he came looking to finalize a deal. Wren wanted my signature on a C Form so I could play for the new Oshawa franchise, which was entering the Metro Junior A League. By signing that piece of paper, I would be committing my future to the Boston Bruins organization, and that was a very big decision.

What Wren didn't realize at the time was that he wouldn't have any trouble convincing Dad or me on the merits of going with the Bruins and playing junior hockey that season. His problem would be my mother. Mom was not willing to let me leave home before I had even completed Grade Eight, and no matter what Wren said, she was not going to budge. As I listened to the negotiations unfold around our kitchen table, my heart sank. I started to realize that this probably wasn't going to happen, and that was tough to swallow. Of course, my mom was absolutely right in her concerns, and eventually everyone involved saw the wisdom of a mother's love.

After much back-and-forth discussion, my dad, the great negotiator, solved the puzzle. Wren wanted me to play hockey in Oshawa but didn't care where I lived. My mother wanted me at home but didn't care where I played hockey. So Dad suggested that I spend the weekdays in Parry Sound, then on Friday, after my school day was finished, we would head to wherever the team was playing. Most of the games in the Metro League were played on Friday, Saturday, and Sunday nights, so my mom could be satisfied that I would be doing my schoolwork, and I would sleep in my own bed most nights. Mom agreed.

Wren got all this down in a handwritten agreement on letterhead from the Brunswick Hotel, where he was staying. It made clear that if I signed with Boston, my mother would have "the Orr house stuccoed" and my father would be provided with a vehicle, "up to a 1956 model, of the father's choice." Plus, we got the grand sum of one thousand dollars in cash. That was a considerable sum of money in 1962.

There was also a small signing bonus for me that Wren agreed to provide: the Bruins had to buy me a new suit. You have to understand, I had never owned a suit before, so this was pretty big news for me. I remember coming home from school, day after day, hoping that the suit would be waiting for me. It was charcoal, and when I finally slipped it on, I felt like the coolest dude in town.

The problem was, though I didn't know it, my new suit didn't fit very well. When I arrived in Oshawa, some of my new teammates with the Generals looked at me the first time I wore it and said, "You have to get that thing altered!" How was I supposed to know how a new suit should fit? In any case, off I went to get it done.

It is amusing to consider the types of bonuses that were paid out back then in order to get a player's signature on paper. It certainly wasn't about the payout for most guys, and it's a good thing, because there simply wasn't much money being thrown around. Imagine one of today's players getting a new suit as a part of his signing bonus.

Apart from the suit and the bonus money, I was guaranteed only one thing. I would get my shot. I had no lock on a job, just an opportunity, and that was all I really wanted. There was no TV coverage when I signed, no fanfare when I arrived in Oshawa. It was all pretty quiet, and that is probably how it should be. In today's game, we tend to anoint players before they play so much as a game as a pro, but in my time things didn't happen that way. Players knew they would have to prove themselves under fire, and no amount of media coverage was going to help you land a spot.

There's a story I have enjoyed sharing over the years about something that happened during my first training camp as a junior player. I was on the ice at the old Children's Arena in Oshawa for what could have been my initial practice with the Generals when my stick broke. I headed over to get a replacement, and when I reached the bench, our trainer, Stan Waylett, checked out what was left of my stick. He looked up at me and asked, "What lie?" I stood there for a minute, thinking about the question. I had absolutely no idea what the guy was talking about. Was he implying I had made up the story about breaking my stick?

It was clearly broken, and he seemed to require an answer of some kind, so, trying to come up with a reasonable response, I blurted out, "Left." Stan must have wondered if the Generals had picked me up after I'd fallen off a turnip truck. He got a good chuckle out of it, anyway. I guess it hadn't taken me long to show I had a lot to learn. (The lie is the angle between the blade and the shaft of a stick, by the way.)

Later that same season, Stan delivered a line I have never forgotten, and it also had something to do with a hockey stick. I had gone to him to complain about some sticks the team had purchased. Once I had finished my little rant, Stan looked me right in the eye and said, "Hey, kid, it's not the gun, it's the gunner." Basically, he wanted to let me know that excuses would not be looked upon kindly and I should just get on with my job. Point made.

The Generals were in their first year in the league, and we actually played our home games at Maple Leaf Gardens. As you can imagine, this kind of schedule meant my family would need some other people to help with driving duties to get me to the games on the weekend. Whenever possible, my dad would drive, but other folks like Bob Holmes or Doug Gignac would bite the bullet and help out. Sometimes Dad simply couldn't make the trip because of work or other commitments, so those gentlemen would help get me to the rink, no matter how far away.

When I look back to some of those trips, I can still visualize that two-lane highway and remember as well the snowstorms we had to endure to get to and from our games. We would leave Friday after school to make the game that night, and I would always have to get back to Parry Sound for Sunday evening, because school was waiting for me on Monday morning. On some of those Mondays, I might be sporting a shiner, or still be feeling a few of the hits I had taken on the weekend. And of course, I can still hear some of the comments my opponents would share with me during those games as well. Hockey players know how to get under each other's skin, and I was a pretty obvious target. They would often remind me to make sure I made it home in time for my Grade Eight classes.

But no amount of chirping or rough stuff was going to change me. Those days represent some of the most exciting moments in my life, because I realized then that I was going to get my shot to play hockey at the highest level. There were no guarantees, and I had no idea if I could cut it, but I was going to get an opportunity, and that was all I wanted. I was anxious for that chance, because when it came to my sport I had a kind of passion that drove me from the very first moments I began to play.

Passion is a key word for any athlete, regardless of the sport. It's important in any profession, for that matter. I'm grateful I had a deep love for the game, and I'm even more thankful that I never lost it. But it wasn't an easy ride. People who look at some athletes and say things like, "It was no problem for him, he's a natural," are way off base. Although all successful athletes certainly have a measure of natural talent, they all have had to put in hour after hour of work in order to bring out their gifts.

Saying that someone is a natural is usually meant as praise, but it is in fact disrespectful to the people who have worked to master any discipline, be it music, literature, medicine, or sports. No one can control what they are born with, but they can control how hard they work. The fact is that talent counts for almost nothing in the absence of hard work. Plenty of gifted athletes never make it. Other guys work their way to the top with very modest gifts. Whether you are talented or not, the only thing that is going to get you where you want to go is hard work.

Of course, the final piece of the puzzle is passion. Without it, the hard work is just too hard. Virtually all of the successful people I have ever met seem to carry that quality with them. I don't care what it is you are pursuing, if you don't have a love for it, I would suggest you should go and try something else, because eventually you will be disappointed. Any skill or skill set is the result of a combination of a couple of things. First, you must have an ability to do it, and second, you must have a willingness to pay the price to perfect it. That is where the passion comes in. At the end of the day, it's difficult for anyone to put in the hours of practice required to succeed at a sport if they don't have an internal drive to commit.

I suppose that whenever you make a run at something in your life, regardless of what that might be, there is a certain degree of selfishness that has to become a part of the quest. Ultimately, your time becomes more and more focused on your goal. If you want to be successful, you also have to be prepared to sacrifice some things as well. Sometimes you forget that not all the sacrifices are your own. Later in your life, you find out what other people were going through while your journey was unfolding.

For example, after my first year with the Generals, when I had moved to Oshawa full-time, I would go home to Parry Sound and visit with my family whenever the team had a day or two off. They were always fun gatherings, and of course questions would be asked about how the team was doing, how I was getting along, and so on. Inevitably, though, I would have to get in a car or jump on a bus and head back to Oshawa.

That was no problem for me, because I was chasing something, and leaving Parry Sound was a part of that pursuit. But what I didn't realize, and what I only found out later in life, was that my departure wasn't as easy for others. As my car would pull away, my mother and sister Pat would stand outside in front of our house and cry. I never knew that at the time. Of course, they never knew that some nights in Oshawa that first year away from home, I would cry myself to sleep as well. You didn't talk about those things, because no hockey player would. You had to learn to handle the loneliness—I signed on for it, because it was the price of pursuing my dream. Everybody paid a price one way or another, but I was paying it for my own benefit. As I see now, my family was paying it, too.

If I told you everything went smoothly that first year in junior hockey, I'd be lying. No fourteen-year-old is going to have an easy time playing against grown men. When I first played for the Generals, I was out there against guys who were bigger than me, faster than me, and more experienced than me. I can tell you, when you really get caught by someone sixty pounds heavier than you, it hurts.

The good thing about competing against older and more mature players is that it makes you pick up your level of play. You have to learn how to sidestep checks, how to shift gears to avoid big collisions. You figure out pretty quickly to keep your head up and not put yourself in vulnerable positions.

You learn those things because you must, in order to survive. And as you do, something strange happens. What I'm about to say might not make a lot of sense to you if you have never competed at a high level in sports. For the highly skilled athlete, the arena becomes a place of comfort. Whether it is a hockey arena, football stadium, or basketball court, many athletes come to feel most comfortable where they do what they do best.

You might imagine a young player trying to cut his teeth at a higher level could get so nervous he couldn't play to his potential. The reality is very different. At least, it was for me. Being nervous before a game is only natural and probably a good thing, because it means you are getting ready to play. Once I got on the ice, however, and the puck was dropped to start the game, I would calm down and everything made sense. I could almost feel a kind of peace come over me. I was in my element. You get to a place that sports psychologists have identified as the "comfort zone." Getting there allows you to play your game at your particular level.

All the practice and training athletes go through over years of playing their sport helps to combat feelings of pressure or fear. I have been told by friends and family members that at certain points watching a crucial game, many of them had to turn their heads away from the TV. They found it that difficult to deal with the tension. But for a player, those are the moments you live for. It's not really all that hard to understand. Although the stakes may be high when you're in the middle of a game, you're in control. You're doing the thing you're good at, the thing you have trained to do and love to do. It may look nerve-racking to an outsider, but that is only because he or she hasn't trained for years, day in and day out, to do the things a player is called on to do during the course of a game.

Those were the times when I most wanted to be on the ice and have the puck on my stick. I can't speak for other athletes, but that is how I felt. Even during that initial junior season with the Generals, when I was overmatched physically, I still felt comfortable on the ice. I may not have been in control of my life off the ice, where, after all, I was just a shy, skinny kid far from home. But on the ice, I was somewhere familiar where I could control what happened. As a result, that whole first year with Oshawa was a great learning experience for me. It went a long way toward building my confidence that I could compete, and maybe even excel, with players at that level.

After my rookie junior season was over, it was decided that I could handle the grind of Junior A hockey. My mother gave her blessing, and I moved to Oshawa in the fall of 1963. I started secondary school at O'Neill Collegiate and Vocational Institute, but not long into that first year I transferred and eventually settled into R. S. McLaughlin Collegiate. The reason for that move was the programming at O'Neill. In those days, it was a particularly academic school and had programs for things such as the performing arts and for gifted students—programs I was probably not able to handle. I was not a gifted student.

The reality is that I was never very fond of high school, though I understood the importance of education. I just figured that the arena would be the principal place of learning for me, not a classroom. I had a responsibility to go to school, however, and so I attended regularly and gave it the old college try. That was expected of all the players on the team—and it was most certainly expected by my mother. My grades were never top of the class, but I kept up, did my homework, and got by just fine. I never did finish high school, because down the road something else would get in the way.

The first priority we needed to take care of as I left Parry Sound and headed to Oshawa was finding a place for me to stay. I moved in as a boarder with a family, just as most junior players did and still do to this day. In my case, that meant a bedroom in the big house of Bob and Bernice "Bernie" Ellesmere on Nassau Street in Oshawa. They also boarded another Generals player, Mike Dubeau, and we would have some great times together, both as teammates and roommates, during that first year in Oshawa.

Mike came from Penetanguishene, Ontario, which wasn't very far from Parry Sound. He was two years older than me. Thinking of Mike brings to mind a particular episode we shared during our stay with the Ellesmeres. As a seventeen-year-old, Mike found himself quite in love with a girl from his hometown, which meant that the courting process was often done long-distance. Mike could never wait to get back home during the season to see his girl, Carol. Sometimes that desire got us into trouble.

Every once in a while, whenever we had a stretch of days when the Generals weren't playing or practicing, we would hitchhike back to our hometowns. The two of us would stand out there by the side of the road, thumbs boldly sticking out, and sooner or later someone would stop and give us a lift along Highway 401. We would eventually get to the 400 and head north together for an hour or so until Mike had to hop out to catch a ride west to his hometown of Penetanguishene, while I would keep heading north on Highway 69 until I hit Parry Sound. In those days, hitchhiking was an accepted way of getting around, and no one gave the practice much thought.

One particular hitchhiking caper stands out in my mind, because it ended differently from the others. It was a Friday night after we had just finished playing a game in Niagara Falls, and things had not gone well on the ice. In fact, the team was on a bit of a slide, and our shoddy play in the Falls apparently really irritated our GM, Wren Blair (who had left the Kingston Frontenacs and taken over in Oshawa). He was so disgusted with our effort that nobody was allowed to go home. That was tough punishment for a bunch of homesick teenagers, because there were no games or practices scheduled that weekend. We were about to have a lot of time on our hands but had been sentenced to house arrest.

It was probably 1 A.M. by the time our bus pulled back into Oshawa that night, and maybe another half hour until we got back to the Ellesmeres' and the comfort of our beds. Mike and I shared a room with bunk beds in those days. Mike had claimed the bottom bunk because he was older and had seniority. For many players, it isn't always easy to get to sleep after a game, and you often end up replaying it in your head. When you have a roommate, it might also mean talking, not only about the game but about other important things as well.

This particular night, hockey wasn't the only thing on my mind, as I was feeling a little bit homesick for Parry Sound. And I knew that the old love bug was biting at Mike as usual. Wren's punishment loomed over us, but I simply couldn't resist tempting the poor guy. I leaned over the edge of my bunk and whispered, "Hey, Mike … you want to go home?"

Before I had even finished the question, Mike had sprung out of bed and said, "Let's go!" Our adventure was on. We actually got Bob Ellesmere out of bed and had him drive us down to the highway, where our trip home was to begin in earnest. I wonder if Bob ever got in trouble with Bernie for that bit of chauffeuring. I wonder if she ever even knew why he got out of bed at close to two in the morning. Regardless, we eventually found ourselves on the side of the road, each with a bag and an outstretched thumb, looking for a ride. As fate would have it, our wait was brief, because the very first car stopped and picked us up.

The driver was on his way to Barrie, so luck had dealt us a good hand. I don't know what time Mike got to Penetanguishene, but I arrived at 24 Great North Road around 9 or 10 A.M., and my mother was shocked to see me. When she learned what we had done, she was beside herself, and made me promise to take a bus back for the return trip. But I had other things to think about. I was soon off to see my buddies and catch up on all the local news. Plus, my older brother, Ron, was playing Junior C hockey in Parry Sound, and his team was scheduled to play a home game that weekend. Naturally, I wanted to head over to the rink and watch my big brother in action.

This is where things got quite interesting and our little scam came back to haunt me. As I sat watching my brother play, who do you think was sitting in the stands scouting the game for the Oshawa Generals? It was our general manager, Wren Blair, the same man who had hours earlier forbidden us from leaving Oshawa under any circumstances. I caught it pretty good for that little bit of poor judgment. I never ratted on my roomie, although I'm sure Wren had it all figured out. It was an experience Mike and I have relived many times and laugh about even to this day. It is worth noting that those trips Mike took back home whenever he could eventually paid off for him in a big way. About eight years later, I would serve as best man at his wedding to Carol, and they have been happily married all these years.

The team had billeted me with the Ellesmere family because their home was situated close to O'Neill high school, where I started out in Grade Nine. When I made the switch in schools that first year, it led to a bit of a transportation problem. Going to my new school, R. S. McLaughlin, meant I would have to find some form of ride to and from classes every day, because McLaughlin was a hefty distance from the Ellesmeres' house.

The obvious solution was for me to take the bus back and forth every day. But if people think I am shy and reserved as an adult, I must tell you that as a fifteen-year-old, I was even more retiring. Talking to strangers was difficult, and riding a city bus became very uncomfortable for me. Sometimes I'd get a ride from the Ellesmeres or guys on the team, but I usually ended up walking the three kilometers each way.

As I began my third year as a player with the Generals, and my second year as a boarder in Oshawa, we all decided it would be best if I changed houses so I could be closer to my chosen high school. As a result, my new parents away from home became Jack and Cora Wilde, and that move to the Wilde house also meant I would have a new roommate. Again, hockey is a small world. Amazingly enough, one of the original members of our pack of wolves from back in my minor hockey days ended up becoming a teammate in Oshawa. Jim Whittaker from Parry Sound would become my new roommate.

It is hard to exaggerate how much this meant to a couple of homesick kids from the same town. Hockey players are supposed to be tough guys who will go into corners against bigger opponents, play with injuries, show no fear. It is easy to look at a young boy who might be big and physically more mature than other kids his age and imagine he is more grown up, too. He might look like a man on the outside, but inside he is still just a sixteen-year-old kid. Coaches and fans sometimes need to remember that.

I can tell you, some players don't move up the hockey ladder not because they don't have the talent or character for the game. Some of them don't get through because they just get homesick. I would imagine that most successful junior organizations today are more aware of that fact and more responsive to players in that regard. The people who run those teams need to have strategies for these types of issues, since you don't want to end up losing a player because he would rather be at home. In the case of a junior player, it is a lot to ask of a sixteen-year-old boy, his parents, and everyone else involved, to have him pack up and leave for a new home. But that is the formula for most hockey players who have serious aspirations for the National Hockey League, and it hasn't changed in a very long time. I don't see that formula changing anytime in the near future, either.

There is one important saving grace for the player in all of this. When you join a team away from home, there is an almost instant bond with your new teammates. They become, by necessity, your new pack of wolves. Those new friends help get you through the early rough patches. That Jim Whittaker was a member of the old pack as well as the new one made life a lot easier for both of us.

At the time, we both thought our billets were far too tough on us. If either of us ever missed a curfew, Jack or Cora would immediately call our coach and report us. We felt that was a little harsh, but looking back I realize it was the best thing they could have done for us. They took their responsibility as billets very seriously, which is exactly the way it should be.

The first season I lived in Oshawa, the Generals played primarily out of a small rink in Bowmanville. We were waiting for the new Oshawa Civic Auditorium to be completed, which it was in December 1964. I would play the remainder of my junior career with the Generals in that facility on some very productive teams. During my time in Oshawa, I was pretty oblivious to all the hype that had started to swirl around me.

All I really cared about was my goal as a hockey player—that was where my attention was focused. I just wanted to play good hockey. If I needed some space to get away from everything, there were always places to go, but at that time in my career, privacy was no big deal. If someone recognized me and wanted an autograph, it was no problem—kind of fun, actually. Of course, with time and more celebrity, I would come to appreciate the privacy I'd had in the past. But as a member of the Generals and throughout my junior career, I never gave the idea of stardom a lot of thought. If it happened, I would handle it, and if it didn't, no problem.

We had some wonderful characters in Oshawa, and some of my teammates became lifelong friends. Because we were all Bruins property, I would end up playing with some of those same players in Boston, including people like Wayne Cashman, Nick Beverley, and Barry Wilkins, among others. Some teammates, such as Jimmy Peters, wouldn't get to the Bruins, but Jim would go on to have a very successful career in Oshawa with General Motors of Canada. He was a teammate in 1962, yet over all of these years we have stayed in touch and remained friends. That is one of the great things about sport in general, especially team sports. Friendships you make along the way often turn into lasting relationships and a link to the past. Jimmy has always been, and always will be, a great friend, and it all began as teammates in Oshawa.

I was extremely fortunate to be with a really good group of guys on that team. Every step of the way, they looked after me, especially the older players, although there weren't many veterans that first year with the Generals. Because we were a new team in the league, we were made up of a pretty young bunch of guys. We were just like any other group of kids our age, with perhaps one big exception. Everybody on that team believed he was getting closer to his objective of reaching the next level in hockey. Most of us, probably unlike other kids our age, were very focused on the course our lives would take. For many teenagers, that's not the case. There comes a time when many kids in their teens kind of slip into neutral. By that I mean they have no idea what they are going to do with their lives. It can be a troubling time, a time of uncertainty.

But I never really went through that phase, because I always knew where I was going to be, or at least I always knew where I *wanted* to be. I had a specific goal and was very dedicated to achieving that goal. In my case, the time of uncertainty wouldn't be in my teens but rather as a thirty-year-old man, when my goals suddenly slipped through my fingers. I guess, sooner or later, at some time or another, everyone faces their own moment of uncertainty.

Some players don't avoid it for long. It is a reality of junior hockey that as the seasons pass, some players will start to realize they are not going to make it in the game. Their dream of the NHL takes a hit, and it begins to lose its pull. If you aren't careful, it is easy to get pulled off track, too, if those players start to lose focus. They have nothing to lose and can get into all kinds of mischief. If you don't watch out, you can get dragged into some of that. Maintaining your commitment is extremely important at such times for any player who has the skills to make it to the next level. Keeping the end goal in mind is vital—and not always easy for a teenager. I was lucky to have had the teammates I did.

In fact, I was surrounded by some great people in Oshawa. We freely give credit to our coaches for their help, and they are certainly deserving of our thanks. But they aren't the only ones who chip in when it comes to developing a young person who is trying to make it in the sports world. There are many others who play important roles, such as our trainers, the guidance counselors at school, or the teachers who go the extra mile to help make up missed schoolwork. For me, it was people like Bill Corella, who managed the arena in Oshawa. I couldn't wait to get to the rink every day after school for practice, and so my routine was to get there as quickly as I could. Bill would open up the facility and turn on the lights for me and anyone else who showed up early so we could get in some extra skating time. We loved the game so much we would hurry to the rink just to have fun. Some afternoons I would strap on the pads and play net—and I learned pretty quickly that was not the position for me. It's not a bad idea to be on the good side of the person who runs the arena.

Then there was Joe Bolahood, who owned a sporting goods store in town. Often on a Saturday afternoon, some of the Generals players would head over to his store and, with Joe's blessing, try on all the brand-new hockey equipment. It was always a special feeling to see and then be able to put on the newest types of equipment available. You could grab a stick, lean on it, and see what kind of flex you could expect in the current models. It was downtime for us, and maybe a bit of team-building time as well. People like Joe helped facilitate that. There was a little restaurant next door to his store, and sometimes a bunch of us would slide over and have a hamburger and fries if somebody had money in his pocket.

But it's not just Bill and Joe, not just the Ellesmeres and Wildes, not just hockey people like Stan Waylett and Wren Blair. When you're part of a team, and part of a community, you're surrounded by people helping out in small ways, making things a little easier, maybe offering encouragement in ways they hardly even pause to think about. You can never thank everyone, but I know how much the people around me contributed to my well-being and success at different times and in different ways.

J ust before I was scheduled to begin playing my fourth and final season for the Generals, my dad decided I wasn't being properly compensated. He got it in his mind that it was time for the Generals to contribute their fair share for gas money and other expenses. If memory serves me correctly, I think we received ten or twelve bucks in pocket money per week. Dad was probably holding poor Wren hostage for about another two bucks.

It was a Friday night, and we were scheduled to open our season that evening, but I had not yet signed my player's card. The rule was pretty simple: if you weren't signed to a card by the time the season started, you simply could not play. I was extremely nervous as I headed to the rink, because I wanted to start that year on time with my teammates, and it wasn't looking good. When I arrived, I went to the dressing room and sat in my stall. My seat was very close to the general manager's office door, and I was getting increasingly anxious as game time approached.

Top: *My father, Doug Orr, on leave during his navy days in World War II. He is second from left. He was very proud to serve.*

Above: *My father and my mother, Arva. I couldn't have asked for better parents.*

Right: *My father always had a smile on his face.*

This is a page right out of our family photo album.

Top left: *That's me as a baby.*

Top right: *That's me on the left with my brother, Ron, and my sister, Pat.*

Bottom left: *Here I am at eighteen at the house on Great North Road, back from Boston and my rookie year with the Bruins.*

Bottom right: *That's my brother, Ron, on the left and me on the right.*

Above: *My brother, Ron, and me (I'm on the far left, and Ron is beside me) with a couple of my buddies on River Street in Parry Sound.*

Right: *My portrait from Victory Elementary School in 1958. I was ten years old.*

Below: *A recent photo of the house on Great North Road. That's the garage where I practiced my shot.*

Above: *From the right, that's my cousin Bruce Abbott, my brother, Ron, Grandma Orr, me, and my cousin Kelly Orr. The Generals were in town for an exhibition game against my brother's team, the Junior C Parry Sound Brunswicks.*

Right: *That's me with Syl Apps. His Scarborough team beat us in a tournament. Do I look like someone who has just lost a big game? We had so much fun traveling and playing hockey that we had a blast even losing.*

Above: *My turn to clean the frying pans after cooking our catch.*

Left: *Me with a couple of speckled trout after my first season in Boston.*

Below: *Enjoying summer in Muskoka.*

Top: *That's me in the front, holding the trophy, with the 1962 fire department midget team. It is probably pretty obvious from how young I look that I was playing up a division. The guy at the very top, on the right, is Jimmy Whittaker, who would be my roommate in Oshawa. The guy to his right is Roddy Bloomfield, who would be Paul Newman's double in* SlapShot. *Front row, second from the left, is Neil Clairmont.*

Above: *Me with Anthony Gilchrist, Bucko MacDonald, and Ivan Nicksy, who was a director of the Parry Sound minor hockey association. I learned a lot from my coaches in Parry Sound, but the most important thing they did for the kids was let us have fun.*

Above: *My student card from Grade 11 in Oshawa.*

Left: *Posing in my brand-new Oshawa Generals team sweater.*

Above: *That's me lined up with Ian Young. He was a great goalie and would have played in the NHL, but suffered an eye injury in junior.*

Right: *My last year in Oshawa.*

Suddenly the door opened and out came Wren, shouting, "Come in here!" He ushered me into his office, stuck out a card, and said, "Sign this thing." Wren knew when to use charm, but he could be forceful, too. My first and only holdout had come to an end. I did what I was told, and my final junior season started up on schedule after all. To the best of my knowledge, Dad never did get that extra few bucks out of Wren. I was just glad to get on with the business of playing hockey. It would be my last season as a General, and it would be a memorable one.

Like all seasons in sport, my fourth and final year in Oshawa would have some highs mixed with some lows. The highs can be found in our team record and the fact that we had a championship-caliber group. The low for me would be the way in which our season ended. It was difficult for me to swallow, both from a team perspective and personally. We had assembled a pretty solid combination of youngsters and veterans, and as the playoffs approached I sensed we would have a shot at a long run, despite having finished fourth in the league. We won the Ontario Hockey Association (now the Ontario Hockey League) championship by beating some good teams in the playoffs, including a great Montreal Junior Canadiens team that featured the likes of Jacques Lemaire, Serge Savard, and Carol Vadnais. That is a pretty solid talent base for one junior roster. And who do you think was coaching that particular team? None other than Scotty Bowman. It seemed like some kind of hockey destiny that our paths would cross again. And it wouldn't be the last time we would square off in a hockey arena.

After Montreal, we followed up with a round against the representatives from the Northern Ontario Junior Hockey League, North Bay, and managed to win that matchup as well. That put us into the Eastern Canada championship against the Shawinigan

Bruins out of Quebec, another tough series, which we also won. All of those rounds led us to the place we had dreamed of getting to, the Memorial Cup championship for junior hockey supremacy in Canada. Back then, it wasn't a round-robin tournament. It was a seven-game showdown between the eastern and western representatives. That year, we came out of the east, and the western representatives were the Edmonton Oil Kings.

The Kings were a great team—it seemed they represented the west in the Memorial Cup just about every year—and had been bolstered by the addition of some key players, such as Ross Lonsberry and Ted Hodgson, right before the series began. A future Boston Bruins teammate, Garnet "Ace" Bailey, was on that team as well. The series was to be played at Maple Leaf Gardens, and the stage was set. Except for one thing. At some point, either near the end of the Shawinigan series or during a practice leading up to the Memorial Cup, I had pulled a groin muscle. It was a serious injury in that it severely restricted my ability to skate. If you have ever suffered through that kind of muscle strain, you know how painful it can be. The only real way to fix it is with extended rest—something that was not an option. It was nothing that would affect me long term. It just hurt a lot. In the short term, however, that kind of injury meant that the Memorial Cup would end up being a very difficult series for me. I had my fair share of injuries throughout my career, but the timing of that particular injury has always baffled me.

Normally, groin problems tend to happen early in a hockey season, perhaps during training camp, as the muscles try to get accustomed to the workload of a new year. I had never experienced that kind of injury and discomfort so late in a hockey season. It was just a piece of bad luck, and that can happen to any athlete at any time, especially when your sport involves a lot of stretching, reaching, and contact. There was nothing I could do about it except try to convince myself that it didn't hurt.

When Mr. Emms, the GM of the Bruins, caught wind of the problem, he told my father he was not going to allow me to play in the Memorial Cup final series at all. There were more important things at stake down the road in Boston, according to him. He didn't want anyone coming to training camp as damaged goods. He wanted to protect his investment. But my father knew better. After my future boss informed my dad of his prohibition, my father looked at him and said, "I don't know about that one, Mr. Emms." My dad was right. There was no way I wasn't going to suit up.

I had spent four years of my junior career trying to get to this point. I was the captain of the team, and even if I had to head over the boards with only one good leg, I was determined to try it. Bep Guidolin, our coach, was caught in the middle. He was employed by the Bruins, so when the boss said not to play someone, I suppose he had good reason to do as he was told. On the other hand, he was the coach of a team in the Memorial Cup. If he thought I could help the team win, it was his job to put me out there. But neither Bep nor Mr. Emms nor anyone else was going to keep me out of the lineup, so he really had no choice other than to put me on the roster.

Allowing me to play probably cost Bep his job eventually. The injury restricted my ability to move to the point where I really couldn't contribute the way I wanted to in that series. We eventually lost in six games. Though we were all disappointed not to have been able to bring that trophy back to Oshawa, it was a great learning experience in high-level playoff hockey. That experience would come in handy down the road during my hockey career.

By the time I finished my fourth year of junior hockey, in the spring of 1966, I had turned eighteen. It was traditional in those days that pro teams would bring prospects at that age to their first pro camp, and so it was with the Bruins and me. In my four years as a member of the Oshawa Generals, I had gained several inches and added some much-needed muscle. Perhaps most importantly, another benefit of my stay in Oshawa was that it had given me the confidence that I could play with the big boys.

Some players, and often their parents as well, seem in a hurry to get to the National Hockey League, even if a little seasoning in junior hockey or the minors might be better for the player in the long run. Some guys step right out of junior and light up the NHL in their rookie season, though they are few and far between. Others, even very high draft picks, take years to develop. Others still, also very high picks, fail completely. If you are a kid who has dominated his peers since playing atom, it can be a real shock to find yourself playing against guys bigger, tougher, and craftier than you. You may not be getting time on the power play or the penalty kill, and you might find yourself sitting on the bench more than you ever have. And you're probably not going to like it. Sometimes, it's just better to slow down the process and develop properly. There is no rush.

I was one of those players who was ready for the move into pro hockey at eighteen, but many more are not. Getting as much seasoning as possible is a smart way to prepare a young athlete for the highest levels of the game. After all, professional athletics is a marathon, not a sprint.

Still, while I was ready for pro hockey from a skill perspective, I have often wondered if one of the reasons I suffered so many knee injuries as a pro was because I started playing against men at such a young age. All the contact against bigger opponents might have caused excessive wear and tear. Add to that the beating my body took as a little fourteen-year-old when I started junior hockey, and it leads you to wonder if I might have avoided some of my injuries if I'd started out along my junior path a year or two later.

But sometimes an athlete has to be moved along in order to be challenged. No one wants to play bantam hockey if he can play junior. No one is going to stick around in junior if there is a roster spot waiting for him in the NHL. I am not the only kid who has been in a hurry to fulfill a dream. In some rare cases, it simply doesn't make sense to hold a player back just because of age. But that decision will not be made by Mom or Dad or the player. It will inevitably be made by the team that holds his rights.

Ready or not, my junior career with the Generals was over. The training I had experienced in Oshawa set me up for the next phase of my hockey life. Four years had gone by in a hurry. Now, it was on to Boston to try to earn a spot in the NHL. My dream was that Boston would become my new home for what would hopefully be a long professional career.

Four

A ROOKIE IN BOSTON: 1966–1967

I never thought there was any guarantee I would play professional hockey. In my own mind, it was never a lock. There is a depressingly long list of highly touted junior players who never make an impact in the NHL, just as some of the very best players were late-round picks, or were even undrafted. Both the unexpected failures and unexpected successes show that scouts' opinions depend on a considerable amount of guesswork. I knew enough then to know that those people who were expecting so much from me could have been wrong. It was up to me to prove them right. I figured I had served my apprenticeship in junior and that the time had come to move on. But that just meant I had an opportunity to earn a job. It didn't mean there was one waiting for me.

I signed my first professional contract in the summer of 1966. I was aboard a cabin cruiser belonging to Bruins GM Hap Emms, on

Lake Simcoe, near Barrie, Ontario. My parents had hired an agent to handle my finances and negotiate that deal, and he was there to preside over the signing to officially launch my professional career. I had known that the day was coming, as I had signed a C Form years before and the Bruins were the only team I could play for. But it was still quite a thrill to get my name on a contract, and I can't say I was disappointed by the salary I would be earning if I made the team: $25,000 as a base salary for two years, plus bonuses for games played (not a suit this time). It was more money than I'd ever seen.

That fall, I attended my initial NHL training camp with the Bruins. Many NHL teams in those days held training camp in cities away from home. In 1966, the Bruins camp was in London, Ontario, at the old Treasure Island rink. At the time, it was the home of the London Nationals of the OHA, now the London Knights of the OHL.

I can remember the anticipation I felt as I headed down Highway 401 toward London and that training camp. An athlete in any sport will experience a variety of feelings when he or she is about to be put to the test. I was about to find myself among the best men of my profession. I was about to enter into a world of people I had read about in the papers, seen on television—in some cases, these were guys I regarded as heroes.

I didn't know what was about to happen. I had been to training camps before, but never a pro camp. I had played the game at a pretty high level, but not the highest. I was still not a match physically for a lot of the people I would be playing against—when I was eighteen, I was still just five feet eleven and 165 pounds. But those junior training camps had at least given me an idea of what was to come, so I had that going for me. I was braced for it. I knew I would be tested along with all the other rookies, just as I'd been tested as a fourteen-year-old trying to make my first junior team in Oshawa. Yes, the talent level would be different, but the process would probably be similar. Certainly, that was what I kept telling myself.

I believed I was far from a shoo-in to make the team, and I didn't have a clue what awaited me if I didn't make the NHL roster. Times were different back then, and players weren't in control of their careers the way kids are now. We didn't understand the way the business worked, because we had little reason to. I didn't know if I could be assigned to one of the Bruins' minor-league teams as an eighteen-year-old, or even where all their farm teams were. I knew that management could always send me back to Oshawa, but I had little interest in spending a fifth year in junior. I knew what I wanted. I went into camp without much of a plan beyond doing whatever it took to stick with the team.

I was in great shape that August. Maybe not the kind of game-ready shape today's players maintain nearly twelve months of the year, but I had spent the summer with training camp in mind. I remember jogging in work boots to build up my leg strength and cardio. Sometimes I'd get on a bike and do some cycling as well, and I don't know how many sit-ups I did (no one called it "working the core" back then). I also used a homemade contraption I developed for strengthening my wrists and forearms. It was a brick attached to a rope, which I tied to a short section of an old broom handle. I would grip the broom handle, hold my arms straight out, and roll that brick up to the top, then unroll it back down. I knew I had to get stronger if I was going to have a chance in the NHL.

I also had a workout bench where I did a few presses and curls. It was always light weight and high repetition. That was about it for my workouts. Most current NHL players take their gym work very seriously—my sessions in the summer of 1966 must look pretty relaxed by today's standards. But those were the times, and that was the way I did things.

As I made my way off the Wellington Street exit ramp into London, it was too late to worry about what I had done to prepare. Whatever work I'd put in would have to do. I was absolutely focused on my first pro training camp, and nothing else really mattered.

My immediate concern was to find the team hotel. I checked in, received my key, and made my way to my room. When I opened the door, there, stretched out before me, resting on his bed and smoking a cigar, was the man who would be my first roommate. I recognized who it was right away. He was the captain of the Boston Bruins, Johnny Bucyk. I walked over to him, stuck out my hand, and said, "Hello, Mr. Bucyk, pleasure to meet you. I'm Bobby Orr."

He looked back at me, gave me that big grin of his, stuck out his hand, and said, "Well, from now on it's Johnny, or Chief, okay?" and that was the beginning of a great friendship. He was low key, considerate, very even-keeled, and he looked after me and many other rookies as well. He made me laugh—something that anyone in a pressure situation will appreciate. We talked often during that first camp, and his words meant a lot to me then, just as they do now. Johnny was a great help to me in making that transition from junior hockey to the pros.

You couldn't have had a finer person as captain than the Chief. He was not a big speechmaker, but he came to work every day and set the standard with his level of play. He always set the bar high for us, and it made you want to follow suit and set your own example for others. Much like my parents, Johnny let his actions do the talking for him. There can be no doubt that his leadership was a key part of the success the Bruins would enjoy in the years that followed.

How he and the other veterans received me was very important, because I immediately felt comfortable in my surroundings, due in great part to their help. Here was a rookie who could possibly end up taking one of their spots in the lineup, yet the veterans welcomed me and almost immediately made me feel like part of the group. The hard reality was that my job was to earn a spot on the team, and their job was to keep the spot they had already won. One guy's victory would be another guy's loss. That is the very basis of pro sport, tough as it may sound. But it's not personal, and no one ever held it against me that I was there to take someone's job.

We used to do a little stretching in the hallway before we skated, and many times a veteran would come over and say a few words of encouragement to me as we got ready for battle. Or someone might give me a tap on the shin pads and wish me good luck.

Of course, the veterans can always read if a rookie comes to camp as a cocky kid, and that can hurt you. If I had been a wise guy, I don't know what the veterans would have done. If they sense that kind of attitude, you can be left behind, but fortunately for me the vets on the Bruins always made me feel included.

In those days, training camp could last upwards of a month—a lot longer than they do today. Many of the vets would arrive in far from peak condition, and they used camp to get back in shape. Remember, a lot of these guys held down blue-collar jobs over the summer. There was no way they had the time to stay in top athletic shape. That's the way it was back then. And let me tell you, the first few days of stops and starts and blue-red-blues were tough.

We wouldn't play any actual games against other teams for perhaps the first two weeks after we'd arrived, except for some intra-squad scrimmages. This meant there was plenty of time to wonder whether you were impressing the brass during practice sessions. Eventually, we played a series of exhibition games in cities across Ontario, places like London, Kitchener, Peterborough, and Hamilton.

As those games piled up, I began to get more and more comfortable playing at the professional level. I had probably started out a bit skittish, but after a few games I knew I was holding on to the puck a bit longer, and maybe trying to beat a guy or make a play I wouldn't have tackled even a few days before. And if a skirmish ever broke out during our exhibition games, I knew that the vets were there if I needed any help. It was comforting to know they had your back.

All the same, I never assumed I was good enough to play. That's not false modesty. That's just the way it was, and the way it had been each step of the way. Like my dad had said so many years before, "Just go out, have fun, and let's see what happens." That was the attitude I took with me to that first camp, and it was the approach that stayed with me throughout my career.

Of course, as training camp wore on, I couldn't help but think about where I was going to end up that season. Toward the end of camp, one at a time, players would be called into the room where general manager Hap Emms and head coach Harry Sinden had established their headquarters. Guys would emerge with their faces betraying the news they had just received. Some were headed to Boston, others back to the minors. Truth be told, though, most players, if they are honest with themselves, have a pretty good idea whether they have the talent to stay at that level. My time was coming, I knew it, and I felt I had a chance.

Finally, my name was called, and I headed in for my own

meeting with Mr. Emms and Harry. That is a tough moment for any young player trying to make it, because you never know if you've done enough. The reality of the NHL in the mid-1960s was that veterans virtually had a lock on their jobs, so beating one out for a roster spot was no easy task. As I walked into the room, I could see Hap seated at his desk. After I sat down on a chair in front of him, he slowly looked up at me, and in a very matter-of-fact tone said, "You'll be heading back with us to Boston to finish training camp." It's funny. All those years of work, and it all comes down to a few words.

Yet, when I left the room, I still didn't know if I had made it. I was relieved, of course. Not being cut was exactly what I had hoped for. I had my chance to make the big club, but there was no guarantee, even at that point. All I knew was I had stepped up another rung on the ladder that would get me to the Boston Garden as a member of the Bruins.

I had many doubts during that entire training camp process, and there is no question in my mind that a little fear can be a very powerful motivator. Many successful people I've met have expressed having a fear of failure, or perhaps a fear of not really belonging to a group or team. Part of that fear is being aware that your job is on the line. There was a certain confidence inside me, yes, but there was always doubt as well. Professional sport is no easy life, and having a healthy portion of fear probably helped push me toward success.

The remainder of that first training camp went smoothly after we returned to Boston. With each passing day, it became clearer and clearer to me that I could hold my own with the big boys, and I believed I could compete at the NHL level. I wasn't dominating anybody on the ice, but I was holding my own.

When it came time to finalize the roster for opening night, everyone was on pins and needles. We all wanted to be in the lineup, and there were more players than roster spots. We could only dress seventeen players and two goalies. Someone was going to be disappointed.

E ventually, it was time to get down to business as we prepared for our regular-season debut against the Detroit Red Wings. My father had made the trip to Boston with some of his buddies, and having Dad there meant a lot to me. He would end up being with me for some of the greatest times in my career. The Boston fans were hungry for a new era to begin for this particular Bruins team.

I was so excited, I arrived just after lunchtime for the 7:30 game. When I walked into the dressing room that day, I was looking for something very important. Back then there were no limits on the number of players a team could carry. Especially early in the season, we found out whether we were playing when we walked into the dressing room and saw if the trainer had hung up our sweater. If you didn't see your number, you were watching from the stands.

And there it was. My sweater (no one called them jerseys) hanging there in my stall. If I remember correctly, I had worn several numbers, including 27 and 30, as well as number 4 for some of the intra-squad and exhibition games during training camp. Back then, there were no names on the sweaters, just the team logo on the front and a number on the back. The number on mine was 4.

I hadn't asked for that particular number. At that time in the league, a rookie wouldn't have thought of requesting a specific number. You were just relieved to have received a sweater with any number on it at all. I had worn number 2 throughout minor hockey and junior, but when they assigned me number 4, I was more than happy to have it. Besides, my old number 2 was not available, because it had been worn by the legendary Bruin Eddie Shore and was now hanging in the Garden rafters in retirement. The season before, 1965–66, number 4 had been worn by Al Langlois, but he was no longer with the organization, so it was available. And that is what someone told the trainer to hang in my stall. I suppose there is a pleasing rhyme between *four* and *Orr*, and it is all the more pleasing in a Boston accent. But trust me, matching that number with my last name was not a plan of mine. I would have worn whatever number they gave me.

That first league game in the NHL was a thrill for me for a number of reasons, not least because I knew I would be squaring off against the guy who wore number 9 for Detroit. It would be impossible to exaggerate the admiration I had (and still have) for Gordie Howe. Everyone coming into the league has to deal with the strange reality of playing with and against guys he grew up admiring, but I had the challenge of doing it in my first game, against the player I think is the best to have ever played.

During that first game, I got into it a bit with my hero. It seems I'd made a couple of mistakes early in the game. The first, as he later told me, was that I'd got my elbow a little high on him (though I like to think I was smarter than that, and that Gordie must have fingered the wrong guy). The second was that I later spent a split second admiring a pass I'd made to a teammate as I cruised into the offensive zone. One moment I was looking at the puck, and the next I was lying on the ice, the victim of a classic Gordie Howe elbow. Mr. Hockey was towering over me, staring down with what can only be described as a stern glare. I understood the message loud and clear: Gordie wanted the rookie to know who the boss was. Five years earlier in Parry Sound, he had warned me to watch out for his elbows after I got to the league. Turns out he hadn't been kidding.

I was a rookie, so in an instant I had several teammates come to my defense. There I was, at the bottom of a scrum, feeling the consequences of my first encounter with one of the fiercest competitors in the game. It wasn't that I thought Howe was a great guy for flattening me. But it also wasn't as though I hadn't asked for it. He was just paying me back, with a bit of interest. So, as I looked up through a maze of legs and arms, I blurted out to my fellow Bruins something to the effect of, "It's okay, guys, I deserved that."

That was the end of the hostilities, and I like to think I gained a measure of respect from Gordie in the process. Those types of things happened often in the old NHL, and I believe it speaks to the respect players had for each other. There were lines you just didn't cross.

Not that I felt Gordie was off limits after that. Later in the game, I got into another minor tiff with him, as did my defensive partner, Gilles Marotte. We both took a bit of a run at him, and I guess Gordie felt he had to deliver his earlier warning again, and perhaps a bit more forcefully. Now, I have always been a firm believer that you should never back down. Backing down only makes it worse. But that night I couldn't think of anything much worse than dropping the gloves with Gordie Howe. At the end of that shift, I looked over my shoulder, and there was Gordie, looming up behind us, looking even more menacing than before and offering us a few choice words. I looked at Gilles and said, "Just keep going ... *get to the bench.*"

I ran into Gordie a few times that first game, and many more times over the years. I don't think anyone ever enjoyed playing against him. He could beat you with skill, he could beat you with brute strength, and that neighborly smile hid a truly terrifying ferocity. But I have wonderful memories of Mr. Hockey, and he remains at the top of my list as the best who ever played the game.

That first game was a victory for us, and I had an assist for my first point in the NHL. The newspaper people wrote it up like it was the greatest assist ever seen in the Boston Garden. I think I was just trying to get a shot on net and ended up accomplishing little more than shoveling the puck toward the goalie. I was lucky that someone was there to jam the loose puck home for a goal. In reality it wasn't much of a play. However it happened, I was happy to have my first NHL point and to get a win.

My first goal came a few nights later, again in Boston. Toward the end of the game, I got a point shot past the Montreal Canadiens' Gump Worsley to tie the game. As a rule, I don't talk about goals I've scored, but I will never forget that one. The fans at the Garden were on their feet, not because the goal was a work of art—it was their way of welcoming me to Boston. Those fans went out of their way to make me feel at home. I always found the cheers deeply humbling. When you hear that, you just want to give back. So that goal was the start of a very special relationship.

I can't say that opposing players around the league embraced me quite as warmly. Right from that very first game against the Red Wings, players came at me to see if I could take the heat. They wanted to see if I belonged. Part of the rookie experience is that players around the league want to know if you will stand up for yourself. While I knew I had great teammates who would come to my aid if need be, I felt I had to make my own statement and that no one could do it for me. Mind you, I never fought unless there was a good reason to, and I never fought unless I was angry. If you mix it up with somebody at that level and you aren't into it, you can get hurt in a hurry.

I guess you could say I was the type of player who was kind of a pain to play against, because I would go after opponents and make contact. I never went looking for trouble, but being aggressive was just the way the game was supposed to be played. I knew perfectly well that if I was going to go after guys, they were going to be that way with me. It works both ways. There were things you did and things you didn't do. So I knew what to expect.

But when I say I liked to play aggressively, I really mean a couple of things. First, I was aggressive in that I wanted the puck on my stick, and that meant I would be in the action for a lot of the time I was on the ice. If you want to carry the play a lot, then you have to expect to be hit. And second, if that aggression took a more physical form, then you could probably expect some retaliation. That was just the law of the land. I didn't expect others to fight my battles for me, particularly since I knew they were coming. They were coming because I was a rookie, they were coming because I got a bit more press than other eighteen-year-olds, and they were coming because I didn't shy away from contact. Other teams had always tried to intimidate me, so it's not as though I was surprised that guys would try to push me around in the NHL. They may have been stronger and punched harder, but I figured there was no way to avoid the challenges, so there was no point trying to. And if you're going to answer a challenge, you'd better go about it like you mean it.

For the rest of the season, we never did have a winning record again after our victory on opening night. Still, I was told to move out of the hotel. When they tell you to go get a place, it means you're probably sticking around for a while, because if the team sends you down after that, they are stuck paying your rent.

Once I got the green light to settle down, I had to decide where I was going to go, and with whom. Joe Watson was my first roommate on the Bruins, but unfortunately that arrangement would only last one season. We lost Joe to the Philadelphia Flyers during the 1967 expansion draft, and he would go on to have a great career in Philly, where he would win two Stanley Cups. But at least for my first year we shared a place together, and often found ourselves on the ice as playing partners as well.

But Joe wasn't my only roommate that rookie year. There were a couple of other players we shared a house with, and they represent yet another example of those times when you realize how small the hockey circle really can be. They were two of the players I had faced off against in the Memorial Cup the previous spring, Ross Lonsberry and Ted Hodgson. They had been playing for the Edmonton Oil Kings in that series, but Edmonton had added them only after eliminating the team they had played for all season, the Estevan Bruins—it turned out that both were Bruins property as well.

The four of us eventually decided to rent a place right on the water in the town of Little Nahant. The guys who took the rooms in the front of the building soon understood how cold the winds could be coming off the water. They would jack the thermostat up so they could at least stay tolerably warm, as those winds blew right through the walls. Fortunately, my room was in the back, and I didn't have to contend with all of that wind. That was the good news. The bad news was that whenever they turned up the heat, my room became a sauna, and I could barely stand it. Unfortunately for Ross and Ted, both players were eventually reassigned to a minor-league team in Oklahoma City, so two of my four roomies were suddenly gone. That's one of the tough parts of being a pro athlete, and having to pick up and move, often on short notice, is just a hazard of the profession.

But for those of us lucky enough to stick with the big club, we were members of the Bruins, living on our own, and enjoying the view. It was all very exciting for a young guy, and those were the best of times as I made my way around the Boston area trying to familiarize myself with the lifestyle of a professional hockey player. It was exciting, but also foreign. The security blanket of a mother and father or billet home wasn't there anymore, and there would be no one doing your laundry at home. Meals wouldn't be cooked, and other details of day-to-day living would have to be figured out, and all of that in combination was quite an adjustment. But to be honest, a lot of our meals, especially on game days, were eaten at the Surf Restaurant down on the waterfront. I mostly went for steak and eggs around noon to be ready to play. While we could all handle a fry pan if we had to, most of us preferred the restaurant fare instead.

There were other little things about the lifestyle as well, like the fact that suddenly there were bills coming in that had to be paid. I wasn't up on that kind of bookkeeping, so I had a lot to sift through in a very short period. I had a lawyer representing me who assured me that many of those little details would be taken care of, and I had no reason to doubt that information. Unfortunately, my lack of attention would cost me dearly in the years ahead. But at that moment I hardly gave money a second thought. All I really wanted to focus on was hockey.

My rookie year would have its share of trials. Like any new player in the league, I had a lot to figure out. Perhaps more than forward, defense is a position you have to mature and grow into. If a forward coughs up the puck, it's a missed opportunity. When a defenseman blunders, the puck often ends up in the back of his net. So rookie defensemen often don't get a lot of ice time, which is one reason they take a bit longer to develop.

I had plenty of ice time, though. In the fall of 1966, the Boston Bruins just weren't very good as a hockey team. A building process had to take place, and the early stages of that process were not very pleasant for the organization. But that meant I would get my chance at lots of ice time in the years ahead. It would be on-the-job training, and I would make all kinds of mistakes. The way I played meant that my teammates would have to figure me out and inevitably cover for those errors from time to time.

There were some frustrating nights. I was aware of absolutely every mistake I made, and it gnawed at me. There were things I could do in junior that just didn't work in the NHL. And when I say that the Bruins weren't a great team that year, I am talking about myself, too. There were games when we were shelled, and it seemed I was on the ice for every goal against. But it beat sitting on the bench, and if it's true that you learn from your mistakes, I certainly had plenty of opportunity that year. But coach Harry Sinden kept sending me back out there, and the Boston fans never soured on me, so I never got gun-shy, which is about the worst thing that can happen to a young defenseman.

Just the opposite, actually. I was getting more comfortable by the game.

When you add my playing time to all the help and guidance I received from a great bunch of teammates and coaches, it all meant that my rookie campaign would be a pretty positive year. Sometimes in life, you just get lucky. I was very fortunate to be part of that particular group at that particular moment, even if we weren't very good as a team.

It was during my rookie season that I suffered my first problem with my left knee. We were playing against the Maple Leafs in early December, and I was on the attack with the puck, trying to slip by the great Toronto defenseman Marcel Pronovost. He had the angle on me, but I tried to squeeze through the shrinking gap between him and the boards. I didn't make it, and he caught me with a textbook hip-check that wedged me up the boards. It was a clean check, but my knee was pinched and twisted under the force of the hit, and pinned there.

I felt an odd twinge of pain. Not agony, but not a good thing. I didn't require surgery after that initial bit of damage, but I had to sit out eight games to let it heal. Of course, I was eighteen, and like a lot of eighteen-year-olds, I thought I was indestructible. I believed I would last forever, that the odd injury here and there was simply the cost of doing business in my profession. I waited until the knee felt better, and then I was off to the races again. But I wasn't as indestructible as I'd imagined.

That first year in Boston, from a personal perspective, was about finding my way around the league. For the team, it was all about building our program and our identity as a group. At that moment, we weren't ready to compete for the Cup. In fact, we were the worst team in the league. For the previous few seasons, the best the Bruins could hope for was to beat the New York Rangers in the race for the second-worst record in the league. Never mind the Cup, even the playoffs seemed an unrealistic dream. The year before I arrived in Beantown, the Bruins had finished fifth in a six-team league, and with my arrival all of that was supposed to change in a hurry. Unfortunately, by the end of my rookie season we had dropped from fifth to sixth overall, with a 17–43–10 record, easily the worst in the league. (New York, by contrast, had escaped the cellar and made the playoffs.) So much for the savior from Parry Sound.

I did win the Calder Trophy for rookie of the year, and I was honored, of course. But not for a moment did I think that trophy made me anyone special. The major triumph, in my mind, was that I'd made the team.

I hated losing. I won some more trophies in the years ahead, but I can tell you that none of them felt as good as winning. None of them even came close. I scored thirteen goals that first season, but not one of them was a game-winner. And we won only seventeen games.

I went back home that summer feeling pretty despondent. There had been a considerable amount of press leading up to my league debut, and expectations had run high in Boston, both for me and for the team, and there was no getting around the fact that we had let people down. Early on during my time in Oshawa, I had played on some teams that lost a lot of hockey games, but eventually, in my final season, we had a run at a championship. It was not easy having to handle a losing record again, particularly since we were all but out of the playoffs by Christmas.

At the pro level, winning is your job. While I was happy to get back to Parry Sound that summer, I couldn't wait for it to end. I wanted to get back to business in Boston.

Five

TOWARD THE CUP: 1967–1970

The league I joined as a rookie was the old Original Six, which had existed unchanged for decades. I was lucky enough to play at the end of an era that included legends. But that summer, the league doubled to include new teams in Pittsburgh, Philadelphia, Los Angeles, Oakland, Minnesota, and St. Louis.

The Bruins lost a lot of players in the expansion draft that summer, including future Hall of Fame goalie Bernie Parent, J.P. Parise, Poul Popiel, Wayne Rivers, Ron Schock, Gary Dornhoefer, Bill Goldsworthy, and Wayne Connelly. As I mentioned, I lost a roommate, since Joe Watson was claimed by the Flyers as well.

I had to look for a new place to live, and ended up rooming with goalie Eddie "EJ" Johnston, fellow defenseman Gary Doak, and John "Frosty" Forristall, our team trainer. Frosty was a great guy and someone I grew close to over my career with the Bruins. He was always a part of the team, as was our head trainer, Dan Canney, and that was how they were always treated. Over the next few years, EJ and Gary both got married and moved out, but Frosty and I were together for a while.

But as deeply as expansion affected the team, there were other developments in Boston that all but eclipsed the changes around the league.

First of all, legendary former Bruins player Milt Schmidt took over as GM from Hap Emms. This was a guy who was already in the Hall of Fame. He had centered Boston's so-called Kraut Line in the '40s, had led the league in scoring, had won the Hart Trophy and the Stanley Cup, and as if that wasn't enough, he had left the Bruins to enlist in the Royal Canadian Air Force to fight in World War II (winning an Allan Cup for the RCAF while he was at it), then returned after the war to pick up where he had left off. It was impossible to get too full of yourself when "Uncle Miltie" was around. Whatever you hoped to do, he had already done. Under his leadership, the team began a steady climb up the hockey ladder.

That climb began in earnest during the summer of 1967. In addition to being a great hockey player, Milt proved himself to be a pretty shrewd hockey mind. In his first deal, he gave up Gilles Marotte, Jack Norris, and Pit Martin to the Black Hawks in exchange for Phil Esposito, Ken Hodge, and Fred Stanfield—three guys who became so important to the Bruins that the deal would forever be known as "The Trade." Even though the deal took place before he was officially the GM, Schmidt negotiated the trade with Chicago, and Hap Emms told him that if the deal was going to make the team better, he had the green light to make it happen.

I was already familiar with Ken and Fred, because I had played against them in junior when they were in St. Catharines, Ontario. I knew Ken to be a big, strong guy who could handle the puck, and he would soon be the right winger on one of the most feared lines in the league. Fred Stanfield was a great two-way player who could kill a penalty and match up against the top opposing forwards. Freddy would also work the point for us on the power play, and would connect with Johnny "Pie" McKenzie and Johnny Bucyk to form a line that would stay together for years.

And everyone knows what a prolific scorer Phil turned into once he joined us. His accomplishments can never be overstated. He had actually already started to put up some impressive numbers in Chicago over the course of his first three seasons in the league. But when he got into a Bruins uniform, Phil became the dominant goal scorer of our era. He never got any style points for his skating, but he had an uncanny ability to get open near the opponent's net. And even when he couldn't get open, he could score with a defenseman on his back.

Of course, I don't think anyone dreamed these guys would perform the way they did right out of the chute. I've often wondered why *where* you play affects *how* you play so noticeably. Certain athletes, regardless of the sport, all of a sudden begin to produce like never before after they get traded from one team to another. (While other guys' performance drops off when they're traded away from a city where they have been playing great.) Some guys just play better on some teams than on others. How could those three players have been viewed as expendable by Chicago and then gone on to have such great careers in Boston? I can't explain it, but it happens more often than you might think. Maybe all it takes is a change in scenery—that's what happened with Phil, Kenny, and

Fred, anyway. Without question, The Trade changed the Boston Bruins into a new team.

But Milt wasn't done. He also brought in Eddie "the Entertainer" Shack. Eddie was productive that year but apparently got into some trouble with the front office. He was a bit of a joker. On one occasion, Milt climbed aboard the team bus a little bit late en route to the airport, something unusual for him, given that he was a very punctual man. As the GM took his seat at the front of the bus, we all heard Eddie yell out in his distinctive high-pitched voice, "Hey, Miltie … are we all going to be fined for being early?" Milt stood up, turned back to Shack, and said, "You'll be gone." Sure enough, Shack was soon traded away.

I always thought Milt had held a grudge over that little cheap shot on the bus, but it turns out I was wrong. Milt eventually told me that the Entertainer had taken to mocking the hats worn by Weston Adams, the owner of the Bruins. Eventually, Mr. Adams got tired of Shack's insults, so he instructed his GM to just "get rid of that guy." Eddie had picked the wrong target for his comedy routine.

There was one more new face on the team that fall—and this was a guy who could steal the spotlight even from Shack. Derek Sanderson swaggered into camp as though he were already a star, courted the press, and even dropped the gloves with Ted Green in practice, which was not for the faint of heart. Not only did Turk (as we called him) make the team; he also became a darling of the fans overnight and won the Calder Trophy as rookie of the year.

Derek was a very gifted player who brought many intangible qualities to the team, and he was a huge factor in the success we achieved in Boston. He was absolutely dominant in the face-off circle, he could shut down the other teams' top centers, and his penalty-killing instincts were like none I'd ever seen. He and Ed Westfall formed probably the finest penalty-kill tandem I ever witnessed in the NHL. I don't know what our PK percentage was during those years, and I don't know how many "shorties" we scored during his time in Boston, but whenever Turk was on the ice killing a penalty, the opposition players were always on their heels.

Even when those Bruins teams were shorthanded, we never sat back and retreated into a defensive shell. We were still trying to carry the play and score. Right or wrong, that was how the members of that team thought, and that's how we all played. I remember during one game against the New York Rangers, we had already scored two shorthanded goals when the ref put up his arm to signal another penalty against us. Once the whistle blew, one of the Rangers on the ice, I think it was Vic Hadfield, shouted, "We decline!"

Turk tells a story about something he and the other guys on the team referred to as the "look." I was never a real rah-rah kind of player, and didn't feel that a big speech was the way to get players going. My belief was that we were professional athletes who were paid very handsomely for our services, so I expected a certain level of performance out of myself and my teammates. I always broke the season into ten-game segments and tried to determine how consistently I'd played over the course of any given segment. I thought that each player should have the same kind of results for eight out of every ten games. You would have to cut a little slack for two of the ten games, because we're all human, and sometimes players are battling illness or injury and just can't clear the bar they have set. When I felt that a teammate was not achieving that level, Derek claims I would sit in my stall and just look at the underachieving player. I suppose it was my way, without singling anybody out, to send a little message that it was time to pick it up.

Derek recalls that one time he wasn't having a particularly productive game. He was living life at a fairly fast clip back then, so perhaps he'd had another late night. As the second period ended, and we all filed into the dressing room and sat down, the Turk could feel me looking at him. He knew he wasn't playing well, and he didn't want to look back in my direction to see me staring at him, so instead he leaned over to the player sitting right beside him, Phil Esposito, and asked, "Is Bobby looking over here?" Espo apparently glanced over in my direction and said, "Yes, he's lookin' here alright." Derek asked, "Is he staring at you or at me?" to which Phil responded, "Well, Derek, I have two goals already tonight, so I don't think he's looking at me!" Derek picked up his play in the third period.

Derek Sanderson was a funny guy and a talented teammate, someone I always enjoyed being on the ice with. But he ended up in a pretty dark place. One day, he was the coolest guy in Boston. The next, he was playing in the World Hockey Association as the highest-paid athlete on the planet. Then he lost it all. Maybe he was too young to handle the money and adoration. Derek had a long way to fall, and he landed hard. But rather than focus on what went wrong in Derek's life after he left Boston, I'd rather focus on what went right. He represents a classic story of redemption, someone who managed to pick himself back up and make a life for himself against some pretty serious odds. At the depths of his fall, he was a real mess and in a whole lot of pain. But with support, and by surrounding himself with people who cared, Derek managed to turn his life around. Today, his wife, Nancy, and sons, Michael and Ryan, give him the stability that allows him to be the man I always thought he would end up being. His life is on track, and I am proud of what he has been able to accomplish.

In any case, that was the team that Milt put on the ice that fall. I have had the pleasure of meeting many gentlemen in the game, but none better than Milt Schmidt. He was always there for advice and guidance, and his influence on my career was enormous. He is one of those people who deserves a big "thank you" for all of the good things he brought to my life.

While the 1967–68 season started on a very positive note for the Bruins, things didn't begin nearly as promisingly for me. I was injured before the season even began. I was dying to get back on the ice after the previous season's disappointment, and when I was invited to play in a benefit game in Winnipeg that August, I didn't hesitate. Maybe it was because everyone on the ice was a little bit rusty, but in the first period I got tangled up on a broken play and awkwardly twisted my right knee. I had to pull myself out of the game, and soon the knee was swollen and very painful. I had it examined at Toronto General, where the opinion was it would recover just fine. But still, I had to keep my leg immobilized. I was furious, of course, and very frustrated. After looking forward to getting back to work after the disappointment of the previous season, I had to miss training camp.

Once I was back on the ice, I felt great. Physically, I was fine, and you could tell that the Bruins were coming together. We didn't feel like a last-place team, and we weren't playing like one, either. At the All-Star break in December, we were playing well. In those days, the All-Star team played the Stanley Cup champions, in that year the Leafs. Frank Mahovlich stepped into me, injuring my collarbone. That kept me out for a few more weeks.

We never really paid much attention to injuries back then. We were pros—all of us were expected to play with some bumps and bruises, and players never made much of their injuries. But still, I knew my knee wasn't right. I can't say that a specific play was to blame, but I knew there was a problem. There was a bit of pain, of course, but it was the increasing stiffness that made it hard to be effective on the ice. There were things I just couldn't do. Finally, in February, it simply wouldn't work anymore. I remember heading out to play at the old Olympia Stadium in Detroit, and as I went to put my skate down on the ice, the knee just locked up. There was nothing I could do but head back to the dressing room.

I flew back to Boston, where the Bruins team physician, Dr. Ronald Adams, opened up the knee and removed two-thirds of the medial meniscus—that's the inner-knee cartilage. He cleared out the joint to restore the range of movement, but that was it for my regular season. I had played only forty-six games.

But it was the playoffs I'd been dreaming of the summer before. The Bruins hadn't made the postseason since 1959, and there wasn't a person in that whole organization who wasn't absolutely desperate to bring that drought to an end. And that year we did. We had some real firepower in that lineup, and more importantly we had depth: seven guys scored twenty or more goals that season. After finishing the year before with the worst record in the league, we were third in the Eastern Conference that spring (the Eastern Conference comprised the original six teams, while the expansion teams made up the west).

We had earned our playoff berth, though our run lasted only four games. We faced a great Montreal Canadiens team, which would go on to win the Cup that year. But it was a beginning for us, a taste of playoff experience. We learned quickly that winning in the regular season was one thing, and winning in the playoffs was something else entirely. We thought we had what it took to compete with the best in the league, but getting swept by the Habs taught us pretty quickly that we had a long way to go.

1968–1969

Whenever you lose that last game of the season, the summer seems a little longer. But our quick exit from the playoffs wasn't the only thing bothering me back in Parry Sound. My left knee had never really recovered from the surgery in February. It was still swollen, stiff, and painful. Soon, I was back under the knife, this time in Toronto. Dr. John Palmer went in to remove damaged articular cartilage—the smooth white lining of the end of the bone. This improved the immediate problem, but when cartilage is gone it is gone.

We were looking to start off 1968–69 with some of the momentum we had from our strong season the year before. We had basically the same cast of characters, and they were all getting better. The year before, we had improved by adding from the outside—now, we were improving from within. We had become a team that could count on scoring from many sources within the room. The team had a hundred-point year, and again we had seven guys who scored twenty goals or more that season. Add all that up, and the Bruins scored 303 goals, the most in the league.

Trust within the group had taken a big leap forward, and the end result was that a solid regular season carried over into a good playoff performance against the Toronto Maple Leafs.

Game one was April 2, 1969, though I'm afraid there are things about it I don't remember. Anyone who has followed my career will know that on that particular night, Pat Quinn put a pretty good lick on me. Pat was a big boy, probably six feet three and 215 pounds, and he seemed even bigger, because he knew how to throw that weight around.

We were up 6–0 with only a couple of minutes left in the second period, so the outcome really wasn't in much doubt. I mention that because sometimes, when you have a big lead, you become a bit relaxed. Perhaps you're not as watchful or prepared for sudden surprises. Maybe I was too off-guard as I picked up the puck behind our net and began a rush. I was being angled toward the boards and momentarily lost the puck in my skates. I looked down for a split second to locate the puck, and I really wasn't expecting anyone to be pinching inside our blue line.

But Pat had other ideas. No one likes being on the wrong side of a lopsided score. Maybe he wanted to let the Bruins know that the Leafs weren't going to bow out quietly. Whatever the reason, he stepped into me, and I took the full force of that hit right on the chin. What happened next is a blur, because all I remember is being taken to the hospital for examination. The doctors figured I had suffered a concussion. You have to remember, back then very few players wore helmets, so from the neck up we were quite susceptible. In spite of that fact, it is interesting that more concussions are reported today than back then. Perhaps it's simply better diagnostic procedures, or increased sensitivity to the symptoms themselves. Or maybe that lack of head protection in the old days made players think long and hard before doing something that might ring a guy's bell. If you did that to someone, retribution was sure to follow.

In any event, we all know that in the modern game, concussions are increasingly causing concern. But I can't recall any other time in my career when I suffered one, and I was hit a lot. While I certainly remember the headache I had the next morning, it didn't stop me from suiting up the following night for our next tilt with the Leafs. I never suffered any lingering effects or showed any of the symptoms we normally associate with a concussion, so I guess I must have been lucky.

Still, the Pat Quinn episode didn't quite end there. I stayed in the hospital overnight for observation. Early the next morning, after I was discharged from the hospital, I had an encounter I have never disclosed, but it is one I'll not soon forget. Once the doctors had determined I was well enough to leave the hospital, I headed back to the hotel where the entire team was staying for the playoff run. The team was staying in a hotel together so we would have as few distractions as possible, even when we were playing in Boston.

As I entered the lobby, a rather tough looking "gentleman," for lack of a better word, walked up to me. I have no idea how he found out where we were staying. To this day, I don't know who he was or what his affiliations were. However, as he came up beside me, he asked, in a very low voice, "Do you want me to take care of Pat Quinn?" It was kind of a scary moment, because the look in his eyes and his general demeanor made me think that the guy meant to do some serious damage. I looked back at him and said, "No thanks … I'll take care of him myself." He walked away, and that was the end of it. I never saw him again after that night, but it is an episode I will never forget.

We started out by sweeping the Leafs in the quarters, but then the Montreal Canadiens got in our way yet again. They were a great team, a group built on speed and skill, and even though they took us out in six games, in a lot of ways we were right there with them. We lost the first two games in Montreal, though both were one-goal games. Then we evened up the series back in Boston. Even when we lost game five in Montreal, we knew we always had a chance to win at the Garden. And we almost did, losing the sixth game in double overtime.

As much as every guy in the room hated to lose, it wasn't hard to see how far the team had come. It was the Bruins' first trip into the semifinals in the new age of NHL expansion. And in spite of not getting to the finals, Espo still finished up with the most points of any player that year in the playoffs, a good omen for things to come. We had been only a few bounces away from beating the team that would go on to win the Cup. In a way, that made it tougher to accept the loss, but it also made it easier to see what we had to do to win.

At that moment, in the spring of 1969, we simply weren't yet ready to be winners. To win a Stanley Cup, or any championship in any major sport, for that matter, you have to be *ready*. By that I mean you have to have the right players in the right spots, the right coaching, as well as a little bit of luck. Without all those pieces in place, you can't become a champion. But it goes beyond mere skill and some good luck. You also have to be willing to pay the price to be a champion, and in our game that price can be pretty steep.

The Stanley Cup playoffs may well be the toughest grind of any sport if you want to go all the way. The long regular season, with all of the endless travel, is followed by a run of pressure-filled playoff games. At the end of a Stanley Cup run, I was always drained, both physically and mentally. That is the process for becoming a champion in hockey. But for our team that year, there were more lessons to be learned before we could make our final push to win the Cup. We were disappointed yet determined, and most of us couldn't wait to get to camp the next year and prepare to do something that hadn't happened in Boston in a very long time. We had our eyes on Lord Stanley.

1969–1970

We now knew we could compete with any team in the NHL. We had depth in the lineup for goal scoring, were solid back of the blue line, and had a goaltending tandem in Gerry Cheevers and Eddie Johnston that was second to none. It was the beginning of the 1969–70 season, and all of us felt we had a great chance to win our first Cup together.

The regular season that year, just like the year before, showed us we could play some pretty good hockey and sustain that level of performance over the course of an entire season. Another six guys would score twenty goals or more and we had ninety-nine points as a team, almost the same statistics as the year before. But something was different. Somehow the regular season mattered a little less to us, even as we took the game a little more seriously. The season was a long warm-up for us, getting us ready for the playoffs. We wanted the regular season over with.

Somehow, the Canadiens, who had stood in our way the previous two seasons, didn't even make the playoffs. Neither did the Leafs. We started with the Rangers in the first round and they pushed us to six games. We won the first two in Boston, lost two on the road, then had to fight hard to take game five back at home. New York threw everything at us, but we managed to take game six at Madison Square Garden to end the series.

Meanwhile, Chicago had swept Detroit and were rested and waiting for us. We knew the series wouldn't be easy. The Black Hawks had finished first overall in the league, and they had Bobby Hull in their lineup. They also had Phil Esposito's rookie brother, Tony, in net, and he seemed at least as good at stopping pucks as Phil was at shoveling them in. Tony had just set a record for shutouts in a season. Also, we were starting the series on the road, and the Hawks were every bit as hard to beat at Chicago Stadium as we were at the Boston Garden. But we won those road games, and once we were back in our barn, there was no way we were going to ease up. Chicago came at us, but the lessons and the discipline we had learned at the hands of the Canadiens probably made the difference. Even when the Hawks got up on us a couple of times, we knew what it was going to take to win. And we did.

A four-game sweep of the Black Hawks landed us in the final. Our opponent was the St. Louis Blues. They were making their third straight appearance in the finals, so it was a veteran group of players with a lot of playoff experience under their belt. The Blues had emerged in a short time as the class of the expansion teams, and we knew this would not be an easy series. You need to remember something here that is very important when it comes to sports and championship-caliber teams. We had been through two very successful regular seasons in a row, and all of us in that room knew we were a pretty good team. But that meant nothing. As long as we thought that being good was enough to win, we weren't going to cut it. You don't win by being good. You win with hard work and sacrifice. Without that, skill is just potential.

Now, our first Stanley Cup was sitting there, within our grasp, just four victories away. We won the first two games of the series on the road, and we took game three back in Boston. That set up a very dramatic game four. What we had in front of us that day, as we prepared for the game that afternoon, was an opportunity to achieve something we had all been dreaming of for years. Let me share how that game developed from where I was sitting on May 10, 1970.

The Boston Garden was packed to the rafters, and everyone had come to the rink anticipating the end of a long wait for the Cup. The Garden was a fantastic old rink, and the fans in Boston had stuck with us even when we were finishing last in the league. By the time we were deep in the playoffs, that crowd kept us going. So, on a hot spring day, in game four, with the Cup waiting for us, the mood was nothing short of incredible.

The last time a Bruins team had accomplished the task was back in the 1940–41 season, so it had been almost thirty years since Boston had last won it all. The drought had persisted long enough—at least in the eyes of the Bruins faithful. As for the players, we wanted it done, right then and there. The chance to sweep on home ice was within our grasp. Of course, people who have played the game, especially at higher levels, will tell you the last game in a series is always the hardest to win. Refusing to lose the series can be as much of an inspiration as wanting to win it. And players hate being swept even more than they hate losing—it leaves a particularly nasty taste in your mouth. We had experienced that taste just a couple of seasons before, so we understood how it felt. They were a proud team, with a great leader in Scotty Bowman, and we all knew that taking the Blues out that night was no foregone conclusion. We felt we were in for their best game of the series.

Just as we'd expected, the Blues came out and gave us everything they had. We got on the board first with Rick Smith, a defenseman not normally known as a goal scorer, giving us the lead right off the bat. But Red Berenson tied it up with under a minute to go in the first. As the second period began, Gary Sabourin (a Parry Sound native, by the way) gave them a 2–1 lead fairly quickly, but Espo tied it again as the period was winding down. It stood 2–2 going into the third, and the already-incredible tension was mounting. They weren't going to roll over for us.

We barely had time to sit down on our bench to start the third when, nineteen seconds in, Larry Keenan gave St. Louis a 3–2 lead and the place suddenly got a little bit quiet. It was fitting that, around the thirteen-minute mark, the old veteran Johnny Bucyk, the first roomie I'd ever had with the Bruins, scored the goal that tied it up. Rick Smith had an assist on that goal, his second point of the night, and it just goes to show how different players at different times can step up and contribute. It was a see-saw battle to end the period, but neither team could finish the job.

It was off to overtime, which is the way every kid wants to win the Cup. No one needed a speech in the dressing room to get motivated to go back out there. Not much was said. At least I never heard much. I suppose nothing really needed to be said. We all knew what was at stake. The deal now was just to go out, each man do his job, and get this over with. Sudden death.

I hadn't scored a goal in the series up to that point. That fact didn't particularly register with me at the time, because in the grand scheme of things it just didn't matter. I wasn't there to improve my stats. I was there to help the Bruins win. I couldn't have cared less who scored the final goal, so long as the player was wearing a black-and-gold uniform.

Harry Sinden decided to start Derek Sanderson's line, consisting of Turk, Wayne Carleton, and Ed Westfall, with Don Awrey and me on defense. Perhaps Harry's decision to go with Sanderson's line and keep the very potent line of Espo, Cashman, and Hodge on the bench might have surprised some people in the stands, or even on the bench, but it made sense to me. Derek and Eddie were both solid two-way players and that was our best defensive line. I'm sure that Harry just wanted to ensure that the Blues wouldn't get one early in the overtime period. He wanted to get that first shift out of the way. He knew there would be nerves.

As play began to start the overtime, the puck found its way into the St. Louis end, and our forwards were on it in a hurry. We had some great pressure on them, and as the play along the left boards developed, Derek eventually picked up a loose puck as the Blues were starting to head out of the zone up their right side. Turk stepped toward the net and let loose a shot that missed the target, going around the boards toward the other corner and heading up in my direction. Remember, even though I was a left-hand shot, I had always played the right point, so I had to stop pucks along the boards on the backhand.

Instinctively, I pinched down. I really can't say why I held the zone, but for whatever reason I gambled a bit. The St. Louis forward closest to me as the puck came around was Number 18, Larry Keenan, who had scored earlier in the game. He got to the puck about the same time I did, and I'm sure Larry had visions of scoring his second of the game as he extended his stick and tried to poke it around me off the boards. If he had been able to sneak it by me, they would have had a two-on-one, or three-on-one, in the other direction, and I would have been caught.

But I managed to get my stick on the puck, and immediately

I slid it toward Derek. By that time, Turk had followed his shot in behind the net and was now standing just below the goal line near the post, a quick pass away. I did what came naturally. Once I chipped the puck in Derek's direction, I went hard to the net. Derek fed it back to me immediately, Glenn Hall's legs opened up in the crease, and bingo, the puck was in the back of the net. I'd like to say I checked first and picked my spot on Glenn, but the truth is it was simply a bang-bang, give-and-go play. I just tried to get a shot on net.

And while I was focused on that, Blues defenseman Noel Picard got his stick on me to slow me down. But he tripped me an instant too late. He brought me down, but not before I'd spent that moment airborne. And as soon as I fell back to the ice, Sanderson jumped on me, and the celebrations began. I was mobbed by my teammates, who poured over the boards. Some of the Boston fans were right behind them. Then, there I was, following Chief around the ice, with him hoisting the Cup over his head. Growing up, lying in bed at night, that was something I had dreamed about.

No words will ever do justice to the feeling of winning the Stanley Cup. So many things come together in that moment. There is, of course, the pure joy of getting something you have wanted for as long as you can remember. Many of those games of shinny on Georgian Bay featured a Cup-winning overtime goal. To actually do what you have dreamed of a thousand times since you were a kid is a feeling like nothing else. But there is more to it than that. Part of the exhilaration is not just getting what you've wanted your whole life, but getting it after years of hard work, and after the gut-wrenching challenge of a playoff run. It wouldn't have felt nearly the same having what we wanted just handed to us. We'd achieved what we wanted with the best hockey players in the world—tough, skilled athletes—trying to stop us at every turn. There wasn't a guy on that team—probably either team—who wasn't banged up after fighting, game after game, for every inch of ice. When you win, all those bruises and stitches just make the thrill of accomplishment that much more powerful.

Still, there was more to the feeling of victory than that. My dad was there at the Garden that night, and my thoughts went to him right away. And it happened to be Mother's Day (someone had hung a banner saying, "Happy Mother's Day Mrs. Orr," behind the net). My thoughts were with her as well. When you win something as big as a Stanley Cup, you can't help but think about all the people who played a part in getting you there. It is a reminder that you really can't take all the credit.

But that doesn't make it less thrilling. Just the opposite. It makes it all feel right. I have won a few trophies over the years, and I never really liked individual honors, because they seem to miss the point. No one guy can accept the praise for the statistics he puts up, because it takes all kinds of unacknowledged help to get there. All the coaches in minor hockey and in Oshawa. All the friends and volunteers, teachers and billets. The neighbors who lent a hand at some point, and the teammates' parents who drove me to the rink. There is really no such thing as individual accomplishment. A team victory means much, much more. I scored only one goal in that series, so there is no way anyone can say I won the series with that goal. I was just helping out at that point. A team gets very close over the course of a few campaigns like that, and I would say that Bruins team was especially close. As an example, I believe we may have been the first team to vote a full share of playoff bonus money to both our trainers. A huge part of the thrill of winning the Cup is knowing that the guys you have fought alongside are also winning it.

In a similar way, it is a real joy to win it for the fans. People talk about sports as though it is just entertainment, but it's more than that. Our fans cared about what happened. They had a stake in the outcome of that season in a way no one does when they go to a movie. We knew that the Bruins meant a lot to them, and that meant a lot to us.

For many years after that goal had been scored, whenever I found myself in the company of Glenn Hall, someone would always bring up the topic of "The Goal" or produce a copy of the photo to be signed. Poor Glenn must have got sick of that pretty quickly, but he took it in good humor. I can remember at one event, he looked over at me and, shaking his head in mock disgust, he asked, "Bobby, is that the *only* goal you ever scored in the NHL?"

Six

HEAVEN IS BLACK AND GOLD: 1970–1975

The years between our first Cup and the end of the 1974–75 season were the best of my hockey life. The core group of guys that came together in the fall of 1967 stayed together through those years, and we had a lot of success. We could play any kind of game our opponents wanted to play, and still win. We had the skill to skate with anyone in the league and put the puck in the net. We had great goaltending. And if anyone tried to intimidate us, they quickly found out we were as adept as anyone with the rough stuff.

People started calling us the Big Bad Bruins, and it's true that it might not have been fun to play against us. But we never set out to be "bad." We just never, ever, let anyone push any of us around. It wasn't so much about deliberately trying to intimidate the guys on the other bench as it was about sticking together as a team. And it wasn't as though we dressed guys just to send them out to fight. We were a tough team, but we didn't have an enforcer. Mind you, toughness isn't just about fighting. It's about going into the corners or the crease—the tough places on the ice. It's about getting knocked down and getting right back up. And more than anything, it's about going *back* into the corner against the guy who just put you on your butt. Just about everyone on that team—Wayne Cashman, Ken Hodge, Ted Green, Johnny McKenzie, and, of course, Derek Sanderson—all knew how to handle themselves, and everybody was there for each other. When guys are sticking up for each other, you're going to win hockey games. And we won a lot of hockey games through those years. Any style the other team wanted to play, we could play.

It may be impossible to say what makes a team a team. Coaches and GMs look for "chemistry," but there is no formula. Sometimes a group of guys will come together and they will want to win for each other. They will anticipate each other's moves, they will have each other's backs, and they will know what role they have to play. It was important that everyone knew his role. We didn't expect any more—or any less—than he was capable of providing. Those Bruins teams had such great chemistry—we didn't even have a captain between the end of my rookie season and the fall of 1973. We all regarded Johnny Bucyk as the leader, and the Chief was the first guy to hoist the Cup, but no one wore the *C* on his sweater. In that sense, everyone wearing the black and gold took his share of leadership one way or another.

The team that showed up in training camp the summer after we won the Cup was pretty much the same team that drank out of it in May. One exception was Ted Green.

Perhaps no teammate I ever played with demonstrated more personal courage, more dignity, and more passion than Ted. In

September 1969, he had suffered a terrible head injury during an exhibition game. He was out for the Cup-winning season, and he'd very nearly died. Most of us viewed his survival as a miracle, and we all would have been more than happy to know he would live a normal life after such a traumatic event. But Ted saw things differently.

He'd ended up with a metal plate in his head, and as he recovered from that surgery, his dream was not simply to get better, to walk again, or merely be able to live comfortably. His single purpose was to come back and play again in the National Hockey League. Not just a ceremonial one-game comeback—he wanted to resume his career. Ted ended up winning a Stanley Cup to make up for the one he missed out on, and would later end up signing with the New England Whalers in the WHA before heading to the Winnipeg Jets. He added three Avco Cups to his accomplishments, and became a very successful coach after his playing days were over. We didn't know all that at the time, though. We just knew that a teammate whose career was supposed to have ended was back on the ice. If the guys needed any inspiration after winning the Cup, Ted provided plenty of it. Ted will always be a special person for me, and for so many others who watched his journey back from the brink so many years ago.

One person who was missing was Harry Sinden. He had been with the Bruins for years, and had been part of my professional career since the beginning. He had coached us to a Cup, and his name was just about synonymous with the Bruins. So it was strange not to see him in camp. In his place behind the bench was Tom Johnson, who had been a pretty good defenseman himself in the NHL. He had six Stanley Cup rings, which was five more than any of us had, so he had a track record of winning.

Sometimes championship teams find it hard to regain their intensity once they're back into the regular season. It is not at all strange for a team that is good enough to win it all in the spring to lose a lot of games in the fall. But we didn't have that problem. We loved winning, and we had a lot of talent on that bench. We finished first in the league, well ahead of everyone else. We had the top four scorers in the league, and ten guys who had scored more than twenty goals. While no one had ever scored 100 points in a season in the NHL, we had four guys that hit that mark that year. As a team, we scored 399 goals and allowed only 244. We set a record for wins. Our power-play was clicking at 28 percent, and our penalty kill was working at 84 percent. We were playing better than we had been the year before, when we won the Cup.

So we were impatient to get the playoffs under way. Our first challenge was the Canadiens. They had frustrated us in previous years, though the year before they hadn't even made the playoffs. At the end of the 1970–71 season, we'd played them twice and dominated them. Maybe it would have been better if we had lost.

Coaches always warn against overconfidence. To win at anything, you have to give absolutely everything. That may be even more true in hockey, where not only are you doing your best, but a pretty good athlete is doing *his* best to stop you. You see it again and again, especially in the first round of the playoffs: a team that plays with determination can beat a team that finishes higher in the standings. The trouble is, no one ever thinks they are overconfident. It is a mistake you never know you are making.

I don't know if we were overconfident going into that series. We were confident, but every team is. To win, you have to believe you can win. But whether overconfidence was the problem, I can't say. It is easy to identify one problem, though. At the other end of the rink, a rookie named Ken Dryden was in net. He had joined the Habs after graduating from Cornell University, and had played only six games in the league. So few, in fact, that he was rookie of the year the *following* season. And there he was, standing on his head. You see it year after year. You can't win without great goaltending. Great goalies give their team a kind of confidence that is hard to explain. And we could feel that Habs team was confident they could beat us, even though we'd handed them a couple of lopsided losses in the regular season.

They did beat us, of course. Far from repeating as champions, we were out in the first round. Every guy in the room knew we had let an opportunity slip through our fingers. Losing hurts, and losing a game seven hurts a lot. But knowing you had what it took to win and you didn't deliver is about as crushing a feeling as there is in sports.

We started the next season on a mission. Again, we had pretty much the same players in the room, so we knew what we could do. There were a couple of additions, though. Ace Bailey joined the team, and my friend and business partner Mike Walton came over from Toronto. Mike was another Northern Ontario guy and we ran a hockey camp together in Muskoka.

It was great having Mike on the team, and more than a little strange having a former Leaf on the Bruins. Games in Toronto were always intense, and particularly after my run-in with Pat Quinn. Toronto fans seemed to dislike me, and they took to booing me whenever I had the puck on my stick. Since I liked to have the puck on my stick as much as I could, I heard a lot of booing at Maple Leaf Gardens.

Mike's mom was one of the sweetest ladies you could ever meet, and she never had a bad word to say about anything or anyone. One night, Mrs. Walton was at the Gardens when the Bruins were in town, and she happened to know that my mother was in the stands as well. Mom didn't come to see me often, but she was there that night. Getting to Toronto was a lot easier for my mother and other family members than having to make the hike to Boston, so on this night she decided to see her son in action. Unfortunately, that meant listening to thousands of people boo him.

As a player, you can't make out specific comments fans direct at you at ice level (though, believe me, when an entire crowd is booing, you hear it). But when you're in the stands, you know exactly what people are saying. Finally, sweet Mrs. Walton had heard enough. She happened to be sitting beside one of the ringleaders, so she turned to him and said, "You really shouldn't be booing Bobby Orr like that."

The guy looked at her indignantly and asked, "Why do you say that, lady?" to which she responded, "Because his *mother* is here." I've always had a laugh thinking of that story, because I can visualize that kind and wonderful lady coming to my defense. Thank goodness for mothers! But the booing never ceased, in spite of her request.

I wasn't thinking about the booing, though. I was thinking about the same thing as everyone else on the team: the playoffs. We were still a great regular-season team, and we loved winning, but if the disaster of the previous season's playoffs had taught us anything, it was that the regular season meant little. We had something to prove in the '72 playoffs.

We faced the Leafs in the first round, and though they gave us a tough series, we won in five. Next was the Blues, who may have been getting sick of us. We swept them in four. Finally, we were back where we had wanted to be for the past two years.

We were up against a great team. The Rangers had taken care of the Habs in six games and swept the Black Hawks. If we had been a little bit full of ourselves the year before, no one was making that mistake this time. The Rangers had proven they knew how to win, and they had no shortage of talent on their bench.

Still, we took the first two games in Boston, and though we lost game three in New York, we held on to win the fourth by a goal. We were heading back to Boston with a 3–1 lead in the series. At least, the rest of the team was.

Back then, the NHL would put on a luncheon during the final series in order to recognize the various award winners from the league for that season. That particular year, they scheduled the affair in New York the afternoon after the fourth game of the series, and I was supposed to be there in order to accept an award. Staying for that luncheon meant I wouldn't be able to head out with the rest of the team back to Boston, and that was not what I had in mind. I wanted to get as much rest as possible, and so I told someone with the team that I would prefer to skip the luncheon.

Apparently, the word of my plan got back to the league president, Clarence Campbell. I happened to see him in a hallway at Madison Square Garden, and he looked at me and asked sternly, "Son, do you think you're too big for this game now?" This was the president of the National Hockey League who was questioning me, and not someone to be taken lightly. He was a Rhodes scholar, had served as a senior officer in World War II, and was already in the Hockey Hall of Fame. (A couple of years later, the league would name the Western Conference after him.) What was I going to say?

I answered, "No, sir!" and promised I would be in attendance the next day.

When I got back to Boston, we had the chance to win another Cup on home ice. You could feel the energy in the city, and since just about everyone on that team knew what it felt like to win, the energy in the dressing room was intense. But the Rangers came out and played brilliantly. It can't have been easy to win in the Garden that night—and all credit to them, that's what they did.

Now it was up to us to do the same in their rink. We just wanted it done. We came out flying, but as great as everyone played, at the end of the game we had to thank Gerry Cheevers. He got the shutout, and with that in hand, the game was ours. And so was the Cup.

That was May 11, 1972. Within weeks, I was back in surgery. My left knee had started to bother me midway through the season. I kept expecting it to improve, but it just got stiffer and more painful as the year went on and we went deeper into the playoffs. Some nights it hurt more than others, but I was usually able to focus on the play rather than the pain, the same way I had always pushed distractions away and kept my focus on what I needed to do. But I began to worry that the knee wouldn't hold up long enough for me to raise the Cup again. Once there was no hockey to focus on, I needed to go back under the knife.

That surgery stuck in my memory in a way that the others didn't—because it cost me in a way that the others didn't. I faced a summer of rehab to get ready for something the whole country was looking forward to: the Summit Series. The idea of matching up Canada's best players against the Soviet Union's was irresistible.

I had played against a team from the USSR back in junior, and knew how different their game was, and how the desire to win takes on a whole new dimension when you play for your country. I wanted to play in that series as badly as I've ever wanted to play.

But there was no way my rehab would be done in time. I went to training camp alongside the rest of Team Canada and skated a bit. But I knew my knee wasn't going to be ready. It was stiff and tender, and swelled ominously afterwards. I held on to the hope I'd be able to play, and I stuck with the team.

The guys in the lineup may not have expected it, but they were getting all they could handle from the Soviets, and plenty more. It was a team we knew very little about. The scouting reports that came back were about players who had been seen individually, not playing together on the national team. Those same scouts told us the Soviets were weak in net. We had watched them in practice before the first game, and they didn't look very impressive. In hindsight, maybe they were setting us up. We thought it was going to be a romp. We had the best skaters in the NHL, yet the Russians were a step faster. We figured out pretty quickly that this was a heck of a hockey team. I would have done anything to help. But there was nothing I could do.

It's difficult to describe the frustration I felt being on the sidelines for that series, invited to travel with the team and not being able to contribute on the ice. It's probably the same for any kid who loves the game. When you see the ice, you just want to play. As a kid, when you look out the window and see the windswept surface of the frozen bay, all you can think about is getting out there. Or when you arrive at the rink for an early-morning practice and see the fresh ice that has been waiting all night, you tie your skates in a hurry, hoping to get just a few extra minutes out there. I wanted to be on that ice for the Summit Series with all the eagerness and impatience of a kid. But I didn't get that chance.

It is a chapter from my playing career that still disappoints me, because that series was a defining moment for Canadians, and I had to miss out.

Would I have loved to be part of that? Absolutely. But missing out on it doesn't in any way diminish my sense of what those guys did. I tip my hat to everyone who made it happen and those players who showed all of us what Canadian pride looked like down the stretch. What our team was able to achieve in that series stands out in my mind as one of the greatest accomplishments not just in the history of hockey, but of all sport. It was an especially impressive victory given that we were able to overcome such great adversity, culminating in our winning the series on foreign soil. The group that was assembled for those eight games will always be special in the hearts of all Canadians, and their place in hockey history has been assured forever.

Heading back to the NHL after a series with that kind of drama wasn't easy. But that fall, the Bruins opening-night lineup included a guy who showed the same kind of determination against seemingly impossible odds.

When our first-round pick, drafted fourteenth overall the year before, showed up at our training camp in the fall of 1971, he was not what everyone had expected. We had already won a Cup, and we had a very established lineup by that time. If any draft choice was going to make our roster, he would have to be pretty impressive coming in. I was surprised, to say the least, at what I saw when Terry O'Reilly stepped onto the ice.

He came to us from my old junior team, the Oshawa Generals, and because he was a high pick, we all figured he would have a very high skill level. But it became obvious early on in our scrimmaging that Terry could not cut it. The guy was a rough skater, and there was simply no way he was ready to play at the NHL level. Frankly, based on what he showed that first training camp, I had my doubts he would ever be ready. Some of us began wondering about our scouting system if that was the best they could come up with.

But the one thing you could see in Terry right from his very first shift was his absolute passion for the game, and it was all expressed through his toughness. Terry was a very tough young man who would not back down from anybody. That first pro season, he had only one game with us in Boston and spent the remaining part of his rookie campaign in the minors with the Boston Braves. But by the start of the 1972–73 season, you just knew there was no way we could keep him out of a Bruins uniform. The rest is history.

Terry had a heart as big as the Boston Garden, and he went on to become a key part of the Bruins organization, so well respected he would eventually have his number 24 retired. And he would go on to coach Boston to the Stanley Cup finals. But not before he had racked up four twenty-goal seasons and over two thousand penalty minutes, and made himself one of the most beloved players ever to wear the black and gold. If you gave me an entire team of players made of the same stuff as Terry, I can guarantee you we wouldn't lose many games. Terry O'Reilly is a shining example of a person who had complete passion for his profession, and his attitude has always been an inspiration to me. If you care about something and have passion for it, you have a legitimate shot.

The players on those teams in those years knew that expectations for the Bruins were high, but that didn't mean we couldn't have some fun. Several of my teammates always seemed to come up with a one-liner at just the right moment to keep everyone loose. One of the best at that was our goaltender Eddie Johnston, also known as EJ—or Popsie, as his teammates called him, because he was so much older than the rest of us. EJ was always looking to put the needle into somebody or would simply try to get you laughing. I could write an entire book on his shenanigans alone.

For example, as my career unfolded, some people in the media took to commenting that the defensive part of my game wasn't what it could be, because I was always up the ice with the puck. I suppose there was some merit to that criticism. EJ picked up on that theme one day just before we started a game. He was in net that night, and, as is customary, the national anthem was being played before the game began. I was in the starting lineup, so I stood at attention along the blue line with my teammates until the music had finished playing. Just before the puck was dropped, I went for a last-second skate toward our goalie to tap his pads and wish him good luck, and he lifted up his mask and said, "See you after the game, Bobby!" I had to talk to myself in order to control my laughter. I'll bet you EJ had been waiting all day long to deliver that line, and the smile on his face as he pulled his mask back down was priceless. (The NHL has never been a place for players with thin skins. You better be able to give and take the inevitable jabs, and it doesn't matter who you are on the roster.)

On another occasion, we were playing in Maple Leaf Gardens. I got off to a great start and had a couple of goals early, but then things started to go south for me. The puck began taking some weird bounces, almost as if the guy responsible for all the pucks that evening had forgotten to freeze them. As the game wore on, I believe I had scored four goals in total: two of them against the Toronto goalie, and two against our own goalie that night, good old EJ.

After I had deflected the second puck past him, Eddie came out of his net, looked at me, pointed to the Bruins crest on the front of his sweater, and shouted, "Bobby ... I'm on the same team as you!" Then, as he turned away and headed back to his net, there was that big grin again that always came over his face. After the game, when he was talking to the press, he deadpanned, "Yeah, you have to watch that Orr all the time."

Yet another time, Popsie waited for just the right moment to get a laugh out of the boys. This happened immediately after I had scored a goal that made me the first hundred-point defenseman in the history of the NHL. The fans were standing and applauding as the announcement was made over the PA system, so there was a delay in the action for a couple of minutes. I remember the play, because Eddie had stopped a puck in behind his net off a dump-in, set it up for me, and then leisurely returned to his crease. I came back, retrieved the puck, and headed up ice with it. I saw an opening, made a move, was soon one-on-one with the goalie, and managed to find the back of the net.

An end-to-end rush that results in a goal is always pretty special, and under the circumstances it was even more special. As the fans continued to applaud, I saw EJ making his way toward our bench. He came over to where I was sitting, lifted up that mask, and in a very matter-of-fact way, stated, "That was a hell of a pass by me on that play, eh, Bobby?" The boys got a kick out of that one. He was just one of those guys who always had something to say, always had a sense of the moment, always had great delivery, and almost always made us all laugh. You need teammates like that, ones who don't take themselves or events too seriously.

Every once in a while during the course of play, the comic relief might come not from your own team, but from an opposition player. Yvan Cournoyer, the great Montreal Canadiens star, had a wonderful sense of humor. Yvan always seemed to be in high gear whenever he played against the Bruins, and he was one of those athletes who would have been the quickest guy on the ice regardless of the era. He could flat out fly when he got it in high gear and was very difficult to defend against because of that blazing speed. One night in Boston, he seemed to be blowing by all of us. While the teams were squaring off for a face-off, Gerry Cheevers, our spare goalie that night, was sitting at the end of our bench and Yvan was lined up on the ice right in front of him, perhaps only two feet away. Gerry leaned over the boards and said, "Yvan, for goodness sake, slow down, will ya?"

Yvan looked back, and with a big grin responded in a classic French accent, "No, no, Gerr-*ie*, I 'av da tail winds tonight!" It cracked up everyone on the bench. Moments like that always helped keep players loose. It can't be all business all the time.

The game is about so much more than X's and O's, so much more than pure skills or statistics. I mention this because of one guy I played against, a fierce rival, in fact, who managed to earn the respect of everyone in the league just by playing the game the way it is meant to be played. I am hardly the first person to praise Jean Béliveau. No one who has come into contact with him over the years can seem to help saying what a great person he is. His dignity, his grace, his skill—there is not much I can add to what we already know about him.

One thing that stands out for me, though, is his humility. He had everything. He was a French Canadian playing in Montreal for the beloved Canadiens, and he was the heart and soul of that team. From the first moment I saw him on the ice, I knew how special he was as a player. He was very strong, and extremely skillful for a big man, which meant he was always tough to defend against. Add in that long reach of his, and he became even more difficult to handle. Jean was Mario Lemieux before Mario Lemieux was born.

Of course, Jean's home arena was the old Montreal Forum. Of all the rinks I played in as a professional, apart from the Boston Garden, I'd have to say that the Forum was my favorite. Not because it was an easy place to play, but because it had such a great history, the ice was great to play on, and you always knew what was waiting for you. The rivalry between the Montreal and Boston teams when I was in the league was intense, and those fans in Montreal always let you hear it. At the same time, they were very fair. They had a wonderful knowledge of the game and always seemed to appreciate a great play on either side of the puck. A big part of the trouble you faced whenever you played the Habs, especially in their building, was that big Number 4 in the other jersey. He was the leader of the team, and played some of his finest hockey whenever he faced the Bruins. Whether in victory or defeat, Jean Béliveau always took the high road and demonstrated a kind of sportsmanship seen far too seldom in professional sports.

Several years ago, I was invited to attend a function alongside Jean. If you've ever seen Jean in person, or caught a glimpse of him on television doing an interview, you will know that he is always impeccably dressed. Knowing that, I decided that if I was going to be in his company I had better dress the part, so I packed my sharpest suit. We were to meet in the lobby of the hotel before heading out to the affair, and wouldn't you know it, Jean showed up in some slacks and a shirt. There I was, all decked out to the nines—and I have to admit that Jean *still* looked better than me!

In retirement, Jean has continued to be a tremendous ambassador, both for the Canadiens and for the game in general. He has retained that old humility so rare in superstar players, and has always remained a gentleman, regardless of circumstances. He is, to my way of thinking, one of the premier players ever to have been in the National Hockey League, and it was an honor to battle against him and those great Montreal teams he so admirably led in the 1960s and '70s.

I've written about some of the players and characters who formed the basis for those great Bruins teams of the 1970s, but I've yet to describe the city of Boston and its fans. For those of us who donned the black and gold of the Boston Bruins, we all came to realize very early in our careers that Boston was a tough sports town, because its fans had such high expectations of its teams. No other city I can think of has had the kind of success seen by Boston over the years in all of its professional sports. The Celtics in basketball were a dominant franchise, and the Red Sox and Patriots were always fan favorites in New England and had won many championships. When you throw in all of the great university programs across the region in multiple sports, you can see that the fans in New England had certain expectations of their sports teams.

The Bruins had not been holding up their end of the bargain for some time, but even so, Boston remained a big-time hockey market. At some point, we would have to reward their faith. Boston was a blue-collar city with blue-collar fans, and if nothing else they always expected that same kind of blue-collar work ethic from their hockey players. Boston fans held you accountable for what you did in one of their beloved jerseys, and my attitude regarding that was very simple.

Whenever I took to the ice, I knew what my level of play should be, and that was my single goal every game. That was my responsibility, because hockey was what I did for a living. I was representing the Boston Bruins, the city of Boston, the entire New England area, and my teammates. I was paid well for my services. But whatever I was making relative to anybody else on the ice on a given night really didn't matter. My play was my responsibility, every time out. It was not the responsibility of my coaches, other Bruins players, or anyone else. My duty was to lead through my play and not be influenced by anyone or anything that might get in the way of that. I've always believed that if you get led down a dark path in life, you have *chosen* to be led. I liked the feeling of accountability when I wore that sweater.

They were not going to cheer you in Boston just because you put on the Bruins sweater. Those cheers had to be earned. My feeling at the time was, if I can't take it, or if any of my teammates can't take it, too bad. I guess we'd have to go play somewhere else where the fans would be easier on us. For those who stayed, for those who were up to the challenge, I can't think of a better place to play during that era. They stuck with us even when things went poorly, and they made the Garden just about the toughest place in the league for visiting teams. And back then, we flew commercial, so we would see our fans in the airport and even end up on flights with them. The rinks were more intimate, and there was a real rapport between the team and the fans. The bottom line was Boston fans demanded an honest effort.

I especially appreciated the fact that our fans knew their hockey and understood the subtle parts of the game that go beyond just getting points. That was a good thing, because I never consciously went out for a game with the sole purpose of scoring two goals, for example. Some of my best games during my time in Boston were ones in which I never even got on the score sheet, but our fans got it. They understood that on the ice you can affect a game in many different ways, and it wasn't always about being a point producer.

As the years went by and they got to know me better, they could also see in some games when things just weren't going my way. If you gain a measure of success in the league, opponents start to pay more attention to you. They try to shrink your time and space any way they can. Some nights, I can remember being almost hog-tied during games, but if you asked the referee if he hadn't seen the holding against you, the response would often be, "Hey, you're a superstar, aren't you? You have to learn to take that." In today's game, players can't get away with as much hooking and holding, but back then it was standard operating procedure for many teams. The rules on interference, holding, and the like were just different back then, and you could get away with a lot more. But as I've noted, our fan base understood those parts of the game, and I was always treated fairly by our people in the stands, even on the tough nights.

And there were tough nights. If it wasn't the other team, more and more it was my own knee that was slowing me down. The feeling in the joint wasn't so much a sharp pain as a dull, constant grind, like a toothache. The soreness and stiffness were never far from my mind, though I did everything I could to push them away. You don't think about the pain, but that doesn't mean it's not there.

I'd play a game, and then the routine would be to get ice on my knee to keep the swelling down. And the morning after a game was always tough, because the soreness would be impossible to ignore. Getting out of bed first thing became a chore, and yet the only way to loosen it up was to get moving.

Back-to-back games became increasingly difficult to handle. I don't just mean the discomfort. Every athlete deals with that. I don't want to make myself into a special case. Guys play with broken bones, with stitches in their faces, with joints taped together by the trainer so they can get through one more game. I've seen guys get up when they should stay down, or play on when they should sit out. So I'm not going to say I'm special because I played through some pain. Some guys may play through a bit more pain than others over their careers, but everyone does it.

What bothered me was the way the stiffness affected my play. Every time I stepped on the ice, I felt restricted. I couldn't play my game. I just couldn't generate the same power in my skating that I once had. When the stiffness in my knee took away the sharpness of my turning, stopping, accelerating, and so on, a big part of the way I played the game was gone.

Professional hockey players talk about going out on the ice and having fun, which may sometimes sound strange to fans, who don't always go to work expecting to have fun. But it's not as strange as it sounds. Enjoying the game meant performing to the top of my ability, and trying to never disappoint my teammates—or the fans.

Like all athletes, I had my own ways of doing things, some based on routine, some on superstition, I suppose. Some writers have guessed that the reason I went with a single wrap of tape on my blade was because it allowed the puck to release quicker, meaning that my shot would be harder. Others have figured I was trying to make some kind of fashion statement. Those are very interesting concepts, but the truth is much simpler. For some reason, when I came into the NHL, I had it in my mind that there was a rule that all players had to have at least some tape on their stick blade. I suppose it was an easy assumption to make, given that everybody did indeed have their stick blades wrapped with the traditional black tape.

In my case, I liked the feel of the puck on the blade without any tape at all. So the idea came to me that if I *had* to have tape on my stick, I would use as little as possible. Over the years, I used less and less until I was down to a single stripe. And eventually I ended up with no tape at all.

Then there was the fact that I didn't wear socks in my skates when I played. Why would someone not wear socks? The answer is that when I played junior hockey, you were responsible for packing your own equipment, and on one trip I forgot to include a pair of socks in my equipment bag. The only option I had was to go without socks—and it felt pretty good. I decided I would just not bother with socks from that point forward. I've been tempted over the years to make up some wild stories about these things, but the truth is they just happened in a natural kind of way, and I never really thought much about it.

One thing I took seriously was my routine. Even dating back to my days in junior hockey, I always liked getting to the rink early on game day to get ready. In Boston, that meant arriving at the rink somewhere round 2 P.M. The trainers eventually gave me my own keys, because on game day I often got there before they did. During those moments, I was alone in my favorite environment and could get ready for that day's game by myself and in my own way. That's an important fundamental for any athlete, finding what works for

Back in Parry Sound with a couple of trophies I won in my rookie year —the Elisabeth Dufresne Trophy on the right, awarded by Boston sportswriters, and the Gallery Gods trophy.

After a win. Notice that I didn't wear shoulder pads. I just had the caps sewn onto my braces.

Right: *Taking a break during practice with Derek Sanderson at the old Garden. The lineup changed a lot in my second year in Boston, but no one was more colorful than Turk.*

Below: *Here I am in a pre-season game in my rookie season, doing my best to clear the Rangers' Reg Fleming from Gerry Cheevers's crease. Note that I am wearing number 27. I didn't put on number 4 until later.*

The 1970 goal from an unfamiliar angle. The first shot captures the moment just after the puck went into the net, but the last one shows what hockey is all about.

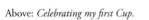

Above: *Celebrating my first Cup.*

Right: *Our trainer and my good friend and roommate John "Frosty" Forrestall.*

Top right: *Derek Sanderson and Shaky Walton in the parade for Bobby Orr Day in Parry Sound. Check out Derek's collar.*

Top left: *That's Eddie Johnston beside me in the convertible.*

Bottom: *That's my mother and father riding in style. It's always great to come home, but it means a lot more to share it with family and friends.*

Right: *The man who turned the Bruins around: Bruins GM and my good friend, Milt Schmidt.*

Below: *I'd take these guys on my team any day—that's me with Phil Esposito, Bobby Hull, and Gordie Howe at the 1971 NHL All-Star Dinner.*

Above: *At my Grandma Orr's cottage—I've got my hand on her shoulder on the far right. I'm talking to my Aunt Margaret and my cousin Joanne. In the back row, from left to right, are my aunt Joyce Abbott, and my cousins Robbie Atherton, Debbie Atherton, and Neil Abbott. You might recognize some of the people in the front row. On the far left is my brother-in-law Ron Blanchard and sister, Penny; my wife, Peggy; and that's Darryl Sittler and his late wife, Wendy, at the right.*

Left: *Boating with Peggy on Georgian Bay along with Eddie Johnston and his wife, Diane.*

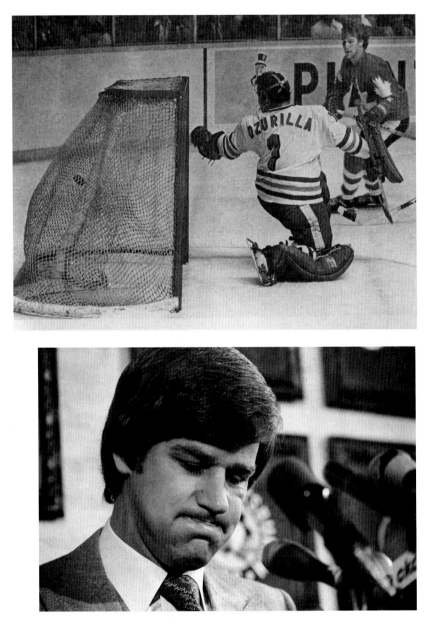

Top: *One of the great thrills of my career was the one time I got to play for my country in the Canada Cup in 1976. Czech goalie Vladimir Dzurilla played great in that tournament, but here I managed to get one by him.*

Above: *At the press conference announcing my retirement, November 8, 1978. You can probably tell from the look on my face that it was a tough moment for me.*

you and then making that a part of who you are. No two athletes prepare the same. Some of my teammates would get to the rink at 5 P.M., having taken a nap after their pre-game meal at midday or early in the afternoon. Others would head out to a matinee movie, because going to a show would settle their nerves and relax them for the game. For every player on the roster, there was probably the same number of different ways to prepare, and no one cared how you got ready just so long as you did indeed get ready. In those days, we didn't focus much on the mental aspect of professional sport, or at least we didn't use fancy terminology for it. But I believe my routine was a great help to me in the mental part of my game preparation.

There were two things I primarily concerned myself with during my playing career. The first was to be as consistent as possible at the level I felt I could attain. The second was to focus on the things I could control and not get wrapped up in a whole bunch of distractions. I tried to play the same game no matter who the opponent might be, and I didn't think much about other specific players or change my game to match up to theirs. I just played my game and let others worry about systems. It's the same game no matter who you're playing against, so worrying about the other guy is only going to get in the way. I can think of a couple of exceptions, though.

Bobby Hull could beat you in so many ways, it was a balancing act to take them all away at once. Let him get outside you, and he was so strong and so fast that there was no way to keep him from cutting back in. Anytime he came over center ice, Bobby was dangerous because of his shot. Generally, you had to stand him up early. There aren't many guys in the league even today who can shoot it the way Bobby Hull did more than forty years ago. Guys like Guy Lafleur and Yvan Cournoyer had truly unbelievable speed and could make anyone look like they were standing still if you played them wrong. No one had a perfect answer for Hull, though.

The other guy I always had to keep an eye on was Stan Mikita. Stan was a truly dynamic player who won more than his share of Art Ross Trophies and Hart Trophies (and even a couple of Lady Byngs, despite racking up triple digits in penalty minutes early in his career), but what I remember him for was his passing. He was probably the best passer in the league. If there was a guy coming late, Stan would pick him up and the puck would be on his stick.

These were a few of the players who got my attention. But of course, if you take anything for granted at the NHL level, you are going to get burned. The best approach is to respect everyone.

Most times, I just thought about what I was going to do. I worried about myself and my own play. That was how I prepared, plain and simple.

Given that I was a professional athlete, my years in Boston meant I had exposure to a lot of famous people, and not just from the sports world. I was fortunate to meet and get to know people in entertainment, the political arena, and so on. My intent here is not to be some kind of name-dropper. Rather, it is to share a few ideas and stories about some pretty impressive people who made an impact on me in various ways. As a part of our growth and maturing, we come into contact with a wide variety of friends, acquaintances, and characters. Many of those people will, either by chance or by choice, influence who we become. That is true whether they are famous or not. It's probably a good strategy to try to associate yourself with as many successful people in this world as you can, and hope that what positive attributes they have might rub off on you, if even just a little bit.

Many of the people I am about to describe understood what professionalism was all about on many different levels, but most importantly they had a keen sense of how you treat others. They showed me certain personal characteristics that I admire, or they lived their lives in such a way as to share values that anyone could learn from. These were people I was a big fan of and admired. That is one of the benefits of celebrity, I suppose—you get some opportunities that many people never have the chance to experience.

I don't want to mention these people in any particular order, but only one was known as the "Greatest." I saw him fight at ringside a few times, and he and I were in Bob Hope's *Gillette Cavalcade of Champions* a couple of times. He was one of my favorite athletes of all time. His athleticism was spellbinding. Muhammad Ali was the reigning heavyweight champion of the world when I saw him, and that title was the loftiest in all sport during that era. Ali *was* boxing! In combination with his good friend Howard Cosell, Ali elevated his sport far beyond what it had ever been.

When Ali stepped into the ring, he had a certain presence that seems to accompany athletes who possess greatness. He gave off that same aura just walking into a room. The man seemed to fill every corner of any place he entered, and that presence would then spill out into the hallways as well. The champ was a physically big man, probably six foot three in his prime, and he carried himself with tremendous self-assurance. He knew who he was, and he possessed great confidence in his abilities.

I've always thought there are certain athletes who are perfectly matched to their sport. There is a match in physical skill, mental toughness, and a passion to succeed that ends up elevating them to the top of their profession. Muhammad Ali was that man in boxing. Like many other great athletes, Ali could have been very successful in any number of sports.

We all know the terrible price that the champ has paid in his later years as Parkinson's disease robbed him of some of his ability. Our paths have crossed a few times over the years, but one memory I will always cherish is of the last time I saw him many years ago in New Jersey. It was a special event with a host of famous athletes and celebrities in attendance, and Ali was in the building. I sought him out, simply wanting to go up and shake his hand one more time. I waited my turn as he sat in a corner of the room until finally I had a chance to step up and say hello. I didn't think he would remember me or the times we had met in the past, and that really didn't matter. But as I grabbed his hand, he looked up at me, gave me that great Ali smile, and whispered, "Kid, you're alright!" Whether he truly recognized me or not, it was still a thrill to see him again and hear him say those words. There have been many great athletes in our history, and there will be many more to come, but somehow I can't imagine anyone being any better at his craft or meaning any more to his sport than Muhammad Ali to his.

There is another king of his sport who taught me what professionalism looks like. I watched him on television for many years before I had the opportunity to meet him in person, and you couldn't help but marvel at how he handled himself. Arnold Palmer was and still remains a pro's pro. If you were to guess that my first encounter with the "King" was at a golf outing, you would be correct. But in the case of Arnold, although I certainly knew who he was in the sporting world while I was with the Bruins, it wasn't until I had retired from the game that I got to meet and spend some time with the legend. It's pretty special when you have an impression of someone and then find, when you finally get to meet and know him, that he actually exceeds expectations. That was Arnold Palmer.

I am especially fond of the memories I have from a gathering I was fortunate enough to attend many years after my playing career had ended. It was held in Brookline, Massachusetts, in 1999. During that particular Ryder Cup competition, there was a dinner at Symphony Hall in Boston. It was a night to honor Arnold, who had just turned seventy, and it was a very special evening indeed. Attendees included the likes of President George Bush Sr., an avid golfer himself, and I recall that the legendary sportscaster Jim McKay was the emcee that evening. Steven Tyler was one of the performers, as were the Boston Pops. So you can see, it was a star-studded evening. I was there along with many good friends, including Dick Connolly, a man who is also close friends with Arnold.

Dick had made arrangements for a few of us to golf with Arnie while the King was staying in the Boston area. I had been at several functions he had attended over the years, specifically at various pro–am events associated with the Champions Tour. I had never spent a lot of time with him one-on-one, however, so being on the course and golfing together was going to be very special for me. We showed up at the designated time at the Kittansett Club in Marion. As I leaned over to put my ball on the tee for my first shot of the day, I was so nervous I could hardly see the ball, let alone swing at it. All I wanted was to get the thing airborne.

I looked over at the King and said, "Arnie, I bet you're really nervous teeing it up with us, eh?" He laughed at that one. I wasn't in my element, and I wasn't on my turf, so as a result it was all quite nerve-racking. Put me on a sheet of ice, and everything is nice and easy. But here, in this world, I was a wreck. Leave it to Arnie to make me feel comfortable almost immediately. That allowed me to laugh and enjoy the moment. He can do what only the truly great personalities can do: make you feel comfortable in his presence. He has a wonderful sense of humor and a twinkle in his eye that just makes you feel at ease.

I would play again with Arnie a few years later at his golf course at Bay Hill during the pro–am portion of the tournament. There was one hole during that round that stands out in my mind. We were on a par-5 hole with a tee shot that had to carry over a body of water, and Arnold hit his drive over the hazard and right down the middle of the fairway. His second shot set him up for a short club into the green. His approach shot was a little wedge that landed about twelve feet from the pin, and everyone in the gallery, his famous "Arnie's Army," was going absolutely bananas. You guessed it—he stepped up to the putt and drained it for a birdie. With waves of applause coming from the gallery, Arnold reached into the cup, picked up his ball, and looked over at me. He had the greatest smile on his face you can imagine, and when I said, "You really are a show-off, aren't you?" he responded with, "Bobby, I used to do that ALL the time!" I've played a lot of golf over the years, but that is a highlight that will be tough to beat.

Arnold has the type of personality that gains the attention of everyone, even his peers. During that pro–am at Bay Hill, as he walked to each tee box, fellow competitors would stop and just watch him go by. They were in awe of him. What has remained consistent about Arnold across all the years is the way he conducts himself so professionally, regardless of his environment. It doesn't matter who he is with, Arnold treats them all in the same respectful way. I have always maintained that the best experience any athlete could ever have would be to spend a day with Arnold so they could watch how a real pro acts around others. In that one day, they would very quickly come to realize that with great success comes great responsibility, *especially* to the fans. Arnold Palmer respects that idea, day after day after day. He will certainly go down as one of the greatest golfers of all time. More importantly, he stands as a role model for how to carry oneself as a pro.

I've also been able to meet some people from the entertainment world. One actor who stands out for me is a Canadian by birth and a man who has demonstrated great courage in his life. When I was playing in Boston, he would have been a ten- or twelve-year-old youngster growing up in Vancouver. I never met Michael J. Fox back then, but I do remember our first meeting at a celebrity hockey function. I was immediately struck by something about him. Here was a very famous TV and movie star, yet he was obviously someone who was very humble and easy to be with. There were no airs when it came to Michael, and I have always enjoyed his company.

But that was some time ago. Since then, I have come to respect Michael on a whole different level. His battle with Parkinson's disease has been an inspiration to millions of people who suffer with this terrible affliction. Rather than go underground, Michael has chosen to take this condition in his life and do something about it for other people. The word I think of now whenever I see Michael doing an interview is *perseverance*, because he just keeps grinding at this disease. Michael keeps working at it and will not allow any setbacks or discouragement to stop him. He is an inspiration to all who meet him. A while back, someone sent me an article in which Michael was asked which living people he most admired. He responded by saying, "Nelson Mandela and Bobby Orr." Imagine him saying something like that. Well, I'll say this: Michael J. Fox is on my own list of most-admired as well. He is a wonderful person, and I am better for knowing him.

Meeting all these people meant a lot to me, and taught me a lot. There was one celebrity in particular who also played in Boston whom I had hoped for years to meet. Our paths didn't cross until I had retired and we both found ourselves at a black-tie fundraiser benefiting Tony Conigliaro, the great former Red Sox player.

On that particular night, April 26, 1983, I was there with Joe Fitzgerald, a reporter with the *Boston Herald*. As I glanced around to take in the sights and sounds, I noticed a man on the other side of the room. He was the only guy not wearing a tuxedo. All at once I could see the profile, and I turned to Joe and asked, "Is that who I think it is?"

It was Ted Williams, in the flesh. Joe told me to go over and introduce myself. I was hesitant. I may have been a Boston Bruin, but this was *Ted Williams*. He was chatting with some other people as I made my way toward him, and when it finally looked like I was next in line, I stuck out my hand and said, "Mr. Williams, it's a pleasure to meet you. My name is Bobby Orr."

He stood up, shook my hand, and without missing a beat replied, "So, I hear you caught a big one this summer, kid. Tell me about it."

Ted was much more than a great baseball player, and actually holds a distinction I don't believe any other major-leaguer can claim: he is the only player named to the Baseball Hall of Fame who is also enshrined in the Fishing Hall of Fame. As much as Ted loved baseball, I know that fishing was right up there as one of his great passions in life. That is something the Red Sox slugger and I had in common.

Although he fished many sites in Canada, Ted could often be found at a fishing camp on the Miramichi River in New Brunswick. As fate would have it, I was fortunate enough to have landed a forty-five-pound salmon that summer, and it was the talk of the town. All of the fishing guides in the area soon heard of this big fish, and the news spread pretty quickly.

Through the fishing-guide grapevine, news of my lunker had even reached the man I still think of as the best hitter ever to pick up a bat. He studied everything he could that was related to his craft, especially when it came to hitting. I once asked him, years later, about a story I had read detailing what was going through his mind as he stood at the plate. It was claimed that Ted could actually see the seams on a baseball as it left the pitcher's hand. He laughed at that one and said, "Look, I studied pitchers. I knew what pitches they could throw, and when they tended to throw them. That stuff about seeing seams is a good story, but just not true."

Just like he studied pitchers, he apparently studied other fishermen as well. He asked me all kinds of questions about what fly I'd used to get my big catch, what the weather conditions had been like, and so on. For those twenty minutes, there was no one else in the room, just him and me talking about fishing. At one point, while I was recounting the story, I made a demonstration of my casting technique. He grabbed my arm and said, "No, no, no! You've got to get your arm more up and back." Right then and there, in a room full of people dressed up in tuxedos (me included), Ted Williams taught me how to properly throw a fly.

What I saw that night from Ted was something all great athletes, perhaps all the greats in any discipline, possess, and that is the ability to focus. We were just talking, and this was probably Ted Williams at his most relaxed, but his eyes bore in on me, and there was nothing that was going to interrupt our discussion.

There have been some tremendous athletes who played in New England. I know all about Larry Bird and Carl Yastrzemski, Bill Russell and, in modern times, Tom Brady. They are all great athletes, without question. But whenever you think of New England sporting legends, Ted Williams has always stood at the top of the heap. As I write this, he remains the last major-leaguer to hit over .400 in a season, a feat that looks more and more untouchable. Given the new age of baseball, with relief specialists and the like, I doubt that .400 will ever be achieved again.

To be able to spend that time with a living legend was a great thrill for me. I was fortunate enough later to actually head out on some fishing trips with Ted and see him in action. He was a master angler, and he always tied his own flies, which tells you a lot about his passion for fishing. He loved my wife, Peggy, who likes to fly-fish. I got to know him pretty well—and I'm not sure I ever saw him in a tuxedo.

I guess you could say Ted Williams was a man's man. He was a big, gruff guy, and a lot of people found him pretty intimidating. But I can tell you, he was a very humble man, with a great sense of humor. If you really want to know what kind of man he was, this is a guy who gave up years, not only when he was in the prime of his life, but in the prime of a record-setting career, to fight for his country. He was a combat pilot in two wars, and was shot down over Korea. Ted was a special athlete, sure, but more importantly, once you got to know him, he was someone it was impossible not to respect. He was someone who always knew who he was and what he wanted. I guess what I'm saying is, there was nothing phony about

Ted. Now that I think of it, there were a lot of similarities between Ted and Don Cherry. Both men had their opinions and stuck to them, and both men did things their own way. Those characteristics have always impressed me. That night, meeting and speaking with Ted for the very first time, stays fresh in my mind to this day.

When I think about the men I have just mentioned, it is obvious that they are role models, especially for young people. If you really wanted to find fault with these men, and were willing to dig deep enough, I'm sure you could. But in the big picture, they all understood their responsibility. What they did in their fields, and what they did away from the spotlight, tells me that they all "got it." There are many other people I could mention, but these are the guys who stand out for me.

Many years ago, a star basketball player claimed he didn't have any responsibility as a role model and that he didn't believe that those types of expectations should be placed on pro athletes. I have to respectfully disagree. To suggest there is no responsibility as a role model is dangerous. After all, it's the fans and the public who inevitably pay the bills, and therefore your salary, so pro athletes need to accept some kind of responsibility toward them. The moment you sign on as a professional athlete, or even at the elite levels of amateur sport, you automatically become enrolled in the "Role Model Club," whether you like it or not. How you handle membership in that particular club is up to you.

If someone is looking up to you as a role model, chances are you have been very lucky in life. You may have worked hard, but you have also received some pretty spectacular gifts. That doesn't mean you're better than anyone else, and it doesn't mean you deserve what you've got. It just means you received a gift. In my view, that means you've got an obligation to share that gift.

Not that anyone should expect an athlete to be perfect. No one is superhuman, and no professional athlete (or a retired one, for that matter!) can be perfect twenty-four hours a day, seven days a week. Athletes will make their share of mistakes. But when you do make a mistake, you own up and accept responsibility. People are very forgiving in most cases and will give a lot of rope to an athlete if they only admit to and accept their faults. I'm no different than anyone else—there are things I did at certain times during my career that I am not particularly proud of. Some of those things happened on the ice, some off it. It's almost as if you go through different stages in your development as a person: your parents first put down a solid foundation for you, you end up making your mistakes, and then you find your way again. You are suddenly hoisted up there on that pedestal, and it can be tough on anyone and can sometimes affect your judgment. I think that eventually, when you end up on the other side of your career, when that pedestal has been removed, you become more centered again and everything turns out alright. At least I hope that's been the case in my life, though I leave that judgment to others.

We won that second Stanley Cup in 1972, but we would not win it again. Of course, I'm greedy. I feel we should have won in 1971, and again in 1974. Once you have a taste of the Cup, you want it again. We started thinking about a dynasty as soon as we were back in the dressing room after our overtime win in 1970. To this day, fans who followed us during that era will come up to me and share their opinion that we should have won more than two championships. I have to agree with them. But we never got to raise the Cup again.

That's not to say the Bruins went into steep decline. We played a lot of great hockey, and Boston was a powerhouse for the rest of the decade. But the ingredients you need to win it all, the good luck and the hard work, and the sense of destiny, just weren't all there. We had a strong regular season in 1972–73, but lost to New York in the first round. The fact that we lost Espo early in that series didn't help our chances.

On a personal note, Bep Guidolin, who had been my coach when Oshawa went to the Memorial Cup, replaced Tom Johnson behind the bench partway through that season. Guidolin had played for the Bruins himself when he was younger (in fact, when he was sixteen he was the youngest player ever to suit up in the NHL). He also coached the Belleville McFarlands to victory at the World Championship, so no one could say he didn't know the game. Harry Sinden was back with the Bruins as well.

On the other hand, the team that won that first Cup was being chipped away, piece by piece. We lost a few guys to expansion, most notably Ed Westfall to the New York Islanders. And we lost Gerry Cheevers and Pie McKenzie to the newly formed World Hockey Association, which had already made a splash by luring away Bobby Hull. Derek Sanderson left for the WHA, too, but came back. Not that anyone in the dressing room judged those guys harshly. We were definitely disappointed to see them go, but we also understood they had to take care of themselves and their families. For most professional hockey players, you have only a very small window of time to play, so who could blame anyone for trying to maximize their financial return. If the NHL wasn't prepared to pay, they now had a viable alternative. But the end result for Boston was that an era was fast coming to a close, and the Big Bad Bruins would never be the same.

Still, we dominated the regular season in 1973–74, and once again had the top four scorers in the league. We swept the Leafs in the first round of the playoffs, and took care of the Rangers in six games in the second. In the Stanley Cup final, we faced the Philadelphia Flyers. Philadelphia may have been an expansion team, but they were not to be taken lightly. In Bernie Parent, they had a goalie who could steal games, in Bobby Clarke they had a captain who would do anything to win. And as a team, they didn't take a backseat to the Big Bad Bruins when it came to toughness. We were the regular-season champions, though, and most of us had a couple of rings already, so we knew we had what it took to get a third.

But we lost that series in six, and we lost on the road, so we saw the Philadelphia Spectrum fans celebrate the way the Boston fans had in 1970, just four years earlier. That series stands as a bitter disappointment to me. Like the loss in 1971, we had that Cup within our grasp and let it slip away. If losing a Stanley Cup final weren't so crushing, winning it wouldn't be so exhilarating.

We weren't conceding anything the following season, either. We still had the top two scorers in the league, and we were still playing with pride. There wasn't a guy in the room who thought he'd never raise the Cup again. But we never did. In the spring of 1975, we were knocked out of the playoffs in a five-game preliminary round by Chicago. And that was that.

We had a great run as a group, with three appearances in the finals over a five-year span, and we had two unforgettable Stanley Cup victories. And though in many ways that season ended in disappointment, I met someone that year who would come to mean a great deal not only to the Boston Bruins and to the game of hockey in general but also to me in particular. It simply wouldn't be proper if I didn't dedicate some space in these pages to him, because he deserves more than a passing mention, and he is going to receive his due. It is rare in sport when a person, regardless of his or her success as a player or coach, ends up being someone that average fans truly identify with. It is rarer still when someone retires from their sport and actually gains in popularity as they grow older. And in hockey, there is one person in Canada most everyone in the country would identify immediately.

In case you haven't guessed, his name is Don Cherry.

Seven

GRAPES

Don "Grapes" Cherry came to Parry Sound for an Easter Seals skate-a-thon fundraiser many years ago. I took him over to meet my Grandma Orr just before he was to leave town. She was in her nineties by then, but Grandma walked right up to Don, looked up at him (though she couldn't see very well anymore), and poked a finger in his chest. She said, "Mr. Cherry, I like you, because you're the only one who always tells the truth."

My grandmother wasn't the only person who has felt that way about Don. I get my fair share of looks from people when I travel, but whenever I'm with him they often walk right by me in order to speak with Grapes. When you are with Don, he is the only person they see. It's truly amazing how recognizable this man is. I've told him that the only reason he gets so much attention is because of those wild suit jackets he wears. You know what I'm talking about, the ones that look like they've been fashioned from odd sets of drapes (seriously, he picks the patterns out himself at Fabricland). But it's not just that. As much as some people may disagree with his opinions, Don is loved by millions, and there is a reason for the adoration. There's a reason he was voted one of the top ten in the CBC's *The Greatest Canadian*. He has a rare quality that few people have the courage to imitate. He tells it like it is.

I know that to this day he takes pride in the fact that average Canadians just like my grandma see that quality in him. Frankly, I wish I had the courage to say some of the things Don has said over the years. I know he has often expressed an opinion when he fully understood that trouble would follow. He may often be out of step with what everybody else is saying, but it is not as though he's unaware he is taking a position others in the media won't share. In Don's mind, the truth is worth the fight that always seems to be going on around him. He is not afraid to go nose to nose with politicians, with the league, with hockey guys like Brian Burke, or even his own bosses at the CBC. He will not change his opinions to suit other people, and I've always respected him for that.

I should be clear that I can't be expected to be objective about Don in this chapter. He is one of my best friends in the world. And yes, he is undoubtedly one of my biggest supporters. I realize there are probably some people out there who do not share my personal feelings about Don. I know he's not for everybody. But even if you don't necessarily like him, or if you disagree with some of his opinions, you must concede at the very least that he shines a bright spotlight on the game of hockey. Even if our feelings about this man differ, it is impossible to deny that he is better known across North America than most players in the National

Hockey League. He's not just a unique person, not even just a good person. He is an asset to the game, no matter what else you think about him.

I'd like to share some insights about the Don Cherry I know. He is a man I have learned to appreciate over the many years of our friendship, and you really should know more about this giant in the game. So, although I may be a bit biased, allow me to share my views on a man I have come to both love and respect.

The first time I met Don was just after he'd been named the new head coach of the Rochester Americans of the American Hockey League. It was 1972, and I was at the induction ceremony for Gordie Howe at the Hockey Hall of Fame in Toronto. By that time in my career, I had played on two Stanley Cup–winning teams and was pretty well known, especially in a hockey-crazy town like Toronto. As usual, the press had gathered for the event, and many of us in attendance were being sought by all kinds of newspeople and fans alike, so much so that it was difficult to get away, even for a quick bite of food.

Don saw that I was being cornered and was unable to enjoy my meal very much, so he walked up to me, introduced himself, and said, "I'll provide some cover for you." He stood in front of me during that luncheon so no one could get to me until I'd finished my meal. It was the first of many times that Don would step up to the plate and help me when I needed a hand in some way.

I had absolutely no idea who he was. He was coming off his first year as head coach of the Rochester Americans, where he had started the season as a player, and he had been a career minor-leaguer, so our paths had never crossed. But two years later, we would meet again, this time in the Boston Garden. Only, on that occasion, he was about to become my new coach with the Bruins.

Don has shared one particular story through the years about the day when he found out he was getting the head job in Boston. He hurried home to tell his young son, Tim, the good news. "Tim, your dad is going to be the new head coach of the Boston Bruins." His son said, "Dad, that's great! I'll get to meet Bobby Orr!" To which Don replied, "Yeah, Timmy—me too!"

And speaking of his son, I'd come to know Tim over the years, too, and spend time with him on some fun outings, especially fishing. It was on one of those trips that I thought Don's beloved dog Blue was going to kill me. We were expected back at Don's house around 4 P.M. that day, but as fate would have it, the fish were really biting. There was no way Tim and I were going to pack up and leave, so we decided to extend the day on the water.

Four P.M. soon became 5, then 6, then 7, and before you knew it, it was about 8 P.M. before we pulled into the Cherry driveway. I guess Don and his wife, Rose, had been getting worried that something had happened, so when we pulled up, the door opened and they came out, relieved to see that their son was still in one piece. Blue came tearing out as well, barking and snarling, making every sign that she was about to attack me, but Don got her under control. Can you imagine the headlines if Blue had sunk her teeth into me? "Orr Out 4 Weeks, Cherry's Dog the Culprit!" (For years after that incident, Rose claimed that Don really wasn't concerned about Timmy all that much. She maintained he was more worried about his defenseman.)

As a leader, Don was what you might call a player's coach, and the guys identified with him on many levels. We immediately saw he was one of us. He had played only one game in the NHL—a playoff game for the Bruins in 1955—but more than a thousand in the minors. Everyone in the room figured this guy had paid his dues. If you ride the buses all those years in several different minor leagues, and move fifty-three times from one unfamiliar city to another, it says something about the passion you have for the game, and it says something about your personal toughness. (The fact that he piled up over a thousand penalty minutes during his career also gives you a good sense of his toughness.) To us, his commitment to play in the American Hockey League demonstrated above all else that Coach Cherry was no quitter, and that is exactly the type of person you want watching your back as a coach. It didn't hurt either that he was coming off winning Coach of the Year in the AHL and had won four Calder Cups as a player, or that he had won a Memorial Cup in junior. Cherry wasn't just stubborn and tough—he was a winner, too. Grapes was finally able to reap all he had sown over those many years as a minor league player when in 1974 he became a head coach in the National Hockey League.

You shouldn't misinterpret the "player's coach" label as meaning that Don was soft on us. He always had a very specific vision of how things should be done, and that vision was nonnegotiable. He was a personality, a forceful personality, and he brought that to the rink every day. He was self-assured and felt he had the roadmap to success, and that was that. There was never a lot of room for discussion when it came to Grapes and the way he wanted to run his team.

He demanded that his players were always prepared to play, and he expected performance on a daily basis. He was a person who motivated people brilliantly. Was he the greatest X's and O's coach in the league? Probably not, but the guys would go through the end boards for him. Don was loved by the vast majority of his players.

Yet he could also be very hard on you if you didn't play to your level. Don and I were on the same page right from the start on that point, because coaches and teammates must be able to trust players to deliver, no matter when. If you didn't carry your weight, Don wouldn't keep you in the lineup for long.

I was lucky in that Don continued a philosophy of coaching I had grown up with from minor hockey. Consistency in coaching styles is, I think, very important, and something I wish more coaches would consider, regardless of the level at which they find themselves coaching. That is, Don allowed his players to play the game their way if that would benefit the team. In my case, that meant puck control and skating. He didn't ask me to dump and chase, or use the glass to get the puck safely out of the zone. My role was to skate and control the puck. Don was smart enough to avoid putting a harness on his players, and instead expected us to get up ice and be creative. He understood there would be mistakes as a result of that style of play. He saw the potential downside, but obviously must have liked the potential upside, too.

I was at a function with Don years after we had both retired from the game, and during a little question-and-answer session, someone asked Grapes about his approach to coaching me while in Boston. In typical Cherry fashion, he had an answer ready: "One thing you don't do is over-coach a Bobby Orr. Imagine me trying to tell Bobby what to do on the ice. How stupid would that be?" The audience loved it, and the truth is that Don did use a hands-off approach—as long as you were doing your job.

If you asked Don today, he'd tell you he had only three rules to guide those great Bruin teams of the 1970s. He'd say something like, "First, in the offensive zone, you can be as creative as you want. Try anything that will get the puck into the back of their net, no problem. Second, in the defensive zone, the exact opposite is true. In the D zone, you do what I tell you when I tell you, and if you don't, I won't argue about it, I just won't play you. And finally, rule number 3, if Orr has the puck on a rush, for goodness sakes don't go offside."

I still get a chuckle out of rule number 3. To steal one of his own phrases, Don is a real beauty! But let's give credit where credit is due. Don attributes a lot of his success to me, but the year he won the Jack Adams Trophy for NHL coach of the year, I wasn't playing for him.

The other part of his personality that has remained unchanged after all these years is his flair for the dramatic. I don't believe I'm exaggerating when I say he is arguably the most colorful coach ever to have stood behind the bench of an NHL team. Don always drew a lot of attention to himself, and in an odd way that allowed his players to fly under the radar and just play the game. He would take the heat from the press when things went bad, but deflect attention toward his players when things were going well. That's the sign of a real leader. Yes, Don enjoyed the limelight, but he used it first and foremost to the advantage of his team.

Consequently, over the years he has been a lightning rod for praise as well as criticism from players, fans, owners, ticket takers, and everyone else associated with the game of hockey. Certainly, public figures have to be ready for that kind of scrutiny, and in Don's case people either seem to love him or hate him. Today, ensuring that people have some sort of opinion about him is a part of his job. But even if you're not a fan of Don Cherry, his good points are not open to debate. As I've said, he is without question the most consistent man I have ever met, bar none. He is a man of absolute honesty, absolute loyalty, and ceaseless friendship. He has a heart of gold, and let me assure you that the sometimes-gruff exterior is a front for a kindness underneath that is beyond description. A thousand times, I have seen him do things for people that never get in the papers, because he insists they stay private. It is impossible to calculate how many times over the past thirty years Don Cherry has called and asked if I could autograph something for a needy child, an adult he's just met, or for one of our troops. He is unbelievable in his giving, and I don't think he receives the credit for it he deserves. He is without question one of the kindest men I have ever known. He's been my coach, my friend, my mentor, and my second father. He has guided me through some tough times in my life and has always been there to support my family. I know he'll always be there for me in the future, too, and that is a great comfort.

A s I write this, Don Cherry is still not a member of the Hockey Hall of Fame, and to me it is one of the greatest oversights in the history of the game. He has left an unequaled mark on hockey over the past fifty years, not just in Canada but internationally as well. He played the game and coached it at the highest level. Of course, younger generations of Canadians know him better as the colorful hockey analyst and main personality on CBC's *Hockey Night in Canada* (no offense to Ron MacLean). His "Coaches Corner" segment during those broadcasts is legendary—it's the most-watched few minutes of television in Canada. Most of us can't even imagine the game without him.

But that is only part of his story. Besides assisting in the growth of the game through his work in the broadcast booth, Don continually goes above and beyond to spread the good word about the game he holds so dear. From hospitals to military bases, from minor hockey rinks to charity events, Don has become an ambassador for all that is good about our game. I know he has never paused to add up all the money he has raised for good causes over the years, but I would guess it is well into the millions. His selflessness in serving the needs of many groups within the hockey community is a testament to his ability to build bridges within our sport. The honored members that make up the Hockey Hall of Fame are all people who have contributed to the game. Don undoubtedly deserves a place in that inspirational group, as his dedication to promoting and improving the game has been unparalleled.

Now, you could argue that Don's career as an NHL player was, to be kind, somewhat abbreviated. Critics might contend that his coaching statistics by themselves don't rank him with some of his contemporaries with respect to wins and losses. (As for his career as an NHL player, it's hard to judge him by the one game he played. But, as he says, "Hey, if you build just one bridge, you're a bridge builder, aren't ya?") When you look at the man in total and across time, however—when you look at his positive impact on the growth and development of the game—his record holds up against anyone in the Hall. If you read just a few of the points that are considered for membership in the Hockey Hall of Fame, Don should have been admitted long ago. For example, the Hall bylaws lay out quite clearly that nominees in the Builder category are considered for their "coaching, managerial or executive ability, where applicable, or any other significant off-ice skill or role, sportsmanship, character and their contribution to their organizations and to the game of hockey in general." In other words, the bylaw could have been written about Don Cherry.

His stature within the hockey community is significant and meaningful, and his importance is as great as that of any player, past or present. Given his long-standing and continuing contributions to the game, both at home and abroad, he is more than worthy of nomination into the Hockey Hall of Fame. And I can tell you, I will most definitely be in the audience that evening when this oversight is corrected. I wonder if he'd be able to make it through his speech should his name ever be called. Certainly, his journey should lead to the delivery of that speech as a new member of the Hockey Hall of Fame.

From all the years I've been friends with Don Cherry, one moment stands out. It happened the day my father was put to rest in Parry Sound.

Of course, Don was there. He and Dad were thick as thieves, and my father's passing affected Don greatly. That my father had made the sacrifice of giving up a hockey career to serve in the military was one of the things that endeared him to Don. Grapes visited Parry Sound often over the years, and he had become a great friend to the whole Orr family. Many is the time over the years that he mentioned Doug and Arva during his hockey broadcasts, and sometimes even Grandma Orr, so you know he had a deep connection with my family. I can still remember being with my parents one summer in their familiar place on the front porch of their home when Don and his son, Tim, pulled up to the house. When Don got out of his car, my mother looked at me and asked, "Bob, what color is that suit?" "Lime green, Mom," I replied, "lime green!"

A lime-green suit in Parry Sound in the middle of summer— now that is vintage Don Cherry! My parents shared a lot of laughs with Don over the years, so when the time came, our family decided to ask Don if he'd stand up and say a few words about our father at the funeral. When it was his time to speak, he made his way toward my father's casket. You all know that Don makes his living by talking—he is rarely lost for words, particularly when there is a microphone nearby. But as he walked up to begin, I could see in his eyes that he was struggling.

As he started to talk about Dad, you could tell the emotions were just too tough to contain. He began by remembering my father in stories, and for a moment I thought he might make it to the finish line. But then, all at once, he just went silent. He stood there, this big, gruff, old-school hockey guy, and he simply could not find his voice. The crowd was silent. He looked out over the mourners, and they gazed back at him, and without any words Don Cherry managed to communicate both grief and sympathy. It was a very moving moment, and one I shall always remember. There are all kinds of images people have when it comes to Don Cherry, but the way he was on that day is the way I still think of him: humble and caring, saddened, but courageous enough to go on.

He was a great coach, and I can tell you, he is an even better person. My dad always said that, as a former member of our military, he'd have wanted Don Cherry beside him in a foxhole, because he is the kind of man that can be depended on. Dad was absolutely right on that point. If Don is your friend, he's your friend for life, and he'll always have your back. As time goes by, I've come to appreciate those qualities of his even more. Being able to count Don Cherry as my friend has been one of the great blessings of my life. I'll take him, weird suits and all.

Eight

THE LAST YEARS: 1975–1979

There is no way to recognize the beginning of the end. Anyone reading the headlines in 1975 would have thought my career was in its prime. Things were going well for me. I led the league in scoring in 1974–75, and more importantly I had managed to stay in the lineup. I missed quite a few games earlier in my career, but in 1973–74 and 1974–75, I hardly missed a game. I played seventy-four games in the one season and eighty games in the next. It probably looked as though my knee problems were behind me.

I knew better, though. I had been playing through discomfort for a few years, and it only seemed to get worse. To be honest, I did not think about pain. When I played, I focused on what I needed to do. I didn't worry about what rink I was in, or who was in net for the other team, or whether we'd had a long flight. And I didn't worry about how my left knee felt. But there were more and more things I simply could not do. The question wasn't whether my leg hurt. Increasingly, it was whether I could skate.

At its worst, the knee would just lock up on me. I might do nothing more than go to stand up and the knee would give out or lock. One moment I'd be fine, and the next I'd have difficulty even walking. Doctor Carter Rowe opened up my knee to remove a loose body in September, and I did manage to take my place in the lineup, but I knew something was wrong.

I remember being in a restaurant in Boston, grabbing a meal before heading to the airport to catch our team flight to Chicago. When I got up from the table and put weight on my leg, the knee was completely locked. The *Chicago Tribune* was planning to run a feature on me when the Bruins were in town, and I had to call Bob Verdi, the great Chicago sportswriter, and ask him not to run the piece, because I wouldn't be there for the game. Even if I could have made it to the plane, there was no way I was going to be able to play.

I never played another game as a Bruin.

Not that I didn't try. I went in for another knee surgery in November to remove a torn lateral meniscus. The team and I were given some hope that I would be back in a matter of weeks. But the weeks added up. The Bruins continued to thrive, and were gearing up for another playoff run, and still I was in no condition to skate.

Meanwhile, the team was changing. In a move every bit as monumental as the trade that brought Phil Esposito to Boston, he was traded away to the Rangers in a deal that brought Jean Ratelle and Brad Park to the Bruins—two guys who would turn out to be cornerstones of the team for years to come. The new Bruins made it to the semifinals, where they ran into the Flyers again. The whole season had come and gone, and I had done little more than watch. I've said that losing is a wrenching disappointment, but watching, and wishing you could contribute, is a special kind of agony.

W hat happened next was something I had never prepared for. I thought of myself as a Boston Bruin. I had done so for years. I had been part of the organization since I was in grade school. I loved the city and the fans. I had been surrounded with great people on and off the ice. I can't begin to explain what that city meant to me, and still does. I wanted to stay in Boston.

That's not the way it worked out, though. For reasons I will come to later, I ended up a member of the Chicago Black Hawks.

B efore I pulled on a Chicago sweater, though, I would have one more chance to play for Canada. My knee was not great, and to be honest I considered declining the invitation to play in the Canada Cup—if the tournament was really going to be the world's best against the world's best, I didn't want to be playing at half speed. That would not have been fair to the rest of the team. But after a couple of workouts, I knew that the chance to play for my country was something I could never pass up. I bitterly regretted not playing in 1972, and had missed an opportunity again in January 1976, when the Soviet Red Army team beat the Bruins 5–2. If there was any way I could play, I was going to play.

My roommate for that series was none other than Guy Lafleur, the great Canadiens player and a wonderful person as well. It was nice to be in the same uniform as him for a change, and not have to worry about how to stop him. If you look at that team roster, you'll know it was a pretty good group of players. Some argue that the '76 team was among the best teams, if not *the* best team, ever to represent Canada in international competition. Of course, you'll get arguments about that, but no knowledgeable hockey fan would disagree that it was a strong team, to say the least. Sixteen guys from that team are now in the Hall of Fame.

If you look at the kind of talent we had on that blue line—Larry Robinson, Serge Savard, Guy Lapointe, Jimmy Watson, Denis Potvin, and Carol Vadnais, my teammate on that '72 Stanley Cup–winning team—it's obvious no one was expecting me to carry them. I wouldn't have to log as many minutes as I had in the NHL, and I could simply make a contribution to the team. All things considered, I couldn't say no to an invitation like that. To this day, I am thankful I had that one opportunity to play for my country, and I wouldn't trade the experience for anything.

Anyone who thinks that was a good hockey team would have to concede that Czechoslovakia sent a pretty good team, too. The Soviets played some good hockey, as did the Swedes. But the Czechs were the only team to beat us in the round-robin. And they played us tough in the best-of-three final as well. Their goalie, Vladimír Dzurilla, managed to shut out the likes of Guy Lafleur, Marcel Dionne, Bobby Hull, and Darryl Sittler in the round-robin, and though we managed to get a few by him in the first game of the final, in the second he was standing on his head again and the Czechs were actually leading as the third period was winding down. But Bill Barber sent it to overtime, which set up one of Don Cherry's great coaching moments.

Don, who was an assistant coach on the team, had been watching the game from the stands. Before the start of overtime, he came down to give us some advice on Dzurilla. He was coming way out of his net to cut down his angles, Don said. If you get the chance, he told us, fake the shot and go by him. Barely two minutes later, Darryl Sittler came down the left wing, wound up for a shot, and when Dzurilla came out to challenge him, took a step to the left and had the whole empty net in front of him.

There is nothing like winning for your country. I have said a lot about wanting to win for your teammates, and for the people in your life and in your community. Sports bring people together, and the bigger the game, the bigger the community. It didn't matter to the guys on the bench what team they played for, or even what league they played in. And on a day like that, for fans and players alike, it didn't matter what province you were from, or what political party you voted for. We were all Canadians, and it was an honor to have been part of something that brought people together like that.

The next day, everyone returned to their NHL teams, which meant that for the first time in my career, I was heading somewhere other than Boston.

B eing a professional athlete is a great way to make a living, but it can be tough when you are not physically 100 percent and ready to play. Injuries will eventually catch up to you. The weak parts of your game get exposed pretty quickly, and your opponents will attempt to exploit those weaknesses. And at that point in my career, my lack of mobility was my weakness. And an injury is a weakness. If the other team figures out you've got a cast on your right hand, you can expect them to start slashing your right hand. If you've got a sore shoulder, they're going to hit you every chance they get. If your leg is hurting and you're sluggish turning right, they're going to go to your right every time. You can't fake it at that level. The opposition is just too good, and all the skill in the world can't overcome a major injury or health issue.

One of the problems when you are suffering through an injury is that it restricts your ability to work out. You just can't stay in top shape, which means you can't keep your game sharp. That inability to keep your body conditioned will inevitably lead to a decline in your play. When I headed to training camp in the fall of 1976 after signing with the Chicago Black Hawks, those were the problems I was facing. I was not able to play up to my own expectations. The knees simply would not allow me to perform in the way I'd become accustomed to.

By the time I arrived at the old Chicago Stadium, the clock was ticking faster as my knees continued to deteriorate. It is difficult to describe the frustration I felt as I arrived in the Windy City, because I really did want to help that proud franchise, and I believed I could. Otherwise, I would never have signed a contract.

Looking back, it's easy to say I should never have gone to Chicago, that I was done before I ever got there. I had missed most of the previous season, had gone through several surgeries on that left knee, and was hobbling around in pain. But really, that had been the way things were for me for years. For the better part of my entire professional career, dating back to the first time I was injured during my rookie season, I had dealt with knee problems.

The reality, though, was that it wasn't this or that game that had caught up with me. It was the style of game I played. I liked to carry the puck, and if you do that, you're going to get hit. That's the way it goes. When you play, you play all out. I didn't want to sit back. I wanted to be involved. I knew the trade-off. I knew that if you invite contact and challenge other guys, you're going to get hurt. I didn't know any other way to play. I didn't even really think about what I was doing on the ice. When I was rushing, I didn't pick a route and then follow it. I just did what came naturally. If I was pinching, or going down to block a shot, none of that was based on some deliberate calculation. Maybe some guys play the game that way, but I let the game unfold the way I had since I was a kid. Now those instincts couldn't help me anymore. They were telling me to do something I just couldn't do.

What I didn't foresee—what maybe no young man can foresee—was the way those injuries would accumulate and chip away at me. Throughout my career, I had assumed I was indestructible. I was only twenty-eight. I certainly didn't think of myself as old. Even with all of the surgeries as the years went by, I felt I could simply put in the rehab work once the doctors were finished fixing me up, and I would go on playing. It wasn't easy to accept that I was wrong.

It's tough as an athlete when you know what you have to do but also know that your body can no longer accommodate it. In that moment, you start to doubt yourself. And if you're not confident as an athlete, you have nothing. Believe me, it's no fun. It torments you.

I feared not playing well every night, and those were the expectations that I lived under from day one. I understood that the key to success in anything is to show up to work every day, whether you are 100 percent or not, and I was determined to do that for my team. There's a problem when you are missing players from your lineup, especially key players, and I always felt that even if I wasn't at my absolute best I should still be taking my shifts. I owed it to my team, I owed it to my teammates, and I owed it to myself.

I never felt pressure when I was healthy. I think of pressure as the fear of letting others down, and that's not something you can control. I believed that if I played the way I could, and took care of the things I could control, pressure was irrelevant. But once I could no longer do what I expected myself to do, I felt enormous pressure, mostly from myself. But by then, things that used to be second nature were out of my control.

As my first season in Chicago began, it became obvious to everyone that I would not be able to follow a full practice schedule along with the rest of my teammates. The knees, primarily my left one, simply never felt right. It was an odd mix of dull pain and a lot of stiffness, sometimes to the point where I couldn't even bend the knee without forcing the joint. I could hardly walk, let alone skate. I wanted to play, but I just couldn't.

In total, that first year, I dressed for only twenty games. Things started out fine in the pre-season, but my knee flared up in October. I tried riding a bike just to keep it flexible, and I had a weighted boot I could use to keep the muscles strong without putting pressure on the joint, but it didn't help. I had a small surgery that month to flush out the particles that were floating around in the joint. But by December it was as stiff and painful as ever. That meant another surgery, and more time recovering.

Recovery had never been easy for me. No athlete wants to sit around, waiting for his body to heal. You want to get back to doing what you are supposed to be doing. But it is one thing going through your rehab when you believe you are on the way back to being as healthy as you ever were, and something totally different when you are forced to confront the realization that things have changed forever. As I rehabbed that winter, I had to come to terms with the fact that I would never play the way I used to, and I started to wonder whether I would ever even play again.

I missed the rest of the season and still wasn't making any

progress. Eventually, I was forced to decide what would be best in the long term both for me and for the organization. I would sit out the 1977–78 season in its entirety and hope I'd be ready to go the following year.

I believed that if I took an entire year to rest and do rehab, there was a chance my knees would finally receive enough time to heal properly. Often, time and rest are the best healers. It was a tough decision to take, because, more than anything, I wanted to be on the ice. I hadn't come to Chicago for a rest. In hindsight, I'd probably rushed back a little too quickly from surgery a few times because I always wanted to play as soon as possible. I was a professional hockey player. That's who I was, and that's what I did for a living, so sitting on the sidelines was never comfortable for me. But over all those procedures, all the damage, eventually I decided I simply could not rush back again. Refusing to rest hadn't helped me. Maybe resting would.

That was a particularly tough time in my life. I was never one who felt a lot of pressure as a player, but for the first time in my professional career I began to understand what pressure was all about. And the pressure came about because of the worrying. I worried that I couldn't live up to the expectations of the Chicago fans. I worried that my teammates would be let down. I worried that the management group who had brought me in would decide that they had made a mistake. That was a kind of pressure that I had never experienced previously. I had to give myself one more good chance to play again, so I made the decision to sit out the year. I didn't accept any salary either. I was paid to play hockey, and I believed that if I wasn't holding up my end of the bargain, I shouldn't be cashing checks I hadn't earned.

I started the 1978–79 season with high expectations. I prepared for that last season like any other. I really thought I was going to go on playing. I had to believe that.

But I played only six games.

I still couldn't practice much with the team, and my ice time wasn't what it used to be. My knee was too sore to allow me to play more, but sitting on the bench just made it worse, as it would begin to stiffen up on me as it cooled down.

I would walk favoring my leg, and going up and down stairs was difficult. I had undergone multiple surgeries on my left knee by that time. Cartilage does not grow back. It just keeps chipping off, leaving more and more of the bone surface exposed. Both menisci were gone, bone was rubbing against bone, and chips were breaking off. Bone spurs and arthritis left the joint swollen and immobile. I couldn't cut, I couldn't accelerate, I couldn't play at the level that I expected of myself anymore. I had always said I would play until I couldn't skate anymore. Finally, I knew that day had come.

I scored my last goal in the NHL on October 28, 1978, against Detroit. Barely a week later, I retired. I just couldn't go anymore.

If I could have played at the pace and with the skill I was accustomed to, I would have been more than willing to put up with all kinds of physical aggravation and discomfort. Was I sore? Yes. Was there pain? Yes. But I would happily have carried on in Chicago in spite of all that if I could have. But I couldn't. I talked about it with Peggy. I told Coach Bob Pulford. And that was it.

Eventually, the day comes when you know you will have to give your skates back. In my case, I had grown up believing I could do whatever I wanted on the ice, and I had convinced myself I could somehow conjure up the will to play through the injuries in order to continue as a pro hockey player as long as I wanted. There was the vision of being a Gordie Howe, someone who could hold up to the punishment year after year. But there is only one Gordie, and no amount of willpower or wishful thinking could prevent the inevitable. Still, I am glad I played those last few games. It was at least a relief not to have to go through life wondering if there might have been a chance I could have kept playing, could have raised the Stanley Cup one more time. I knew, without a doubt, I was no longer able to play.

On November 8, I had to do what I knew had been coming for some time. We held a press conference and I gave them back my skates. What I had started on the bay back in Parry Sound had come to an end in a conference room at the Chicago Stadium.

Though I have never found it easy to be open among strangers, I cried that day. I was surrounded by cameras and microphones, but there was no point trying to hide the fact that I was devastated. Hockey had been my life. I was only thirty years old—an age when many defensemen are in their prime. Anyone who has dedicated their entire life to something only to have it taken away knows it isn't as simple as just saying goodbye.

The tears expressed something more than sadness, though. As I faced the end of my career, I came to appreciate more than ever the people around me. People had stuck by me even when I was less than I had once been. There were my parents, who had supported me from the beginning. There was Peggy, who was there when I needed her most. My teammates, and other people around the game. The journalists. The fans. I received hundreds and hundreds of letters in the weeks that followed, and I'll never forget those acts of kindness.

I had always taken my role in the game as an important responsibility. Just then, facing those microphones, I felt more than ever that it was an honor.

At the same time, despite the warmth and respect I received, retirement was lonely. I had lost something I didn't think those around me would understand. My health, my career, my place in the game—it had all slipped through my fingers.

I would soon discover I had lost more than that.

Nine

ABOUT
ALAN EAGLESON

To this point, I have not mentioned Alan Eagleson by name, and there is a reason for that. I didn't want his name strung through the fabric of this book. If I had the choice, I wouldn't write another word about the man for exactly the same reason I rarely talk about him. That is, Alan Eagleson is no longer a part of my life—he is just a bad memory. But the truth is, at one point he *was* a part of my life, a very important part, and at a critically important time as well. And so, it is only appropriate that I include my thoughts about him.

Nevertheless, this will not be easy to write. I am both angered and embarrassed by my memories of Eagleson: angered by what he did to so many people, and embarrassed that I was one of them. The fact that two courts of law in two countries convicted him, and that he was sent to jail for embezzlement and fraud, should say all that has to be said about Eagleson. But it doesn't come close. The reality is that none of our dealings ever entered into the charges that eventually resulted in his convictions and imprisonment. I was betrayed by someone I had trusted from the time I was just a kid. Though he has paid a heavy price for many of his crimes, he has never had to answer for that.

Anyone can commit a crime and be convicted of it. There is nothing special about that. But to be stripped of honors like the Order of Canada and membership in the Hockey Hall of Fame is a punishment reserved for a particular kind of criminal. It means you have done great things in your life—and it means your misdeeds are bad enough to overshadow those great accomplishments.

No one can deny that Alan Eagleson did some great things. He almost singlehandedly changed the game by empowering players and developing international hockey. He engineered what may be the landmark sporting event of the twentieth century in the Summit Series. He brought the Canada Cup into existence. Without him, Foster Hewitt would never have shouted, "Henderson has scored for Canada!" and there would have been no magic from Mario Lemieux to beat the Soviets in 1987.

I mention this not to make the case that Eagleson was a hero. Far from it. The only reason to remember any of this now is to show just how dark his crimes had to be to overshadow accomplishments like these. In the end, many of the very best things he managed to do were corrupted. The memory of everything he ever did to earn the respect and gratitude of the people around him has soured. He has had to watch everything he was proud of turn into a monument to his greed.

The same is true of my relationship with him. When he came into my life, I thought I had a friend. More than a friend. I trusted him with everything. Imagine having a friend you would entrust *all* of your financial dealings to without question. Trust doesn't get much more complete than that. It is a rare and precious thing. Like everything good he did over the course of his career, though, Alan Eagleson turned even trust as great and rare as that into something foul and regrettable.

The first time I met Alan Eagleson was during the summer of 1964. I was all of sixteen years old and had been a member of a championship baseball team. At the end-of-season banquet and awards presentation in the tiny town of MacTier, not far from Parry Sound, Eagleson stood up and spoke to the players and parents in the crowd. He was an impressive man and very self-assured. He knew how to speak to a room and sway people to his way of seeing things. In fact, that was his job as a lawyer and as a member of Parliament.

Our first contact with Eagleson was after the festivities in MacTier. That's where the relationship began. It didn't take long for all of us to be impressed by the man. It was Mom and Dad who were making the call on this matter, and both of them felt very comfortable with Alan Eagleson. The truth is, so did I. Love him or hate him, Eagleson could sell—and he could especially sell himself. It was my mother who would ask him the toughest question: What would he be charging for his services? He responded with a look of great sincerity and answered, "Mrs. Orr, I'll make money only if your son makes money." And that was true.

If there were other agents back then, we didn't know about them. Pro sports during the 1950s and '60s were run with an iron fist by the men who owned the various franchises. Regardless of whether the sport was hockey, basketball, baseball, or football, the conditions were basically the same for most players. Management made all the rules and set the salaries, and players were forced to accept whatever offer was put on the table. The pensions were very small, and medical coverage was there only when you were playing for the team. Many players worked blue-collar jobs in the off-season to pay the bills. And once they retired or were forced out of the game, they were on their own.

In a six-team league, in which the teams had players' rights contractually stitched up, and the owners held all the cards, there seemed to be nothing any player could do about it. There are stories about players trying to stick up for themselves, or squeeze a small raise out of an owner or a GM, and just as many stories about guys getting buried in the minors or traded to a rival team. A player might even have found the courage to step up and talk about becoming a part of a players' association—such as Ted Lindsay did in the late 1950s—only to find that the league wouldn't even allow players to look at the books of their own pension fund. Lindsay and fellow organizers Gus Mortson and Ferny Flaman were promptly traded for their efforts.

It was an environment where players didn't know much about what others were making, and very few dared to rock the boat. No one wanted to end up being the guy who got shipped out of town. I was a small-town kid who hadn't played a game in the league and was dreaming of getting into the NHL. I wasn't very interested in negotiations or that part of the game. Still, it was obvious to my parents and me that we would need help if we were going to deal with the men who ran the NHL. Eagleson may very well have been the only agent in our sport as I was getting ready to sign a professional contract. He already had a few clients by the time we met up, including people such as Bob Baun, Carl Brewer, and Bob Pulford. But he was just getting started.

Timing and circumstance all seemed to point in one direction for me, and that direction was clearly toward Alan Eagleson. It appeared to be a great match. The Bruins had made no secret of the fact that they wanted my name on a contract, but they were not accustomed to negotiating. They were in the habit of dictating terms to hockey players, and my parents just didn't have the kind of boardroom skills it took to sit across the table from a bunch of veteran hockey guys and team owners and force them to see things their way.

One thing you could tell about Eagleson when you met him—he would not be intimidated by anyone. He was an impressive personality, especially to people such as the Orrs, who frankly did not have a lot of experience with these types of matters. And it should be noted that he more than delivered on his promise. When I signed my first contract with the Bruins, it was for several times more than what Hap Emms had initially offered. There seemed no way to deny that Eagleson was doing something right.

It was not long before Eagleson's career and mine were tightly bound. He was on the rise, smooth and confident with the media, able to go toe-to-toe with the owners in the boardrooms of the league. As the most recognizable agent in the game, he was soon handling dozens of clients. And in 1967, the National Hockey League Players' Association (NHLPA) was launched. By 1972, he was a household name, and possibly the most powerful man in hockey.

That is the big picture. On the smaller scale, Alan Eagleson came to play a role in every aspect of my life, and in none moreso than my finances. I was not especially gifted when it came to numbers and found the whole process around finances to be rather boring and time-consuming. The money side of things just wasn't all that important to me, in part because I'd never had any. Financial matters were a distraction in my life, and in Eagleson I had what I considered to be the top of the heap as a financial advisor. His job was to handle all of those distractions.

From the moment I signed my first NHL contract as an eighteen-year-old, right through most of my time as a pro player, Alan Eagleson was there by my side. He handled all of the details related to my finances. And as our time together in those early years unfolded, he did his job as I expected he would. I played hockey and he put contracts in front of me to sign from time to time. Endorsements rolled in. And the more successful Eagleson was, the more confident I became that he knew what he was doing—and the happier I was to have a guy like that in my corner. I had more than I needed, and every assurance from someone I trusted that my future was well safeguarded.

It was about as tight a working relationship as any player and representative could have, and there was no reason to doubt his counsel. We were business associates, yes, but it went much deeper than that. We were close friends. When your close friend is shrewd and powerful and gets things done, if he says something is taken care of, it's easy to assume it's taken care of. The fact is, I wasn't going to tell the biggest deal-maker in the game how to handle money. I figured he would do what he was good at, and so would I.

But there were some signs he was not the most scrupulous of businessmen. Eagleson owned a cottage near Orillia, which is not too far south of Parry Sound. He decided in 1969 that we could do a tremendous business in the summers in the Muskoka area north of Toronto if we put some time and money into developing a sport camp.

Exactly whose time and money it was emerged only later. My partner Mike Walton and I took the whole thing very seriously, because, after all, our names were on the marquee. We never cut corners and worked many of the on-ice sessions—we wanted things done right. Eventually, several members of Eagleson's family were on the payroll. His father-in-law was hired to build the facilities. (In fact, the same guy was contracted by Eagleson to build the new house I wanted to provide for my parents in Parry Sound once I'd turned pro and had some money in my pocket. I'm guessing there wasn't a competitive bidding process for that job.) In addition, he suggested certain people come in and act as instructors, for which they would receive a fee. Of course, they were always Eagleson clients or players he was courting. He was distributing perks to all these people, and Mike and I were helping to pay all of his bills.

That's not to say the camp was a disaster. Most of the players he brought in were pretty good guys and were willing to put in a solid day's work at the camp. But if I had seen things a bit more clearly, I would have noticed that Eagleson leveraged the camp and many of our other business ventures as a means of compensating family or friends—and the best part for him was that he never had to foot the bill.

After a while, I began to believe that Eagleson wanted to control not only the purse strings attached to his clients, he wanted to control their relationships as well. He wanted to run the show, and he worked to diminish everyone else's influence. He seemed to want total loyalty on all levels, and would insert himself into other friendships.

For instance, he started playing a kind of psychological game with me with respect to other people in my life, among them family friends such as Bill Watters. He would say things to me about Bill in the hope of creating some sort of tension between us. Eagleson told me that Bill really didn't want my father involved in any aspect of the hockey school operation or any other businesses we were engaged in. The story was a complete lie, but Eagleson used those types of tactics to keep people on edge and cause them to lose trust in others. He wanted me totally dependent on his advice and his friendship, and that left little room for others. The moment he suspected someone was getting close to me, such as Bill, the stories would start.

One of my great regrets is that it worked. There were friends and teammates over the years who didn't like or trust Eagleson. But I was his friend, so I defended him, even against people who were looking out for me. I would pay dearly for this friendship.

As he grew more powerful, he became harder to take. I grew to dislike the way he treated people in public. I will never forget a lunch meeting Eagleson and I had with Paul Fireman, who today is one of the richest men in the world but back then was an up-and-coming businessman from the Boston area. He wanted to talk about a potential sponsorship deal with his new sporting goods company. The three of us met at a nice restaurant, and we had barely sat down before Eagleson started ranting to the point where I could see poor Paul was quite taken aback. Eagleson wasn't just aggressive—his language was rude and totally vulgar. I suppose he was trying to intimidate Paul, but all he managed to do was offend him, along with everyone else in the restaurant. Perhaps to further insult Fireman, Eagleson marched out of the restaurant to make a call from a pay phone in the lobby, leaving Fireman in stunned silence. I'd had enough. I called over the manager, apologized for the bad language and disruption Eagleson had caused, and shortly thereafter the meeting was over.

Paul would tell me years later Eagleson's behavior was about the worst he had ever seen. The company he went on to found was Reebok, and Fireman maintains that after that first meeting with Alan Eagleson, he decided he would never work with him or his clients. As it turned out, Paul and I became good friends many years later, but that meeting could have burned a very important bridge for me and certainly cost me an opportunity at the time.

Eventually, I couldn't go out to a restaurant with Eagleson, because he often became rude and belligerent. For a long time, I didn't have the nerve to say anything. I couldn't find a way to get myself out of his clutches, because so much of my life was tied up in him and his company. I was in a situation over which I had very little control, and the relationship left me feeling helpless. I had allowed him to dominate to a point where getting out from under his shadow would be a difficult thing to do. He controlled my money, he controlled my schedule, and in my mind he was in control of my life. I was afraid to make a move.

In spite of all the problems, in spite of the many warning signs, a lot of people, including me, chose to turn a blind eye when it came to Alan Eagleson. You have to consider that I was riding pretty high as an athlete at the time, and the future looked very bright. I believed that because of where I was as an athlete, my financial world had to be in good shape as well. The two went hand in hand, as far as I was concerned, and that was especially true because of the man I had at the helm of my business dealings.

There is no way to deny that Eagleson knew how to negotiate a contract. From the time I first laced up in the league, I was among the very best-paid players. That is because most guys, especially early on, were underpaid. But as salaries rose, mine rose along with them. My second contract was the first million-dollar deal in the game. Eagleson could be ruthless and was not afraid to tangle with anyone. So, even though Alan Eagleson's personal shortcomings became obvious to me over the years, it was reassuring to know I had a guy like that looking out for me.

For me, the whole thing with Eagleson primarily began to unravel during my time in Chicago. Eventually, I just couldn't stand to be in his presence. It got to the point where I simply had to get away from him, and it didn't matter to me what the cost would be, financial or otherwise.

The fact is, I wouldn't have been in Chicago if I hadn't trusted Eagleson completely. My heart was in Boston. I didn't go to Chicago for the money. I went there because that was the advice I was getting.

As the world knows now, it was terrible advice. Not because I have any complaints about the Black Hawks—rather, because I never got the truth about Boston's offer. What I kept hearing from Eagleson was that the Bruins had given up on me, that they were ready to discard me. I was offended that the team I cared about so much figured my value was going down.

But I wasn't getting the whole story. Eagleson conveniently forgot to disclose to me what exactly the Bruins new owner, Jeremy Jacobs, was offering. The truth is that Eagleson never even discussed the Bruins' offer with me in detail. Rumors began to circulate, and when I started hearing some things, I asked him about it. He told me that the Chicago offer was simply the best one. Period.

No point talking about it. In hindsight, I should have pushed him on the details, but I thought I had no reason to. He knew how to negotiate a contract and get the biggest bang for the buck that he could. And when he became the head of the NHLPA, he became the man responsible not just for my well-being, but the well-being of every player in the league. It would have been difficult for anyone to believe in those days that Eagleson was not to be trusted.

The final irony is that the information Eagleson was withholding came looking for me—but I wouldn't listen. I remember being on a bike in the Bruins dressing room one day rehabbing my knee, and Paul Mooney, the president of the team at the time, came in and asked to chat with me. I brushed him off. He asked me if I knew the substance of the offer the team had made. I told him that he was trying to drive a wedge between Alan and me and that it wouldn't work. That was the end of the discussion. When I found out what he had wanted to tell me, it was too late.

Jeremy Jacobs had been prepared to offer me a part of the team to ensure I remained a Bruin for life. They had plenty of money on the table, but much more importantly they were offering me an ownership position. The kind of stake they were talking about represented a huge investment back then, and an exponentially bigger one thirty-five years later. It would have been big money.

The offer from Chicago amounted to roughly $500,000 a year for five years, certainly nothing to sneeze at. I was honored to sign that contract. But even someone with my limited financial skills would have known which offer would have been the most lucrative in the long haul. If I had ever been presented with the choice, that is.

Any representative or advisor who receives that kind of offer needs to disclose all aspects of it to his client so that every detail can be studied. I was getting near the end of my career, and considering my medical condition, my future earnings as a player were questionable. Eagleson knew that. It's obvious what his advice should have been.

Eagleson told me only those parts of the negotiations that he wanted to share. Why? I can only assume it was to get the outcome that would most benefit him, not his client. There were all kinds of stories in the press about my contract negotiations—apparently, other people knew all about the Bruins' offer. How could I possibly have been in the dark?

The reality was that Alan Eagleson often used the press to his advantage during contract negotiations. His clients never knew whether what appeared in the paper was fact or just another of Eagleson's ploys to gain the upper hand at the bargaining table. Anyone who knew him knew not to believe many of the things he told a reporter.

I believed what he told me, though. There was no reason to doubt him, and no reason to even consider that he wasn't hammering out the best deal he could make for me. After all, he wasn't just my representative. He was a valued friend.

I still don't know why he did what he did. I can't see what he could have gained from that betrayal. People have guessed he was doing the Hawks' owners a favor, and it is true that he was friendly with the Wirtz family. But he was friends with me, too, and it is not clear that he did either party any favors by sabotaging the Bruins' offer. I suppose I'll never have all the answers, and it really doesn't matter. In the end, what really matters is that someone I trusted betrayed me. This close friend, someone I paid to take care of my financial interests, turned out to be the last person I should have trusted. Eventually, I knew I had to get as far away from the man as I possibly could.

Finally, in the spring of 1979, I decided to schedule a final face-to-face meeting with Eagleson to clear the air. Peggy and I met with him at a mutual friend's apartment in New York City, and it was not a pleasant afternoon. By this time, it had become very apparent to me that in his capacity as my representative on all matters relating to my contract negotiations and other aspects of my financial affairs, Alan Eagleson had misled me. That realization was a difficult one, first to understand and then to cope with. But it had become obvious what had transpired, and a break was inevitable.

Even as we gathered for that final meeting, he kept up the classic Eagleson bravado and told me that if I stayed with him all would be well. He had the gall, even at this late stage, to try to make me believe it would be in my best interest to remain part of his "team." He looked at me and said, "It would be a mistake to leave me." I looked at him and said, "Alan, I don't care how it turns out. I have to get away from you." It was tense, and I couldn't wait to leave the room and him behind when it finally ended. I simply had to get away from him for my own sanity.

My sanity was just about all I had left. It wasn't just that Eagleson had hidden from me the opportunity to be a part-owner of the Bruins. It was that he had left me practically broke. I didn't grow up with a lot, and I knew kids with less, so I shouldn't use the word *broke* lightly. And I don't want to get into an inventory of my assets and liabilities at the time. But I had played over a decade of pro hockey, and during that time had been one of the highest-paid players in the history of the game. I had no shortage of endorsements. Yet when I retired from the National Hockey League, I was not in the financial position I had expected to be in.

For years, Eagleson had told anyone who would listen that "Bobby will be a millionaire by the time he's twenty-five years old." That didn't quite work out.

Where all the money went, I will never know. A huge part of what remained was eaten up by unpaid taxes. Whether this was due to incompetence, greed, or malice on his part is impossible to guess. At this point, it doesn't matter. What mattered to me then was that I was watching what remained all but disappear.

I was not the only hockey player to be affected by Alan Eagleson. *Every* professional hockey player paid a price. Obviously, along with many members of our players' union, I failed to do my due diligence on Alan Eagleson. Time would expose a lot of the inconsistencies in his dealings, but it is his personality that I will never understand.

He had everything a person could possibly want, but apparently it wasn't enough. For instance, during the Canada Cups, the players and team personnel would be outfitted by a Toronto tailor named Marty Alsemgeest. All this work was paid for with gift certificates Eagleson had bought with Team Canada funds. But according to Marty, friends of Eagleson who had nothing to do with the team would walk into his shop with those gift certificates. Eagleson's buddies were benefiting from that friendship, but it was the players who were picking up the tab.

This kind of practice by Eagleson was common during that time. I remember on several occasions being at functions at Eagleson's home in Toronto. Inevitably, the guests would receive a bag full of gourmet food and presents on the way out the door. We soon came to realize that those goody bags were full of gifts he had managed to accumulate from various companies that were involved with his long list of clients. He was always scamming one way or another and just couldn't do a deal and be up front and honest about it.

In his book *Game Misconduct*, Russ Conway documents all kinds of examples of Eagleson's conflicts of interest. I won't try to list them. But one thing stands out for its pettiness. When the NHLPA moved its headquarters, Eagleson seized the opportunity to rent out ten parking spaces—when only four were available. The NHLPA and Hockey Canada picked up the tab.

My old teammate Gerry Cheevers came up with a famous line shortly after Eagleson negotiated a new contract on his behalf. Someone asked him how much more money he got due to Eagleson's efforts, and Gerry responded that "he got me another $1,500, but when I got his bill I owed him $3,000."

It is tough to summarize a person like Alan Eagleson in just a few words. He appears to me to have been someone who, above all else, was driven by greed. That word *greed* always seems to come up in any conversation you have with people who knew the man. He always wanted more, and it didn't seem to matter how he accumulated it, or at whose expense it came. But there is another word that I now associate with him.

As I think back on so many incidents that I witnessed during my time with him, I realize that Alan Eagleson was the worst kind of bully. He used power to get what he wanted from people and wasn't afraid to threaten in any way necessary to achieve his goals. I don't know how you define a bully, but that seems like a pretty good description of one in my estimation.

I don't bring any of this up looking for sympathy. I don't want to present myself as a victim, because ultimately only I was responsible for myself and my finances. I handed off a lot of responsibility to Alan Eagleson, but it was still mine. That lapse in judgment, the total faith I put in him, is all on me. I've come to understand that I didn't take care of my own business, and I can't blame anyone but myself for that mistake. Eagleson would slide legal papers in front of me and tell me to sign them—and I would sign, believing I had no reason not to comply. He may have abused that trust, but it was still my signature.

My focus at the time was on one thing and one thing only, and that was to be the best I could be at the game I loved. Most everything else to me during that period was little more than a distraction. That was a mistake, a very big mistake, and that was my mistake alone.

What Alan Eagleson did hurt me in any number of ways, financial and otherwise. But it especially hurt because of the relationship we had developed. We were friends. We were a team. We were brothers. To be disrespected in the way that Eagleson betrayed me is probably the most bitter of all pills anyone could ever have to swallow. I'm no psychologist, but I believe that what transpired during that time fundamentally changed who I am. I became much more guarded about those around me, about their intentions as well as my own decision making. The entire episode made me less willing to open up to people. As time has passed, I have also become far more appreciative of qualities such as trustworthiness and loyalty. Those are the qualities that mean the most to me now, and they are at the center of all of the meaningful relationships in my life.

There was a time after his betrayal when, had I found myself in a room alone with Alan Eagleson, I don't know what I would have done. He caused my entire family a lot of pain, and the anger I experienced over that ate at me for a very long time. Those feelings have now passed.

In the end, of course, Eagleson was brought to justice. He was forced to step down from the NHLPA in 1992 amid charges that he had been abusing his expense account. And from there, the cracks spread as journalists picked up the story. He seemed to be protected by his money and connections, and, were it not for the efforts of the American prosecutors in this case, it might all have been neatly swept under a rug. I certainly didn't have the finances to go after him, nor did I have the desire. I just wanted to be rid of him. So I have always been thankful for the way the US justice system fought for his extradition from Canada to face his crimes.

In 1994, the Federal Bureau of Investigation charged Eagleson with thirty-four counts of racketeering, obstruction of justice, embezzlement, and fraud. In 1996, the Royal Canadian Mounted Police charged him with eight counts of fraud and theft. It would take several years to get him into a court, but eventually, on January 6, 1998, he was convicted in a federal courtroom in Boston. He pleaded guilty to three counts of fraud and was fined US$697,810, or CA$1,000,000. Shortly thereafter, he was returned to Canada and again pleaded guilty to three more counts of fraud. Those charges landed him with an eighteen-month prison sentence. His legacy will forever include the words "convicted felon."

As a matter of course, he was disbarred from the legal profession in Canada. He had his Order of Canada revoked. And his hockey legacy was taken from him by the people he had trampled. After Eagleson's conviction, a roster of legends—including Brad Park, Gordie Howe, Bobby Hull, Johnny Bucyk, and Ted Lindsay—and I announced that if Eagleson were permitted to remain in the Hockey Hall of Fame, we would resign from it. Before he could be kicked out, he resigned.

The fortieth anniversary of the Summit Series may have marked the final reminder of the way Alan Eagleson dishonored the games he once seemed to have done so much to promote. As the players and coaches prepared to gather to celebrate what was probably the most thrilling hockey ever played, Alan Eagleson had his invitation revoked by the team. The man who had been so instrumental in creating that series, a watershed moment in Canadian sports history, had become an embarrassment. While it is true that some players still stand behind the former head of the NHLPA, there was simply no room for the person who had robbed his own friends. Certainly, had Eagleson been allowed to attend those celebrations, I know I would not have taken part.

But enough is enough. That's all over for me now. Alan Eagleson changed the course of my life. That is undeniable. But that was decades ago. He has not been a part of my life for a very long time. The good times during that era are what I choose to remember. A lot has happened since then. I have more than recovered. And justice has caught up with him.

To this day, though, I can't help but wonder how he rationalizes many of his actions. It's difficult to imagine how, or whether, he has taken account of the hurt he caused so many people. I just don't understand how he can sleep at night. Yet knowing the man for what he is, my guess would be he has no difficulty sleeping at all. He probably couldn't care less.

Ten

FINAL ACT
AND BEYOND

It was Halloween night, 1980, and we were dishing out candy for the neighborhood kids. Peggy stood there with a bowl of goodies and handed out the treats as each child came to the front door. I was hanging around in the doorway so I could catch a glimpse of some of the costumes, so I was nearby when three little ghosts and goblins came up the steps, accompanied by their father. As Peggy stepped forward to hand them their candy, their father caught a glimpse of me standing in the wings and immediately said to the kids, "Do you know whose house this is?"

Without missing a beat, they all blurted out, "It's Scout's house!" Then they got their candy and went on their way. Scout was our family dog. Apparently, he was quite popular with the neighborhood kids. So much for my fame and fortune. My number 4 was hanging in the rafters of the Boston Garden, but my dog was the celebrity of the household. Things were changing quickly in my life.

It's not easy to describe the anxiety you feel when the one thing you are good at is taken away from you. I know I'm not the first guy who has ever been out of work. I can sympathize with anyone who has been laid off for what seems like no good reason, men and women who suddenly feel they have nowhere to turn. I had no real education, and what schooling I did have hadn't prepared me for any trade or vocation. The only experience on my resumé were the jobs I'd held as a kid. I was thirty years old and completely unprepared for the real world, which was now breathing down my neck. I had to go to work.

What had been a day-to-day reality for me just months before now seemed like the distant past. Hockey had never felt like work to me. As hard as I played, it had always been a game, and I had always considered myself lucky to be paid to play it. The lifestyle of a professional athlete is pretty special. But nothing could ever take from me the important things I had been lucky enough to experience. Yet it would be dishonest not to admit that when I saw so much had changed in my life, it was frightening. At the moment my health left me, I lost my money, an important friend, a lifestyle I had grown accustomed to, and a career that meant everything to me. Ahead of me was only uncertainty.

What I found, though, was that what I'd always thought to be true—what my parents had taught me, what coaches had instilled in me, and what I had seen for myself—was true whether I was a hockey player or not. The important things in life don't change when your luck turns against you, and those things are no different for celebrities than they are for anyone else. No one is going to succeed without taking their lumps. No one is going to succeed on their own, either—what sometimes looks like an individual accomplishment is always the result of a team effort. And when you get knocked down, there really is only one thing to do.

I believe, without any doubt, that if you approach anything with discipline, you've got a chance to succeed. But that confidence comes from looking back. Looking forward, it wasn't nearly as clear that I'd find my way out of the mess I was in.

The Black Hawks tried to help me land on my feet by offering me a job. I certainly wanted to do everything I could to help the team. I felt I had let them down after they had shown such confidence in me. But I found it very difficult to be around the team. People told me it would get easier as time went on, but I found that the longer I was away from the dressing room and the routine of preparing for and playing the games, I missed it more and more. I wanted to help the team, but more than anything I wanted to help them on the ice. I would watch the games, see the play unfold, and feel in my heart that I should be out there. The more I watched, the harder it got.

A few years later, I did some consulting work for the Hartford Whalers. My old teammate Eddie Johnston was the GM there, and he figured we might capture some of our old magic if we put our heads together. I must have thought so, too, or I wouldn't have taken the job. But once again, I found that involving myself in the game from anywhere but on the ice was agonizing.

It is probably also fair to say I was never cut out to be a coach or any kind of manager. Because, as much as I loved the game, I didn't really *think* it. Hockey is fast and complex—you can never anticipate exactly where everyone is going to be at any moment. You can't plan for something you can't foresee. I made all my decisions the moment I had to make them, not the night before. So it was difficult for me to expect to show up and tell others how to play or run their teams.

When I had entered the spotlight of professional sports years earlier, I was extremely shy. I never really came to love being in front of microphones and cameras, but after more than a decade I could at least handle myself in a variety of social and business situations.

The fact that someone as shy as I am would take a job on television is a good sign of how much I needed the work. I am uncomfortable enough in a small group, but there I was on the CBC doing color commentary for *Hockey Night in Canada*. The guys in the booth always took care of me, and I remember that Danny Gallivan especially was always trying to help me out in any way he could. I would be in the broadcast booth, and the veterans would sort of hold my hand by feeding me good questions while keeping me on track. There was always a three-man crew: the play-by-play announcer and two color commentators, of which I was one. But one night in Edmonton, I'm in the booth, but it is just me and the play-by-play guy. I'm looking around for the other color commentator, but he was nowhere to be seen. For a moment, I thought I was going to pass out. I figured out pretty quickly that being in the broadcasting business was not for me.

Still, as I'd grown older, I had started to become more comfortable in the company of strangers. The idea of speaking in public when I was a young man would have been frightening. But when you are in the public eye there is no way to avoid speaking to crowds or making conversation with people you don't know, whether you're appearing as a volunteer or being paid for your time. Either way, if you're going to do something for the public, you should either do it right or not at all. It isn't good enough to sign on to appear at a function and then try to slide out the back door at the earliest opportunity. That isn't professional, and it isn't right, yet I've been at events where people have done just that.

I have tried to be true to that concept, and have shared that philosophy over the years with my friends and colleagues. For example, Derek Sanderson and I were two celebrities among others at a golf event several years ago. After we finished up the round, I was taking my clubs to my car when I noticed that Derek was already in his own car, preparing to leave. I asked where he was going, and he told me he was heading home. I pointed out that he had played golf with only three people that day, so only three people had got to meet him. One hundred and twenty other folks had missed out. I said we should go back and meet some more of the group. To his credit, Derek did come back inside, and many more people got a little piece of him that day, as well they should. Unfortunately for Derek, he had left his car windows open when he walked back to the clubhouse with me. It rained cats and dogs while we were inside. Poor Turk had to ride home waterlogged, and I don't know if he's forgiven me to this day.

Growing up, I would never have guessed my future would one day depend on talking to people. In those years after I left Chicago, I came to understand that talking to people didn't have to be a torment. It was an opportunity—and one I couldn't afford to do without. I was fortunate enough to become involved with some wonderful companies after my playing days, and those associations helped ease my transition. Companies like Bay Bank, Standard Brands (which would eventually become Nabisco), MasterCard, and General Motors of Canada all provided me with business opportunities.

I've been very lucky to have known some outstanding business people who helped me along my path after my playing days were done—and again, I credit the skills and lessons I learned in hockey for much of my success in various business ventures. Then, in 1991, the world of professional sports would come calling again, when I joined Woolf Associates to help recruit players. Bob Woolf was a pioneer in the agenting business, and the company already had a sports and entertainment roster that included Larry Bird and Larry King, but one thing they didn't have was hockey players (despite the fact that they were based in Boston). Along with some partners, I bought the company in 1996, and Rick Curran joined us in 2000. In 2002, I separated the hockey operation from the rest of the firm. That was the beginning of the Orr Hockey Group.

It's no secret that I didn't have the best possible experience with an agent. Parents and players know that. I suppose there is some irony that someone who lost so much to an agent would become one himself. But on the other hand, I think parents recognize that my experience has shown me a side of the game that not a lot of people have seen.

One thing we never do is handle clients' money. Any player, whether he is a client or not, should learn from my experience and realize that he is ultimately responsible for himself and should not give complete control to anyone for any reason. The money a player earns during his career is *his*, and it is his duty to learn to protect that income. It could mean taking a class to understand how to read a financial statement, or developing the ability to ask appropriate questions about potential investments. After all, if a player's hard

Left: *With my wife, Peggy, on our wedding day in Parry Sound.*

Below: *This photo was taken on Orr Night in Boston in 1979. The Bruins retired my number before a game against the visiting Soviet Wings. Here I am shaking hands with Al Secord, Terry O'Reilly, and Peter McNabb before the opening faceoff.*

Top: *Here's my dad with Walter Gretzky at the annual Skate-A-Thon for Easter Seals in Parry Sound. Walter also comes to the golf tournament every year in support of the Bobby Orr Hall of Fame.*

Middle left: *Here I am with King Arnold at a senior event at the Nashawtuc Country Club.*

Middle right: *With Michael J. Fox at a benefit in Boston.*

Above: *With Frank Sinatra at a benefit for Tony Conigliaro in 1983.*

Above: *At the outdoor game in Boston with two of my favorite Bruins, Cam Neely and Ray Bourque.*

Right: *With my friend Ace Bailey, who we lost on 9/11.*

Below: *With Boston sports legends Ted Williams and Larry Bird on the set of Bob Lobel's Sports Final. It was an honor to be there with two guys who made the kind of mark on their respective sports that those two did.*

Top left: *Salmon fishing on the Cascapedia River with Fraser Baikie and Ted Williams.*

Top right: *Bass fishing on Lake St. Francis in Quebec.*

Above left: *Salmon fishing on a trip with my father and friends in northern British Columbia.*

Above right: *On the water with my family. Peggy and my sons, Darren and Brent, are all accomplished anglers.*

Top: *Arm wrestling with Don Cherry at the Prospects Game in Calgary.*

Above: *That's Don and me at the tee of my annual golf tournament in Parry Sound. Grapes comes every year. You wouldn't believe how excited golfers are when they come around the corner and see Don standing there.*

Right: *At my sweater-retirement ceremony in Oshawa. Grapes was a surprise guest.*

Below: *Possibly my fondest memory from childhood is playing hockey outdoors, and I'm always happy to share that experience with others. Here I am (below left) at the rink at Fenway Park with my friend Dave Harkins on my right; his son-in-law, Jeremy Styles; and Dave's grandchildren, Logan and Sadie. And here I am at Fenway again (below right) with the grandchildren of my friend Phil Morse. From left to right, that's Sawyer, Ben, Ryan, Will, and Annie.*

Top left: *Here are my sons, Brent and Darren, when they were just kids.*

Top right: *Here they are all grown up at Darren's wedding. We were thrilled to welcome Chelsea into the family, just as we were to welcome Kelley, Brent's wife-to-be (far left).*

Center: *Here are Chelsea and Darren with the next generation, my grandchildren, Alexis and Braxton. There is no thrill quite like being a grandfather.*

Bottom: *Here are Kelley and Brent with some of their boarders at Paws 4 Play, their grooming and boarding business in Jupiter, Florida.*

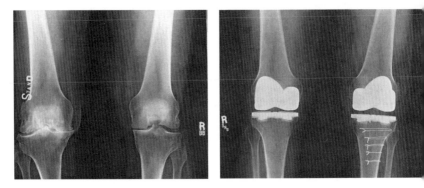

Above: *My knees, before and after. You don't have to be a doctor to see there wasn't much cartilage left in the joints. I had eight more surgeries between 1982 and 2002. Finally I bit the bullet and had a total knee replacement in 2004. I should have done it a lot sooner.*

Below: *Here's the statue outside the new Boston Garden. The Bruins mean a lot to the loyal fans of Boston.*

work is squandered because of bad advice, it will be the player who pays the price. Professional athletes who accumulate wealth need to take the time to do their homework.

As a business, we're not just looking for good hockey players. We're looking for kids with good character. I've said before that the mental part of the game is the toughest part. Talent can take you only so far. We're also looking for parents who understand, because when you take on a player as a client, you're taking on his parents, too. This is always a family deal. Kids in hockey have enough people telling them what to do. They don't need their parents barking at them, and they don't need me doing it, either. I often point to families such as the Staals, from Thunder Bay, Ontario, as shining examples in that regard. Both parents, as well as all the hockey-playing brothers, have the kind of personalities and characteristics that help to ensure their long-term success. When I get to work with families such as the Staals, my job becomes a real pleasure.

I know I keep saying I have benefited from the lessons I learned from the game—the fact is, I am lucky to be able to work every day at a job where those values make sense. No one succeeds without a team around them, and everyone needs teammates to step up for them once in a while when they get knocked down. I've had clients win the Cup and had kids go first overall in the draft, and I am personally thrilled for them. That's not just professional joy, that's the real joy anyone feels when something great happens to someone they care about. And I've seen clients' ugly contract disputes play out unfairly in the media, or taken calls from guys who got sent to the minors. And that feels personal as well. I always went to my teammates' defense without question, just as they came to mine. That's how I do business, too.

I know I've been lucky twice: once as an athlete and once as a businessman. And both times, my good fortune was to have quality people around me. Success is important, there's no point denying that. But the company you keep is more important. My greatest blessing may be that I have known both.

Now, past disappointments have all but lost their sting. I've made up my earlier losses and recovered in other ways. I can't say it was easy, or that it happened quickly. In fact, it took a generation to unfold. When I was struggling in Chicago, my sons were just little guys. There is not a father in the world who doesn't want to do the best he can for his kids. The thrill of victory means more when you share it with those you care about—but then, the bitterness of disappointment tastes that much worse when you have to share that with those you love.

Now, though, there are kids in my life again. When you talk about thrills in life, I suppose I've experienced my share as a hockey player. But the most overwhelming joy I've known is not winning a Stanley Cup or any individual award. I'm talking about the absolute thrill I've experienced in becoming a grandparent. There is no way to describe the feeling of holding a grandson or granddaughter, to see the looks on their faces and watch them grow. Many people tried to tell me about the joys of being a grandparent before it happened for Peggy and me, but I always assumed they were exaggerating. I understand them now, because I'm one of those fanatics who carries pictures of both my grandkids everywhere I go. It is, without question, the thrill of a lifetime to have someone call you Grandpa.

Eleven

State of the Game

I joined the National Hockey League in an era that included legends like Gordie Howe and Jean Béliveau on the ice, Punch Imlach and Harry Sinden off the ice, and Foster Hewitt and Danny Gallivan above the ice. It was a six-team league when I started, but by the time I finished, the league had expanded to eighteen—and it's nearly double that now. Back then, guys made a very good working-class salary playing the game. Now third-line players are millionaires. At a glance, it would seem that it's a different game.

But it's not. What makes hockey great—what makes a team great, or an individual player, or a specific game—is no different today from what it was when I was a kid. You win by skating. You win by controlling the puck. You win by standing your ground. One key ingredient binds all these together and ultimately determines success or failure. Passion. That is something that doesn't change over the course of a career. It doesn't change from generation to generation. Many times over the years, I have seen how passion can change a game or a series. I've seen careers built on it, teams built around it. When you've got it, you can do anything. When you don't, you'll be lucky to get anywhere at all, even with all the talent and coaching and dry-land training in the world.

Like most kids, when I started skating at age three or four, it was just for the pleasure of being on the ice. I'm told my first game of organized hockey was at age five, though I have to admit I can't remember it. But what I do remember is how much enjoyment skating and playing hockey brought me almost instantly. There wasn't a day that went by when I wouldn't somehow find my way to the ice. Those long hours skating during those cold, dark days of winter instilled in me something I couldn't do without. They turned me into who I am. I was shaped not by what anyone else wanted me to be. I was shaped by my own passion.

There is no question in my mind that any success I enjoyed in hockey can be traced back to that passion. It is a simple word but a very important concept in all aspects of life. I've heard it said that if you really want to be a successful parent, you should just find out what your children have a passion for and then back them in that area. Maybe that's easier said than done, depending on what the passion might be, but the parents who stifle their kids' passion are going to find life even harder.

Too often, I see talented players have their passion slowly drained from them as their life in athletics becomes what can only be described as a means to an end. Some get it taken from them early, and we never get to see the player they might have become. Too many simply walk away from the game. How do they end up in that state of mind? Whenever I have an opportunity to meet leaders in a profession or business, I always hear the same kinds of stories and philosophies about what got them to the top. They talk about getting up each morning and heading to the office, or rink or ball field or whatever, and making a conscious decision to try to be at the top of their game. Fortunately for me, no one took away any of my passion for hockey.

That kind of attitude doesn't mean you are never going to make mistakes. It doesn't even mean you'll achieve a personal best every day. That's not very likely. But if you try, the negatives are going to be outweighed by the positive things you accomplish. If you can do that, your passion won't just propel you along. It will make everyone around you better as well. That is one of the indescribable things about being on a team fueled by passion. When every guy in the room is inspiring everyone else, there is almost nothing you can't do.

That passion is the constant in the game, and that's why hockey hasn't really changed. The arrival of composite sticks and mandatory helmets doesn't change anything fundamental. In fact, so little has changed that the player I admired most when I was a kid is the fellow I admire most today: Gordie Howe.

There have been many players before him, and many players since, that fans might argue were better than Mr. Hockey. Here's all I can say, having played against him. If you wanted to play a finesse game, he had world-class skill. The numbers don't lie: Gordie finished in the top five of all scorers in the league for twenty years in a row. Nothing could stop him. He could control the puck in traffic. He had a deadly shot from anywhere in the offensive zone. So he could beat you with skill, no question. And if you wanted to play a grinding game, he was built like an ox and could make his living patrolling the side boards in every area of the rink. Similarly, if you wanted to rough it up, he was happy to oblige. (He used to say he considered himself a religious player in that he felt it was always better to give than to receive.)

He had the whole package. Basically, he could play any style of game you wanted, on any given night, and play that style better than you. How do you top that? In addition, Gordie was able to do something I never could, and that was stay healthy in a very physical sport for a very long time. It's not as if he played around the edges and avoided corners in order to keep his health. We all know what a warrior he was, so when you add his longevity to his impressive list of abilities, he is clearly the one player who stands above the rest. Have there been guys with softer hands? Probably. Have there been better skaters? Maybe. But has anyone played with a more powerful, more sustained passion for the game? No. After his career, Gordie has remained loved by his fans because of the kind of man he is and the values he stands for. There will never be another one like him. It was a privilege to face him as an opponent, and I count it as one of my life's great honors to be able to call him a friend.

It's more than just friendship, though. To me, Gordie Howe represents all that is good about our game. I don't want to sound like one of those old-timers who always looks back nostalgically at the game and assumes everything was better in the old days. Certainly, there are many aspects of hockey that time and experience have helped shape and improve. There is no doubt that, for the most part, guys shoot the puck harder these days. For the most part, and for a number of reasons, the games are faster. Goalies are more athletic. It's fair to assume that the average player is bigger, stronger, and in many cases more skillful. Players are generally better coached than they were back then. They are in better shape. We cannot discount those facts.

Having said that, I think it's fair to ask if all of this adds up to make hockey *better*. From a purely personal point of view, I have to wonder if any coach today would let me play the style of game I was comfortable playing during my time in the league. Today, so many defensemen are told, beginning at a very early age, that the only smart play to get the puck out of the zone is the simplest play. Don't take risks. Just chip the puck off the glass and out. For me, that is just boring.

Sure, modern players may have better conditioning than their predecessors, but they are hardly ever on the ice for more than forty seconds. They may have impressive skills, but for the most part they are forbidden to make anything but the safest play. While coaches might be better at their craft, they may have helped shape the game in a way that isn't always for the better. Think of the number of times you watch a game and for long stretches nothing really happens. The games I watch today tend to be played in tight spaces along the boards, where there is less risk of a turnover. There is little or no emphasis on creativity, because, above all else, the game is about systems.

There are two things I think may be stifling the game. First, I keep hearing from people close to hockey that the size of the contracts players are signing has fundamentally changed the game. If you give someone everything he wants, the reasoning goes, you have taken away his motivation. And if that contract is "long term and guaranteed," it affects the attitude a player brings to the rink. At first, I resisted this notion, because I couldn't bring myself to believe that a professional player wouldn't want to be the very best he could be, night in and night out. Not just for himself and his own pride, but for his teammates, the fans, and everyone else associated with his organization. But the more you examine the idea that money can change a player's attitude, the more the evidence starts to present itself.

When I know what a player is capable of yet only see it every third or fourth game, it concerns me. When I see a player doing very little for a prolonged period, then suddenly have a "career year" as his contract is about to be renegotiated, that sends up some red flags. I watch a lot of hockey, and I see a lot of ups and downs. I suppose the logical question to ask is, "If it isn't the money that has changed attitudes, what is it?"

I can't speak for everyone, and there's no way I would accuse a whole generation of players. I work with some real warriors, who play through pain, who stick up for their teammates when it would be easier to skate away, who would carry their teams on their backs if they could. That's the way it should be. That's the way that hockey players are. Still, I do sometimes wonder whether, overall, there is the same urgency in the game that there used to be. Understand one thing: the amount athletes make today doesn't bother me in the least. What concerns me is whether they earn it every night.

The second point to consider involves the fundamentals surrounding the game. The reality is, for the huge majority of young players, there will never be a paycheck from hockey or the possibility of a spot on the Olympic team. The numbers are overwhelming. Putting kids into hockey in order to make them into millionaires is a bad investment—not just because the odds are against you, but because hockey is not an investment.

I've been asked many times what my most special memories of hockey are. Certainly, there are a few easily identifiable ones from my time in Boston, but if I was forced to single out one specific thing, it would undoubtedly be those days skating and playing as a child. It is no exaggeration to say that those hours on the ice in Parry Sound are every bit as precious as my happiest hours with the Bruins. No parent can guarantee their kids the joy of winning a Stanley Cup, but they can guarantee them the opportunity to find their passion for play.

Mine are the kind of memories that I wish for every child who laces up a pair of skates, because it is in those times that we learn our passion for the game. Unfortunately, many people don't get to hold on to a passion like that. How many folks go to work every day and hate what they are doing? I am not so naïve to think we can all drop what we are doing in order to pursue a lifelong passion. But I do wonder why anyone would want to turn childhood into preparation for a job.

My two sons never really got into hockey as kids, but they were certainly active in other sports, whether it was baseball, soccer, or football. As their parents, Peggy and I both watched as Darren and Brent gained valuable experiences through their time in minor sports. I never pushed them into anything, but I didn't want them to miss out on the kind of people they would meet playing on teams, or the lessons that would serve them well into adulthood. I fear that not all children involved in minor sports can say the same thing.

As a former player, and as someone who is still close to the game, I meet some truly fantastic people. But I do wonder why some kids take up the game in the first place, and why some people decide to become coaches in minor hockey. Most of the time, the answer is easy. A lot of people love the game the same way I always have. But sometimes it's not as obvious. Sometimes kids don't seem drawn to the game the way my friends and I were. Sometimes they seem pushed into it. And in my view, if a kid has to be pushed into hockey, he might as well be playing something else. He or she might want to play another sport. Or maybe it's music. Or drama. What's important is that kids are doing something they love and that they are with their friends.

If nothing else, I hope that bringing up these ideas might spark some further discussion among all the key stakeholders in minor hockey. I'm going to begin with a program that is dear to my heart—a program that speaks to the basic needs of young boys and girls who play hockey, but which I believe should be the basis for all youth sports. If we start our children out on the right track, we have a better chance of keeping them involved in sport for a lifetime. We can't confuse a game played by children with a game played by men for money. The vast majority of hockey players are kids, so let's start with them.

SAFE & FUN HOCKEY

During the spring of 1998, I grew more and more concerned with many of the headlines I read about problems within several minor sports in North America. Some of these problems were quite shocking to me. Many of the headlines that caught my eye referred to events such as parents of very young players being involved in post-game brawls, and even a death resulting from parents of players fighting in the stands in the Boston area.

To me it signaled a real need for action and education, and that is when I approached my friend Dick Conlin, who was a VP at General Motors. When I mentioned my concerns about the decay of values in youth sports, he agreed, and then asked, "So, what can be done about it?" That was when Chevrolet Safe & Fun Hockey was born. I suggested to Dick that we couldn't cure all ills associated with all sports, but we could try to make a dent in the hockey community across Canada.

That is exactly what we did. Since 1999, the program has touched hundreds of thousands of players, parents, coaches, and officials, and I am extremely proud of the message it brings. Along with Hall-of-Famer Mike Bossy and Cassie Campbell-Pascall, formerly of the Canadian women's Olympic hockey team, who speaks to the needs of the young girls who are playing the sport in ever-increasing numbers, the program has advocated for change within our minor hockey systems. Our instructors are not just teaching hockey; we are using hockey as a platform for teaching important values.

Hockey can give kids the experience of sportsmanship, dedication, and commitment. That's true for parents and coaches as well. We produce manuals and instructional videos for all participants. But the kids are always the focus. It's tough to get across to kids in only a few words what the overall perspective is— and after all, they are there to have fun, not listen to lectures—so we use two value-based words to frame the intent of our program. We call them our "two *R*s": respect and responsibility.

In my mind, respect is a cornerstone concept, not just for minor sports, but for living in general. Whether it's toward teammates, coaches, rink attendants, teachers, or whoever, basic respect is something everyone deserves. It's something we should see everywhere, not just on the ice. But on the ice is a great place to teach it.

Like respect, responsibility is something every young athlete can and should apply off the ice once it has been learned in the rink. Once a kid learns not to blame others for his mistakes, or not to be selfish when others are counting on her, he or she is not just a better teammate, but a more complete person. One of the best-known elements of our program is the work we put into getting kids to be careful when they see others in a vulnerable position. Hitting from behind is dangerous and irresponsible, and if we can help get it out of the game, we know we've done something we can be proud of. Away from the rink, responsibility may mean being accountable for your grades, helping parents with household chores, or doing the right thing in the playground at school. These are life lessons that can be learned through our sport.

We do a little homework exercise with the kids at our camps. We ask them to draw us a picture of anything that they associate with the word *responsibility* or *respect*. It is always amazing what they come up with, whether it's taking their dog for a walk or cleaning their rooms (responsibility) or shaking hands with an opponent at the end of a game (respect). At one session a few years ago, we told the kids on the ice before they drew their pictures that it was very important to listen to their coaches while they were playing because it showed respect. Of course, when the pictures were drawn, we saw many examples of that.

But we also saw some ideas that we couldn't quite make out, and they seemed to be associated with school. When we asked what the pictures were about, the kids said, "Don't bully anyone." It turned out that school had just started and these children had received an anti-bullying presentation from their teachers. Obviously, they were listening, something we sometimes fail to realize. Very young children hear the messages that we as parents send, and they hear them very clearly. Our goal at Safe & Fun Hockey has been to keep providing positive messages for our young people in the hope that, over time, a culture shift will happen. We have heard some great feedback over the years, and we are all encouraged by that. But the message of respect and responsibility needs to be kept in the forefront in order to reach not only children, but parents, coaches, referees, and administrators within the game as well.

Marc Comeau is now the man who champions the program at GM. Like his predecessor, Marc sees great value in the message the program brings. At the heart of the program is Harold Konrad, the program director and a dear friend. Harold is one of those people who just gets things done. He has been a great resource person for all of the major innovations over the years in Safe & Fun Hockey, and without him we simply could not carry on. My hope is that as the years go by, we will see fewer and fewer of the headlines that spurred us to create our program. My hope is that all kids who participate in minor sport will have the same kinds of fun experiences I enjoyed as a kid in Parry Sound. That was one of our main reasons for creating the Chevrolet Safe & Fun Hockey program: to let children have fun with the game in a safe and secure environment. But there is still much work to be done.

YEAR-LONG HOCKEY PROGRAMMING

I've mentioned that I didn't attend hockey school until I was eighteen—and that I was there as an instructor not a participant. I mention this with a specific thought in mind. While no one can really object to a young player heading off to a hockey camp for a week or two during the summer, I don't believe that summer is the time to train kids to play a winter sport. You might think, if they want to go to camp and they like hockey, why not? Let them play. I loved the game to the point that I could hardly think about anything else when I was a kid. If I had had the chance to play during the summer, maybe I would have. In any case, I can hardly say there is anything wrong with a kid wanting to play a little more hockey. But I see very young children shipped off for long stretches by parents who seem to think the hockey school environment will "make them a player." The fact is, no one can make a kid into a player if that is not the kid's passion. And really, why would any parent want to?

But the real point is that, whether we're talking about summer hockey school, spring leagues, or private lessons, some parents feel their kids have to stay on the ice year-round or they will lose ground. But do we need to keep kids on the ice twelve months a year in order to keep grooming them? I think there is something very wrong about that. From my perspective, a brief summer experience on the ice should be as much a social time as anything, because the truth is the instructors at any hockey school, gifted as they may be, will not make your son or daughter a top-level player. And no kid should head off to camp thinking he or she needs to come back a more accomplished athlete.

My preference would be to see kids play other sports, especially during hockey's off-season, be it lacrosse or soccer or rugby, or any other activity they enjoy. I played a lot of baseball, and that was a different experience than hockey, including a different pack of friends for at least a couple of months a year, and that can be only a good thing. There is something to be said for what we now refer to as cross-training, meaning that kids should be involved in sports besides hockey. It means you are becoming an *athlete*, not just a hockey player. Youngsters involved in multiple sports get the opportunity to experience a broader range of skill development, and that will only help them when sport specialization starts later in their teen years. I believe that those types of rounded athletes have a great advantage over other players in the long haul.

If the point of keeping kids on the ice twelve months a year is to turn them into hockey players, the plan may backfire anyway. Children who get pushed into year-round programming can end up with hockey fatigue. Many promising kids just get sick of being driven to the rink to put on their gear in the middle of summer when they'd rather be throwing a football around or going mountain biking.

Not every kid is going to be gifted in the sport their parents happen to have in mind for them. In fact, most kids won't be gifted in any sport at all. But sports are not there for the gifted. They're there for everyone.

TRAINING

I understand the importance of training for the sport, and I know that teams have high expectations for their players in that regard. I have certainly spent enough time in gyms and weight rooms to know that you can get only so far without putting in the effort. But I have come to wonder in recent years if over-training isn't actually hurting many players. First, hockey is about strength and power—no one who has played the game would try to deny that. But hockey is not weight lifting, and players need to watch that their training sessions don't turn them into athletes whose bodies are more suited for wrestling than hockey. There is strength, and then there is "hockey strength." It isn't so much about brute force on the ice, because if that were the case we would see only giants participating. And giants do have some advantages. But the list of top-ten scorers on any given week doesn't include many giants. Defensemen tend to be bigger, but with few exceptions even the top defensemen aren't beasts.

What players need is the right *kind* of strength and power. That includes learning to understand that leverage and positioning can be just as important as raw strength when it comes to winning battles in the game. It's more about timing and athleticism—and avoiding injury—than it is about how much you can bench press. I don't know how many times I've seen a guy with the physique of a defensive end line up a guy half his size, only to bounce off when he connects. Sure, there is room in the game for big guys who can throw their weight around. But for the most part, players are smart enough to see them coming—and strong enough to protect the puck when they arrive. There are trainers out there who know how to develop hockey-specific strength—though a trainer can help only if a player follows the program. All too often, I've seen players sign up with the best trainer, but not show up for their workouts and never reap the benefits.

Often, when I'm on the ice with Safe & Fun Hockey, I'll have a little boy or girl come up and angle me into the boards. The point of this demonstration is to show that even though you might have a physical disadvantage in terms of your size, proper technique can help you overcome any size deficiencies you might have relative to your opponents. Putting on muscle is no substitute for learning the game.

The second point to be made about training is that I firmly believe at some point athletes need to rest both body and soul.

That's right, just rest. They must allow their bodies to heal up, especially after a long campaign when perhaps they've gone deep into the playoffs. Some youth teams play upwards of one hundred games a season, and even though they have lots of energy, kids do get tired. Would you prefer your child performed when rested or fatigued? I've done both, and I can tell you, I always played a lot better when rested. And remember, tired players are more prone to being injured, so keep that in mind as your son or daughter moves up the hockey ladder. The human body needs some time to heal from that kind of physical output. It's important to calm the mind and get away from the mental stress associated with the game. You might believe that mental stress is only for the pros, but the pressures put on many children by the volume of games and by coaches' and parents' expectations all come with a cost. And those players have school and other activities as well. We should never forget that these are just children.

THE ROLE OF PARENTS

Watching a child move into the top levels of hockey can be both an exhilarating and confusing time for parents. While previously they were in control of most aspects of their son's life, parents must eventually cut the strings and let him go. They can't dictate terms. "Johnny" isn't going to be guaranteed power-play time, because at elite levels of the game Johnny is going to have to earn that privilege. So what advice would I give parents as they enter into this often-stressful time for their family?

I always go back to that discussion my folks had with the Lindros family, because I truly believe the wisdom of Dad's comments. You simply have to get out of the way and let them stand on their own. You can't push them where their talent wouldn't have taken them anyway. You should be forewarned that everyone thinks, as a player moves up the hockey ladder, that communication will get better and everything will be understood by all parties involved, but that isn't necessarily the case. Where once a player was a big fish in a small pond, that same player must now come to grips with the reality that he or she will be competing against the world. Players, and parents of players, must be mentally tough. Nothing is given away, because hockey, especially at the professional level, is big business. The player's ability to *produce* will determine his success, and no one can talk his way onto a roster. Merit is the only way.

If I had a son or daughter who was pushing forward in the game, I would also be very conscious of what I said when things were not going so well. For example, telling your child that the coach doesn't know what he's doing may feel like a way of cheering up a dejected kid who didn't get much ice time. But it's only going to make things worse by furnishing the player with a ready-made excuse: "It's not my lack of effort. The coach doesn't know how to use me!" Probably not a great strategy, even if, in some cases, the coach may be partly to blame.

We teach our children at a very early age about things like responsibility and accountability, so parents shouldn't make less of their child's need to accept responsibility for the quality of his or her play, even if it makes the kid feel a little better for a while.

The reality is that as a player gets deeper and deeper into elite hockey, parents basically become fans. Certainly, as a parent, you shouldn't let anyone take advantage of your child. You always have to know what is going on. As I said before, everyone has to do their homework so as not to become a victim of an unscrupulous person or program. But after the decisions are made, the best thing a parent can do is slow down, relax, and remember that it is a marathon, not a sprint. And besides, you aren't the one running the race.

THE ROLE OF COACHES

During my time as a hockey player, I was very thankful to have had a series of coaches who were wonderful role models and guided me right up until I retired. You should never underestimate how important a coach can be in a young person's life. If nothing else, this is the person who controls ice time, and that means he has immense power over your child's development. A coach's job is also to figure out how to motivate your child, how to get the very best out of him or her. Coaches need to learn what drives each player and develop a very intimate relationship. Today, players don't simply nod their heads and say, "Yes, Coach," when someone tells them to do something. Current players want to know *why*, and aren't afraid to challenge authority. If a coach is doing the job right, he or she will come to know every player on that bench, and will know how to talk to them.

The relationship is built on trust and shared values. What those values are, and who your child comes to trust, are things that will shape them. That makes coaches some of the most important people in your child's life, and the further he or she goes, the more important that relationship—and the relationship with the team—will get.

I won't go into the abuses of power by coaches we have witnessed in the past, but we have all read about them. Hopefully, these are isolated cases, but I do believe that in some cases the culture of hockey has contributed to these abuses of power. How? Well, coaches often seem to be running their teams in order to achieve immediate success. They are thinking of survival in the here and now instead of having the confidence to do what's right for a program down the road.

I understand the "win or get fired" pressure that many coaches are under. Unfortunately, that kind of thinking is not restricted to the professional ranks, because even at basic levels of hockey I see coaches who are in survival mode. I have always thought that if we develop people properly we will have a greater opportunity of producing more accomplished players, and our coaching jobs will actually become more secure. There are no shortcuts in this game. Players need time and nurturing to develop, and the driver of that bus is always the coach. It is a serious responsibility.

Unfortunately, if you get a coach who thinks he or she is on *Hockey Night in Canada* when in fact they're standing behind the bench of a novice team, no one is going to have any fun. Winning can become a sort of drug for coaches, and they like the feeling of that high. But it has consequences for kids in minor sports. I would ask coaches not to get hooked on that winning drug and ask themselves instead why they are coaching. If you have any reason for coaching other than wanting to develop better people through minor sports, you should probably step aside.

And coaches, one more thing. If in any given year you find yourself with a team that can't seem to win, then you need to set a goal other than hoisting a trophy at the end of the season. The challenges under such circumstances can be difficult, but I've always felt that truly great coaching can happen even when a team doesn't have a winning record—and not every team can have a winning record. The most skilled coaches will always find a way for players to have fun, even if that trophy is nowhere in sight. Creating little victories within the bigger defeats is a mark of excellent coaching, and to those who follow that path, I applaud you.

WHICH ROUTE TO TAKE?

In my position as a representative for many talented players from around the world, I have seen firsthand the whole range of leagues and programs players come through. I've seen players who went undrafted shine when they got their shot in the NHL, and all too often I have seen blue-chip prospects wash out before they made it to the big league. But there are two main routes to the NHL: Major Junior in Canada and the National Collegiate Athletic Association (NCAA) in the United States. Just about every player in the league has come through one of those systems. And it's not about nationality. More and more, we see American and European players coming to Canada to learn the Canadian game and get Major Junior exposure. And we see all kinds of highly ranked Canadians playing for American universities. The current captain of the Los Angeles Kings is an American who played junior in Canada. The captain of the Chicago Blackhawks is a Canadian who played NCAA hockey in the United States. I am often asked which system is better. And, of course, there is no simple answer.

For one thing, the two are very similar in an important way: they are both big business. There are careers at stake, and money to be made and lost. If a player can help a coach or a program get ahead, he will have people on his side. If he can't, he likely won't. And that is as true of Major Junior as it is of college hockey. Minor hockey exists for the kids. But at the next level, it's for the fans.

Several years ago, Rick Curran, my partner at Orr Hockey, was attending the annual meeting of NCAA hockey coaches in Naples, Florida. One of the head coaches from a high-powered NCAA team accused Rick of approaching players who he thought were still too young to be considered by a player agency. Rick had been having conversations with the parents of a fifteen-year-old player, and the coach wanted him to know he thought that was far too young for us to represent.

Rick pointed out that we do not "represent" players at that age. We provide advice when asked, as is permitted by the NCAA. It is all within the very carefully defined rules. Rick then asked a question of his own: "If it is so wrong for agencies to talk to fifteen-year-old players, how can schools commit a scholarship to someone that age?" The reality is, talent always draws a crowd, and if you are not proactive then you will not get the best talent available. I guess you could compare it to my days as a twelve-year-old, because one organization, the Bruins, did a great job of laying a foundation of trust while other teams showed little or no interest. That is the way the business works, so you have to be prepared for that.

If I were deciding where to play my amateur hockey as a means of preparing for a potential career in the sport—which not all players are—there are several things I would take into account. Initially, a player needs to consider how he feels about pursuing academic studies. It's a waste of time for all concerned if a young player decides to go the university route while the whole time he knows in his gut that school is not his cup of tea.

It's a matter of motivation, not intelligence. I was never particularly fond of school and couldn't imagine having to sit through four years of university to get a degree. So the first question you need to ask yourself, and you need to answer this honestly, is whether school is a viable option. I definitely think players should go to school—you need to get some kind of education as a backup should things in hockey not go your way—but that's an argument for education as something you need in itself, not just as a means of getting onto a hockey team.

Next, players need to consider their developmental timeline. By that I mean, if you develop very early in terms of talent and potential, say at fourteen or fifteen, then you may not want to wait until you are eighteen to go off to school. You probably want to be challenged right away. As an example, if you were the parents of Connor McDavid, who first played Major Junior hockey at the age of fifteen, what would you do? "Too good too young" sometimes has to be a consideration. Others might be late bloomers who could use a little more time developing at lower levels before moving up. Major Junior players are twenty and under, though the elite players have jumped to the pros long before they hit twenty. But college hockey starts and ends later. So a guy who might not have been ready to play junior may be able to take advantage of those extra years to get stronger and polish his game.

Another area worth investigating is the lineup you are joining. While this may not be the biggest part of your decision, it should be a consideration. For example, if I am a defenseman and the program I'm looking at has seven returning veterans in that position, I have to consider my chances of getting ice time. You can be joining a NCAA championship team, or the winners of the Memorial Cup, and that is wonderful. But if in the process you never get the chance to dress for a game, then your development will be stunted and you probably won't be a very happy camper. It is something you need to consider. Many players who have had solid pro careers have come from small programs at the university or junior levels. You don't always have to come from a top program to succeed.

It isn't a simple decision. What is a great situation for one person could be a disaster for another. And remember, when you're being recruited, you're going to be told a lot of things you want to hear. But things almost never come as advertised. And be ready, because nothing will be handed to you. The decision as to which hockey route to take is a difficult one, and it requires serious consideration. Use all the resources at your disposal to gain the necessary information to assist you in making an informed decision, including asking questions of previous players associated with a given team. Know that when the decision is made, it will have a dramatic impact on the rest of your life.

THE ROLE OF ADVISORS
(REPRESENTATIVES/AGENTS)

I made a very conscious decision in 1991 to make a career move into the player-representative business, focusing specifically on hockey players. It's no secret that I didn't have the best of all possible experiences with an agent during my playing days. Many players and their parents I am in contact with today are aware of that fact. No doubt, they all realize that my experiences have shown me a side of the game that few people have had to endure.

Representing clients who aspire to be professional players has been a very interesting journey, and I have met some inspiring young men and their families. Unfortunately, I've also met others who seemed to have an attitude of entitlement. They are the type of people who feel they are owed something yet don't act with the kind of responsibility you would expect. The old saying, "To those whom much is given, much is expected" is something all athletes should remember. I'm always amazed how some people feel this entitlement when, in reality, they simply have not earned it.

As a company, we get close to our clients and their families. I want what is best for them. When things don't go well for them, I am frustrated. If a GM or a reporter is giving them a hard time, my instinct is to come to their defense. And sometimes I do, but more often, and especially with young players, my job is just to try to keep them on the right path. A player can have it all, but if he doesn't have discipline, it is all too easy to let everything slip away. And once he does have representation, he has someone who can help him make the most of his talent. That doesn't just mean making sure he has the best possible contract. More than anything, it means helping him to do the right thing. And it means helping him understand what it takes to be a pro.

A few years ago, I handed out a letter to our clients at a hockey camp in which I tried to get across the idea that the journey they were on, though filled with many potential rewards, was a very difficult path indeed. It's a journey that requires a special type of person, someone who is able to navigate the highs and lows, all the while keeping an even disposition in order to move forward and get better at their trade. That letter follows below. I would like to thank Dale Dunbar, who has done work for the Orr Hockey Group over the years, as the originator of the earliest draft of this document. I believe it still has relevance and may allow players and parents to see more clearly the life they are choosing.

So You Want to Be a Professional Hockey Player ...

As the old saying goes, "If it was easy, everyone would do it!" So it is for professional athletics as a career choice. What follows are some questions and thoughts that everyone preparing to pursue a life in sport should consider before committing the time and effort necessary for success. It would be irresponsible on your part to be caught off guard with what is about to happen in your life simply because you did not do your homework! Please read on and contact us directly if you have any questions pertaining to the following information:

- Are you willing to move away from home at a relatively young age, perhaps fifteen?
  - this means potentially having to look after yourself for some meals, which have previously been prepared by one of your parents.
  - this means you may have to do some laundry, something that was probably also done for you by a parent.

- this means living in a billet home that may have young children and where you may not have all of the conveniences of your own home, all the while with total strangers!
- this may mean being homesick.

- Are you prepared to work hard at each and every practice and game and always give your best effort regardless of how much ice time you get?
- Are you willing to pick up pucks after practice, load the bus for road games, sit next to another first-year player on the bus, and generally do all of the things expected of a rookie, as this is considered part of the game?
- Are you prepared to get limited ice time and possibly be a healthy scratch on occasion because you are the youngest player on the team?
- Are you prepared to play for a coach who is extremely angry because your team just lost or played poorly? You may be benched or not dressed for the next game without any communication from the coach. This could make it appear that you are the cause of the loss or poor play.
- Are you willing to accept that this is the first rung of the ladder of pro hockey and that everything is about winning?
- Are you able to remain positive and work hard if every time you make a mistake it results in you being benched?
- Are you prepared to move to another team with new teammates, a new coach, and a new billet if you are traded?

- Will you be able to disregard any negative remarks made toward you during a game or in the media?
- Are you prepared to live your life in a fishbowl where everyone knows everything about what you do or say?
- Are you prepared to go to school every day and do your very best to succeed?
- Will you have the courage to tell teammates or friends that you are tired, or you have schoolwork to do, or you need your rest when they ask you to go, for example, to the movies?
- Will you have the courage to say no to any form of alcohol or drug that is offered to you?
- When everyone around you is having a beer, will you be able to say "no thanks"?
- When you are invited to a party and you know that it isn't where you should be, will you have the courage to say "no thanks"?
- If a teammate or friend is doing something that is wrong, will you have the courage to tell them it is wrong and distance yourself from them?
- Will you have the courage to walk away from any situation that could be detrimental to your health, welfare, or reputation?
- We all know that it is human nature for most people not to want others to succeed. There will be some who are jealous of you and want you to fail. Will you be able to stay away from this group of people?

These are some of the issues you may encounter as you pursue your dream, and we want you to be ready for whatever may come up.

If you are one of the lucky few that make it, I can assure you that the life of a professional hockey player is wonderful. Don't cheat yourself! Do things right. Make good decisions to give yourself the best chance to realize your dream.

Some of the preceding information may in part appear to paint a negative picture of a life in sport. In reality, professional athletics has many distinct advantages for its participants, but it is never an easy process to make it to the top. As such, if a player *is* going to commit his energies to this pursuit, I feel that it becomes *vital* that he considers these ideas very carefully! Why? Because down the road we do not want him to be among that group of foolish athletes who make headlines for all the wrong reasons.

If you want to be successful, you must be prepared to sacrifice some things, and professional athletics is no exception. I often read media accounts of professional athletes who have embarrassed themselves and their sport and I can't help but wonder why. Why do these people view themselves as bulletproof? Why didn't someone sit them down early in their career and give them the necessary "what for" with respect to the path they are following? It's one of the reasons that we have tried to keep the lines of communication open with our clients right from the beginning within my own company.

They need honest and reliable information if they are going to adjust during their transition into professional sport. Our clients inevitably gravitate to different men within our organization because they feel comfortable with them. But in the end we all share the same message. That is, we try to be honest and forthcoming in order to help them develop as athletes and people. Of course, it's a two-way street. Parents and players need to communicate, as well.

We can't guess that something might be wrong. I've actually had parents say they don't want to bother me with little problems. But they should. They need to.

Once you become a pro, other issues will arise, many related to performance. Because the hard reality is, if you contribute to a winning program you retain great value. If you are associated with losing, your value decreases. You can't control what the people around you do—except by example. The thing you can control, though, is your own consistency. During my time in the NHL, I had all kinds of teammates with all kinds of skill levels. The most frustrating thing as a player, and I know that this drives coaches mad, is to have an athlete who performs at a world-class level on one day then a recreational level on another. It all relates to consistency and this is a key to long-term success. It isn't that everyone has to or even can perform at the level of a Gordie Howe. That isn't the point of consistency. The point is, *whatever your performance level and whatever positive skills you bring to the team, you must demonstrate those skills game after game.*

There is nothing worse than having a teammate whom you cannot trust with respect to their level of play. Eventually, that player will be left behind. On our old Bruins teams, Pie McKenzie was the same player every night out, we always knew what Dallas Smith would do on defense, and Eddie Johnston or Gerry Cheevers gave us NHL-caliber goaltending regardless of who was between the pipes. In order for us to become champions we all had to contribute consistently. A great example is my late teammate Ace Bailey.

Ace couldn't play at the level of a Gordie Howe—of course, not many could. And teammates never expected him to. But we did expect him to bring whatever his particular level was night after night, and that he most certainly did. Ace ended up scoring some big goals for us, especially during the run for the Cup in 1972. Great coaches don't try to get anything out of their players other than that which they are capable of. They are supposed to know at the pro level what you can and cannot provide for the team. The key is to bring what you have every day.

It is a lesson that all young athletes should be aware of, because inevitably they are going to be judged in no small measure on how consistently they perform over time. During my brief stint in the coaching ranks with the Chicago Black Hawks after my playing career was over, I remember having a discussion with a young player who was not living up to expectations. After I had shared my ideas about consistency with him, he looked at me and said, "Ya, that's easy for you to say but I can't play like you." Fair enough, but the whole point was that I didn't expect him to play at any level that he was not capable of, only that he should play at *his* level, whatever that level might be, night after night.

RULES

There have been some rule changes in recent years that I'm not sure have made the game better or safer for our players. In my view, player safety should be the top priority. Of course, hockey is a physical game played by big men. There is no out-of-bounds to escape to, and it is played at high speed. When you add those factors up, it's easy to understand there will inevitably be injuries. Whether you are talking about hockey, football, rugby, or any other contact sport, casualties occur, and there is nothing that can ever stop that. When you examine what has happened to the game over a long period, however, you have to question some of the changes that, in my opinion, might have damaged, rather than advanced, the cause of preventing injuries. I'd like to share my views on several of these changes.

For example, many of the new rules that prevent impeding opponents make me wonder if I'd want to be a defenseman in the current NHL. I think if I were playing in today's game, whenever the puck was dumped into my corner I'd just let the opposition go get it. Call me chicken if you want to, but going back there with absolutely no time or help seems a little bit crazy to me. I'd rather be a chicken and not have to worry about another concussion, thank you very much. Even a split-second of interference on an opposing forechecker can allow a defender to get to a puck, make a play, and then brace for contact. I'd feel the same way even if I wasn't the guy going back in the corner. You have to allow me to protect the health of my defense partner. In the current game, however, there is no allowance for impeding an attacker who is speeding to the corner, and as a result we see defensemen being forced to choose between making the play and getting rammed into the glass. Taking the hit is part of any contact sport, and those acts of sacrifice are exactly what are needed to win. But it is shortsighted to change our game in such a way that the players' instinct to make the play, no matter the cost, puts them in danger night after night.

The other part of this problem can be traced to the loss of the center-ice red line. If I were commissioner for a day, the first thing I would do is bring back the center red line as one way to reduce high-speed collisions. Again, no one wants to see hitting taken out of the game. Players love taking the body, and fans love to see it. Hockey is a tough game, and that's what attracts a lot of people to it. But when you have freewheeling players skating at twenty-plus miles an hour gaining speed through the neutral zone without any offside worries, then guys are going to get run over. It's inevitable. Yes, players should keep their heads up. And they do. But the better the player, the more he's going to be carrying the puck. Eventually, maybe at the end of a long shift at the end of a long road trip, he is going to misjudge the gap between himself and a defenseman in the neutral zone, and suddenly both teams are looking on as a player is lying unconscious on the ice, the victim of what might have been a perfectly legal hit but one that happened at a dangerously high speed.

That is exactly what we've been seeing over recent years: previously unheard-of numbers of concussions, often involving top-end players, and regrettably often with long-term implications. It's one thing to have your knees beaten up through wear and tear. But the brain is another issue altogether, and I have a feeling that we are hurting rather than helping solve the problem with these rules. With the size and speed of modern players, we must have some barriers.

Another way to help protect players in such a high-speed environment would be to get rid of the trapezoid rule for goaltenders. As it currently stands, goalies have very little room to maneuver when helping their defensemen on a dump-in. This rule allows a goalie to handle a loose puck below the goal line only in a small, restricted area behind the net. When the attacking team dumps the puck into the corner, the goalie can't play it. This automatically puts defensemen in that vulnerable position against attacking forwards, because their goalie can provide little assistance.

Controlling the puck is a skill that is all but lost for many goalies today, yet it can be a tool for any team—a good puck-handling goalie used to be like a third defenseman, starting the play with a smart pass out of the zone. I understand the intent of this rule, but I believe it has done more harm than good and should be reversed.

In the interest of reducing injuries, another rule change I'd like to see would be to introduce automatic, or no-touch, icing. Frankly, I can't understand the reason for the delay in changing this rule. My understanding is that the league is hesitant to adopt no-touch icing because it will slow the game down by causing more whistles for icing. But how many times does a forward outrace a defenseman for the puck as the rule currently stands? We are putting athletes at risk in what is almost always a meaningless footrace, as the icing occurs anyway. The number of injuries that have resulted from players racing to touch the puck on an icing call is well documented. The rule needs to be changed immediately. And there is another rule associated with icing that I have trouble understanding as well. Not allowing the defending team to change players when icing occurs means that you are going to have tired players on the ice. Again, while I can see the reason for originally adopting the rule, the reality is that fatigued players make mistakes, and often those mistakes can lead to injuries. The game is tough enough without having tired athletes on the ice who can't perform to the desired level of play.

There are a couple more things I'd like to get off my chest. In the past few years, we've seen rule changes I just can't agree with. If I were a player on the ice, I would hate to see the outcome of a game decided by a power-play goal scored when someone was in the box for something like flipping the puck over the glass by accident or batting the puck with a glove in the face-off circle. That would be a tough way to lose any hockey game, never mind a Stanley

Cup playoff game. Pucks go over the glass by accident all the time. Come playoff time, one idea would be for teams to get at least one "get out of jail free card" for the over-the-glass call.

Of course, many of these tweaks were brought in to increase offense. But we need to stop worrying about creating more offense, because offense takes care of itself. Whether two goals are scored or six, there is going to be offense. Look at teams as they get ready for the playoff run. There are great games played all around the league on any given night, and no one is talking about how many goals are scored. I've never seen a baseball fan walk out when a no-hitter is being pitched because there isn't enough offense. I've never seen football fans walk out because their team's defense is holding their opponent scoreless. And I've never seen hockey fans protest because they are being forced to watch a fast-paced, end-to-end, 1–0 hockey game.

It is interesting how one rule change can lead coaches to adjust their team's style of play, which will affect many other parts of play. For example, we've taken out the red line to increase the speed of the game, the idea being that more offense could be created. But coaches have adjusted to that change by setting up a more trapping kind of neutral-zone defensive system. The result? In my opinion, it's often boring hockey where a lot of the play ends up going back and forth between the blue lines. Shoot it in, shoot it out. And speaking of blue lines. When the league moved the blue lines out four feet, not only did they clutter up the neutral zone and increase the frequency of high-speed hits, but they also gave the point men a lot more time and space to load up huge slap shots. It's probably no accident that we've seen a lot more injuries from shot-blocking and pucks deflected into guys' faces—coaches have figured out how to use those extra four feet.

In my mind, the three most important things we can do to make the game safer for our players are 1) bring in no-touch icing, 2) get rid of high blind-side hits, and 3) get any kind of hitting from behind out of the game.

No one wants to see radical innovations in the most exciting game on the planet. If we change anything, let's move cautiously. Let's not try to fix what isn't broken.

FIGHTING

The opinions I'm about to share need to be understood in the right context. Allow me to begin this section by noting that fighting in minor hockey is something that should not be tolerated. Two peewee teams engaged in a bench-clearing brawl is something that simply has no place in our game, and shame on those people who allow such things to occur. I once heard a mother say that she and her husband were considering having their son learn boxing so he could defend himself properly in his league. The boy was seven years old. Something is wrong there, because no child should ever have to step onto the ice worrying about having to fight.

You might think this is an isolated incident, but I recently read about a minor hockey coach who was suspended for giving one of his own players a concussion while teaching the team how to fight. It doesn't matter what kids see on television—we *can* and *must* control our own minor hockey systems. If enough parents, coaches, and administrators determine that fighting will not be tolerated, it can be eradicated from minor hockey. It's up to all of us to relay that message to our children. After all, we are supposed to be in control of the games they play.

However, there's always another side to every story, and so it is when it comes to fighting in pro-level hockey. In "pro level," I include all professional ranks plus the highest levels in Canadian junior hockey as well. I include junior here because the players in those leagues are there with the main purpose of apprenticing for the next level of play. They need to be ready for what is to come, and fighting is a part of it.

Of course, no one wants to see a goon in junior hockey. I applaud the graduated scale of suspensions the junior leagues have brought in to deter the chronic offenders. For example, in the Ontario Hockey League, once a player hits a certain number of fights in a season, he gets an automatic two-game suspension for every fight after that, and that goes up to four games if he is the instigator. To me, that seems appropriate action for any league to take should a team or individual become too focused on fighting or intimidation as part of their game plan. And as far as staged fights go, I'd be all in favor of an automatic ejection. There's no room in our game for any of that stuff.

But I would be very hesitant to take fighting out of the pro levels of the game, and here's why. As a young player in the NHL, I was called out on certain occasions and responded to those challenges to fight because I felt it was my duty to do so. I didn't particularly enjoy fighting, but I understood its place in the game. I never wanted or needed someone covering for me when the rough stuff started, and as a result I believe it helped me over the course of my career, both with teammates and opponents. My first fight was against Ted Harris of the Montreal Canadiens. He wanted to see what I was made of—that happens to every rookie. If you answer the challenge, you will have the respect of both your teammates and your opponents.

It is a tough sport, a sport that requires physical play, and sometimes that can lead to frustration. Speaking as a former player, whenever those situations occur on the ice I would much rather face an opponent man to man in a fight than have to deal with sticks to the face as well as spearing to other areas of the body. Similarly, hitting from behind is a cowardly and careless act that has resulted in far more significant injuries than those resulting from fighting, at least in my estimation. If respect for the guy between you and the boards isn't enough to stop you from running him, maybe what will be is the fear of the retribution that is sure to follow.

A lot has been said in recent years about fighting and its place in hockey. True, the pro game can be cruel to those who choose fists over skills, and it is a tough way to make a living. But the more I look at the current state of the game, the more I realize a simple truth about it. The threat of a fight, or the fear of doing something that might trigger retaliation, is a powerful deterrent. It always has been, and it always will be.

Historically, skilled players were considered "out of bounds" when it came to fisticuffs, and that was respected around the league. Call it honor among thieves if you like, or the law of the jungle, but it worked. Often, in the current game, I see little pests with face shields or visors acting like tough guys and not having to account for their actions. Those pests take away from the honor of the game and actually help create more opportunities for injuries. Their job is to provoke retaliation, and they are almost never the guy paying the price.

I know that hockey fans are very interested in the arguments for and against fighting. On one side of the argument you have Don

Cherry, who is very much in support of the tough guys. Others call it barbaric and feel it should be banned. The various kinds of data and statistics brought forward either to support or condemn fighting are often viewed with skepticism regardless of which side of the argument you might be on.

But I would say this about the place of fighting in hockey. I believe that especially at the pro level you need to be held accountable for your actions, and the threat of a fight can accomplish that. The truth is, you couldn't pull the gloves off certain players if a fight was in their future, yet many of those same players in the modern game take liberties with others simply because they can. That is not right, and players should not be allowed to have it both ways. It leads me to the notion of what is commonly referred to as the "enforcer."

Take the great Jean Béliveau. Do you think he would have been as useful to the Canadiens if he'd spent more time in the penalty box because he'd had to defend himself through fighting? Obviously, the answer to that is a resounding no, and the Habs appear to have agreed. They hired John Ferguson to take care of that part of the game for him. "Fergie" was an enforcer, no matter how you want to define the term, yet he also had some twenty-goal seasons for Montreal, which goes to show that tough guys can have more than one dimension. But goal scoring wasn't his main purpose. John was there to make sure no one took liberties with any of the Habs' star players, foremost among them Mr. Béliveau. You could bump Jean and take him out during the course of normal play, but go over the line and sooner or later you had to deal with the "law." John Ferguson knew his job and was not an antagonist, but rather a type of insurance policy for his team.

Now, fast-forward to the modern game and ask the same kind of question. Would you rather see Sidney Crosby performing on the ice or sitting in a penalty box after a fight? Again, the answer is obvious, but today the rules have changed. He doesn't have a John Ferguson, and that means Crosby is vulnerable. The opposing teams take all kinds of liberties with him, and if no one is going to stop you, why not do whatever you can to slow down a player like that? The outcome of that vulnerability has become all too evident in the series of injuries Sidney has endured. I don't want to watch Sid fight his own battles. He's our best player, and I want to see him healthy and on the ice, not sitting in the box.

Of course, the star players today have a role to play as well. If someone like Sid is going to take a poke at the opposition with his stick, or trash talk while on the ice, then there will be some kind of retribution. You get what you go looking for in this game. But the main point is, if a player of Sidney Crosby's stature had an enforcer, a true enforcer, whose main job was to protect the star player, then perhaps some of the physical punishment he's gone through might never have taken place. Enforcers have a very practical role to play. If the league really wants to see its stars shine, one of the best ways is to give them more time and space to be creative. And that is the enforcer's job description.

Unfortunately, the game seems to be moving in the opposite direction by forcing the referees to call each game by the book. Not long ago, they had much more room for interpretation and could call the game as much by their sense of justice as by the black-and-white of the rule book. What might be deemed roughing in a clean game one night, might not be in a chippy contest the next. Refs could call the game according to what was fair. But in the search for standardization, that discretion has been taken away from the refs, and, along with it, a lot of their feel for the game.

Of course, officials shouldn't go looking for penalties to call.

Just observe, don't infer. There are too many cases where referees are reacting to a player falling to the ice or reaching for his face rather than to the high stick that may or may not have come up. Just because a guy goes down doesn't mean there was a penalty.

Being a referee is a very tough job, and I think they do good work in a very demanding environment. They have to make split-second judgment calls in front of thousands of very partisan fans—millions, if you include television. It's a fast game, and players are smart enough to know how to take advantage when the refs aren't looking. Refs are never going to catch everything. But if officials were allowed a bit more discretion on calls, as they once were, I believe a lot of the silliness that sometimes occurs on the ice could be taken out of the game. If an agitator goes after a skilled player, then, according to the code I played under, there was always someone waiting to even the score. In today's game, the lines are blurred, the agitator turtles when justice comes calling, and suddenly the victim's team is shorthanded and the agitator is on the bench laughing while his team goes on the power play. In other words, this arrangement rewards injustice. Not long ago, a ref might have looked the other way when the agitator got his due. That may have been a very inexact form of justice, but it did keep the game cleaner.

It works the other way, too. Sure, there are things the refs need to get rid of. But there are other things they should keep their hands off. Specifically, there has been a lot of attention paid lately to big open-ice hits that have left guys injured. No one wants to see anyone lying injured on the ice, whether he's a teammate or an opponent. But if it was a clean hit, it was a clean hit, and the officials need to let them play on. You can't penalize guys for unfortunate outcomes, and you certainly shouldn't suspend anyone on those grounds either. After all, he was playing by the rules. We need to allow our referees to use that common sense and judgment. They are not robots and will never be perfect, but I would prefer to give some rope to a well-trained official and let him use his discretion when situations require it.

TO CONCLUDE

I began this chapter by talking about how the game never really changes, and ended by talking about how I would change it. But I'm not advocating any radical overhaul or any bold experiments. Really, what I have in mind is what the game has always been. As a fan of the game, what I want to see on the ice is what I saw when I was on it myself.

I'd like to see a game where out referees are allowed discretion. I'd like to see a game where barriers exist to allow for greater skill development and to protect player safety. And I'd like to see a game where respect dictates that blindside hits and hitting from behind are not longer accepted.

That's the way hockey should be played. When guys are playing with passion, you see what the game is really about. Players don't get paid a salary in the playoffs—just a very small bonus for getting there. And look how much more intensely they compete. Players don't get paid to suit up for the Olympics or other international tournaments, yet that is often where they play their best hockey. They don't do what they do in order to get rich. They do it because they love it, and they do it *the way* they do it because that is just how the game is meant to be played.

The creativity, the competitiveness, the physical battles, maybe even the fighting—that's the game at its best. We just have to get out of the way. While the game does change in small, unimportant ways, I've come to realize that no owner, no hockey executive, and no player is bigger than the game itself. Eras come and go, yet the game always manages to move forward. That is a testament to the integrity of the game itself, and to the passion of the people who love it, whether they are on the ice or off it.

Let's keep it that way.

EPILOGUE

Where has the time gone? From Parry Sound, to Oshawa, to Boston, and beyond, it sure went by in a hurry. I think back to that time just a short while ago when that statue made its debut in front of the new TD Garden in Boston. That event is now in the rearview mirror as well, and the clock just keeps on ticking. You come to realize how very quickly the better part of a lifetime can be lived.

As I look back on the process of putting this book together, I'm struck by how many wonderful people I have had the good fortune to meet over the course of my life, both inside and outside of hockey. It's been a heck of a ride so far, and doing this project has allowed me to recall people and events from the past while reliving some very satisfying memories and friendships. However, sometimes in the rush of living we lose track of, or simply don't keep in touch with, people who have done so much for us and our families, and that is unfortunate. Of course, looking back on your life can also come with a cost. It makes us look at the tough patches, and that includes examining our faults. The memories might lead you to consider what you would change if you could do it over, and how those changes might have benefited those closest to you. Seriously, anyone who says they have no regrets either isn't looking at everything they've done or they are glossing over reality. In my own case I know I made my career a priority for several years. It's true I gained a measure of fame as a result of that dedication to my career, and I managed to fulfill a lot of my own goals. Yet the truth is, there is always a cost to that kind of pursuit.

Like many, I can't help but have some regrets about all the time away from loved ones that my career necessitated. When I watch my son Darren interact with his son and daughter, my two grandchildren, I must admit I feel a bit envious. I say that because Darren has had more time with his children than I did as a father when my boys were that age, and that is something I regret now.

As I think about that era in my life, I am struck yet again at how supportive Peggy was through all those years. She carried the mail for a long time, especially when it came to raising our children. In writing these thoughts, it strikes me that I'm using my career as an excuse for my shortcomings as a father, and frankly that's a bad crutch to lean on. It's your family, and you should be there for them. I suppose I just wish I had a few of those days back, that's all. Times have changed a great deal on the parenting front. Many modern families need two breadwinners to get by these days. Sometimes it's the dads who stay home, and today's fathers on average probably see more of their children than in generations past. I think that is a very good thing. The good news is that I get another chance to spend time with some little ones who are very special to me.

All this talk of parenting brings me back to my own parents, and specifically my father. I remember the last time I ever fished with him. It was on one of my favorite rivers, the Cascapedia in Quebec, and although it would end up being our last trip together, it was actually the first time my dad had ever tried fly-fishing. It was quite a day, watching him trying to throw that fly. It was a great day in my life, a memorable day. With age, you become far more aware that times such as those were never about money, or fame, or statues, or success. Those memories are the most important ones, because they speak about family, about love, and about sharing. And while those occasions are unique and special to everyone on a very personal level, they are probably similar in many ways for most of us as well. Their value runs deep. A fishing trip with a father, comfort from a mother, pride in children, these represent the fabric of a lifetime. We should celebrate those moments, enjoy our successes, and learn to forgive ourselves for our failures.

SOME AWARDS AND RECOGNITIONS: A PERSONAL PERSPECTIVE

When your career finally comes to an end, one thing always remains: career statistics. Those numbers can be rather cold things. They hardly tell the human side of the story. Your final numbers are what your final numbers are, and you can never get away from that. But there is a lot more that goes into any player's career besides just those numbers. The stats can't relate any of the ideas or emotions that went into the creation of those final numbers, and they can't expose the feelings an athlete had at particular moments. I am often asked questions about my career that the numbers simply cannot account for. I was fortunate to play on a team that ended up having some pretty good success in the NHL, and as a result of that team success I was honored with a few individual awards over time. While I have no interest in discussing those individual awards in any detail, there are some things that are special to me, and I'd like to share with you a few personal insights about them. Yes, the numbers are the numbers. But here are some comments as to what the numbers and the recognitions mean to me.

Winning the Stanley Cup

If you are a young boy growing up in Canada and play the game of hockey, you almost certainly have the dream of someday winning the Stanley Cup. I was no different. It's difficult to put on paper what it feels like at the moment you suddenly realize that you did just win it. I can tell you that it was a mixture of excitement and relief, and winning it the first time only made me want to repeat the experience again and again. Regardless of your profession, when you get to the top of your chosen field, however you measure that, it is a thrill you'll never forget. In the world of hockey, the top of the mountain was, and always will be, a Stanley Cup Championship.

Canada Cup Champion

The year 1976 will always be a memorable one for me, because it marked the first and only time I was able to wear the colors of my country. I must confess that by that time I was having a lot of problems with my knees, but it's amazing what you can do when the adrenaline kicks in. That excitement afforded me the opportunity to play, and although I was limited in what I could do, it was fun to contribute to that amazing group. It is an experience I will always cherish.

James Norris Trophy

I'm proud to have won that award. But the Norris Trophy I most remember was the one I didn't win. During my rookie season, I finished second in voting to the great Harry Howell. After he accepted the trophy that year, he said some very complimentary things about me and what the future would hold, and I remember thinking to myself, "Hey, that's Harry Howell saying those things about me!" Given who he was, those comments meant a lot. I was able to win the Norris because teammates and coaches let me be me, and by that I mean that through their support I was allowed to play my style.

All-Star Selections
When you step on the ice and you're surrounded by the likes of Gordie Howe, Jean Béliveau, Ken Dryden, Yvan Cournoyer, and so many others, it hits you how special the moment is. To be included with that cast of characters is something I never took for granted and always appreciated.

Member, Hockey Hall of Fame
In 1979, the NHL did something very kind. They waived the normal time requirement in order to induct me into the Hockey Hall of Fame when I was thirty-one. I was especially honored to have been introduced by Weston Adams's widow. Mr. Adams owned the Bruins when I was a rookie. She was the first woman ever to introduce a member into the Hall of Fame. I think that being a member of that very prestigious group has grown more meaningful to me over the years. As I've gotten older, I have started to appreciate it more, perhaps because its meaning changes. At the time, when the ceremony is held, it all goes by pretty quickly. Speeches are made, you receive your ring, and then it's over. But with time and distance comes a different feeling, and you realize just how special it all is. Every time I have occasion to be in that great building in Toronto, with all of the likenesses of the members

around me, I know again what an honor it is to be one of them. It is a recognition that means a lot to my entire family.

Order of Canada

That was totally unexpected. To think that someone like me from Parry Sound would grow up to have such an honor given to him during the course of his life. The motto for the Order of Canada is, "They desire a better country." You learn in sport that you can always get better, but I have to say that, as a nation, Canada is a pretty solid country. If my involvement in hockey has helped in some small way to make it better, then that makes me happy.

Lester B. Pearson Award
(now called the Ted Lindsay Award)

In winning this, you are being recognized by your peers, and that gives this award extra meaning. To have the respect of your colleagues is something any professional athlete tries to achieve, so winning the Pearson Award was pretty special.

Lester Patrick Trophy
(Service to Hockey in the United States)

The list of names on that trophy makes it a unique honor. The NHL has done a good job of growing the game in the United States, and quite a bit of that expansion took place during my time in the league. It has been wonderful to see how hockey has taken off in many places across the United States.

Bobby Orr Elementary School

This great school in Oshawa, Ontario, is filled with dedicated professional educators and a terrific bunch of kids. I have been able to visit a few times over the years, and of course the kids don't know me, but that's okay. It's wonderful to be associated with such a school by having my name on the outside. I am especially touched that we have a special-needs section of the facility that helps so many deserving children in so many unique ways.

Bobby Orr Hall of Fame

The creation of this hall of fame is an honor I would never have dreamed of when I was growing up in Parry Sound, in part because it keeps bringing me home. The Charles W. Stockey Centre, which comprises a performing arts center and our hall of fame, is a very functional facility and something I'm very proud to be a part of. Each year at the hall, we honor a select few deserving recipients. Honorees are men and women who have made outstanding contributions in the community and region, and the list to date is quite impressive. It is a pleasure to participate in recognizing so many people who have done so much for others.

"The Goal" Statue, Boston

It's nice to know that this moment in time has been captured in this way, and that the legacy of that team will live on through the statue. It's very humbling.

Number Retirement, Boston Bruins, and Oshawa Generals

It's a great feeling to know that those two organizations think highly enough of my contributions that they would retire my number. I'm sure a lot of people didn't realize that in Oshawa it was number 2, not 4. I went there as a boy in 1962, and I really grew up in that city. I still have many dear friends in the city and region. I am still connected with General Motors of Canada as well, so Oshawa has remained a big part of my life.

As for the Bruins, the day they hoisted my sweater to the rafters was pretty emotional. It happened to be an exhibition game against the Russians that night, and the ceremony took quite a long time, as the fans would not stop applauding until I put on my old Boston sweater. I'm sure the Russians were asking each other who this Number 4 guy was. But my best memories are of those Boston fans—the best fans in the game.

Olympic Flag-Bearer

That was quite a view walking into the Olympic stadium for the 2010 Winter Games carrying one corner of the Olympic flag. Getting to meet and chat with the other participants in that ceremony was something I'll not soon forget. The late Betty Fox, Donald Sutherland, Anne Murray, Jacques Villeneuve, the late Barbara Ann Scott, Senator Roméo Dallaire, and Julie Payette: my fellow flag-bearers all deserve to be mentioned. As I've often noted, I had the opportunity to wear the colors of my country as an athlete only once, in 1976, so carrying the Olympic flag was another chance to represent Canada, but in a different way. It will go down as one of the greatest experiences in my life. Mind you, I have taken some heat from family and friends for the white suit and shoes I was asked to wear that day!

CONTRACTS

Brunswick

MOTOR HOTEL

TELEPHONE 746-5834

PARRY SOUND, ONTARIO

Sept. 3/62
Parry Sound ont.

Mr. & Mrs. Douglas Orr,
21 Great North Rd.
Parry Sound ont.

Dear Mr. & Mrs Orr.

This letter will serve as agreement made between you (on behalf of your son Bobby) and The Boston Professional Hockey Association Inc. regarding Bobby signing a Jr "A" playing card with the Oshawa Jr "A" Hockey Club, sponsored by the Boston Bruins. Under terms of this agreement the Card to be signed on this date.

Terms

1 - That Bobby will play four (4) games only of Jr A hockey coming until Nov 4th of this coming 1962-63 hockey campaign. Upon completion of these four games the Boston Bruins agree to release him back to the Parry Sound Minor Hockey Ass for the balance of this season. Bobby will reside in Parry Sound and will commute week-ends for the aforementioned four games.

2 - That in consideration of signing the Junior A. Card on this date, the Boston Bruins will pay to Bobby Orr, one Thousand (1000.⁰⁰) dollars in trust.

3 - Further to the above the Boston Bruins will pay to have the Orr residence at 21 Great North Rd. stuccoed in full at a cost of approximately

BRUNSWICK HOTEL (PARRY SOUND) LTD.

(over)

This is my first contract, handwritten by Wren Blair on stationery from the Brunswick Hotel. Dated September 3, 1962, this document commits me to playing for the Oshawa Generals for at least four games in the upcoming season, in exchange for $1,000 and $12 per week. In addition, the Bruins were to pay to have our house stuccoed, "in full, at a cost of approximately $850," and my father was to receive a used car, "up to a 1956 model, of the father's choice."

II

850.⁰⁰

④ - After Bobby has been released back to Parry Sound, he will return to Oshawa next season to play Jr. A hockey, where the Boston Bruins will pay his school tuition completely through high school, pay his room and board through the full school terms, buy his school books throughout school, and pay him a weekly sum of money for pocket expenditures throughout the entire school terms. Weekly sum to be $12.⁰⁰ per week, for pocket expenditures

⑤ Signed card not to be registered until all requisites for Orr to return and play Junior Hockey in Parry Sound out.

⑥ The Boston Bruins agree to provide a car up to a 1956 model of the father's choice (Douglas Orr) to be purchased by Mr. Orr and paid for by the Boston Bruins as an integral part of this contract

Wren A Blair
per Boston Professional Hockey
Associating Inc.
Personnel Director

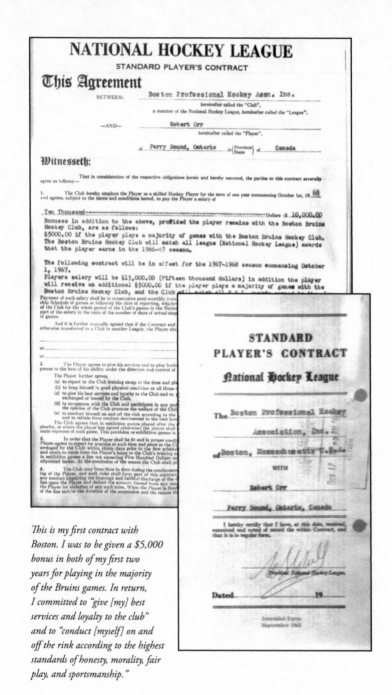

NATIONAL HOCKEY LEAGUE

STANDARD PLAYER'S CONTRACT

This Agreement

BETWEEN: **Boston Professional Hockey Assn. Inc.**

hereinafter called the "Club",

a member of the National Hockey League, hereinafter called the "League".

—AND— **Robert Orr**

hereinafter called the "Player".

of **Parry Sound, Ontario** in [Province/State] of **Canada**

Witnesseth:

That in consideration of the respective obligations herein and hereby assumed, the parties to this contract severally agree as follows:—

1. The Club hereby employs the Player as a skilled Hockey Player for the term of one year commencing October 1st, 19 **66** and agrees, subject to the terms and conditions hereof, to pay the Player a salary of

Ten Thousand————————————————————————————Dollars ($ **10,000.00**

Bonuses in addition to the above, provided the player remains with the Boston Bruins Hockey Club, are as follows:

$5000.00 if the player plays a majority of games with the Boston Bruins Hockey Club. The Boston Bruins Hockey Club will match all league (National Hockey League) awards that the player earns in the 1966-67 season.

The following contract will be in effect for the 1967-1968 season commencing October 1, 1967.

Players salary will be $15,000.00 (Fifteen thousand dollars) in addition the player will receive an additional $5000.00 if the player plays a majority of games with the Boston Bruins Hockey Club, and the Club will match all N.H.L. awards earned by the player.

Payment of such salary shall be in consecutive semi-monthly installments following the date of reporting, whichever is later, and to the Club for the whole period of the Club's games in the National League part of the salary in the ratio of the number of days of actual employment of games.

And it is further mutually agreed that if the Contract and otherwise transferred to a Club in another League, the Player sha

or

or

2. The Player agrees to give his services and to play hockey games to the best of his ability under the direction and control of

The Player further agrees,
(a) to report to the Club training camp at the time and pla
(b) to keep himself in good physical condition at all times d
(c) to give his best services and loyalty to the Club and to g exchanged or loaned by the Club,
(d) to co-operate with the Club and participate in any and the option of the Club promote the welfare of the Club
(e) to conduct himself on and off the rink according to the and to refrain from conduct detrimental to the best inte

The Club agrees that in exhibition games played after the charity, or where the player has agreed otherwise) the player shall mate expenses of such game. This provision on exhibition games is

3. In order that the Player shall be fit and in proper condit Player agrees to report for practice at such time and place as the C arranged by the Club within thirty days prior to the first sched and meals en route from the Player's home to the Club's training or in exhibition games a fine not exceeding Five Hundred Dollars m stipulated herein. At the conclusion of the season the Club shall p

4. The Club may from time to time during the continuance ing of the Player, and such rules shall form part of this contract any conduct impairing the thorough and faithful discharge of the fine upon the Player and deduct the amount thereof from any mo the Player for violation of any such rules. When the Player is fined of the fines and/or the duration of the suspension and the reason th

---

STANDARD PLAYER'S CONTRACT

National Hockey League

The **Boston Professional Hockey**

Association, Inc.

of **Boston, Massachusetts U.S.A.**

WITH

Robert Orr

Parry Sound, Ontario, Canada

I hereby certify that I have, at this date, received, examined and noted of record the within Contract, and that it is in regular form.

President National Hockey League.

Dated _____ 19___

Amended Form
September 1965

This is my first contract with Boston. I was to be given a $5,000 bonus in both of my first two years for playing in the majority of the Bruins games. In return, I committed to "give [my] best services and loyalty to the club" and to "conduct [myself] on and off the rink according to the highest standards of honesty, morality, fair play, and sportsmanship."

5.   Should the Player be disabled or unable to perform his duties under this contract as shall submit himself for medical examination and treatment by a physician selected by the Club, and such examination and treatment, when made at the request of the Club, shall be at its expense unless made necessary by some act or conduct of the Player contrary to the terms and provisions of this contract or the rules established under Section 4.

If the Player, in the sole judgment of the Club's physician, is disabled or is not in good physical condition at the commencement of the season or at any subsequent time during the season (unless such condition is the direct result of playing hockey for the Club so as to render him unfit to play skilled hockey, then it is mutually agreed that the Club shall have the right to suspend the Player for such period of disability or unfitness, and no compensation shall be payable for that period under this contract.

If the Player is injured as the result of playing hockey for the Club, the Club will pay the Player's reasonable hospitalization until discharged from the hospital, and his medical expenses and doctor's bills, provided that the hospital and doctor are selected by the Club and provided further that the Club's obligation to pay such expenses shall terminate at a period not more than six months after the injury.

It is also agreed that if the Player's injuries resulting directly from playing for the Club render him, in the sole judgment of the Club's physician, unfit to play skilled hockey for the balance of the season or any part thereof, then during such time the Player is so unfit, but in no event beyond the end of the current season, the Club shall pay the Player reasonable bonus provided for and the Player releases the Club from any and every additional obligation, liability, claim or demand whatsoever. However if upon joint consultation between the Player, the Club's physician and the Club General Manager, they are unable to agree as to the physical fitness of the Player to return to play, the Player agrees to submit himself for examination by an independent medical specialist and the Parties hereto agree to be bound by his decision. If the Player is declared to be unfit for play he shall continue to receive the full benefits of this Agreement. If the Player is declared to be physically able to play and refuses to do so he shall be liable to immediate suspension without pay

6.   The Player represents and agrees that he has exceptional and unique knowledge, skill and ability as a hockey player, the loss of which cannot be estimated with certainty and cannot be fairly or adequately compensated by damages. The Player therefore agrees that the Club shall have the right, in addition to any other rights which the Club may possess, to enjoin him by appropriate injunction proceedings from playing hockey for any other team and/or for any breach of any of the other provisions of this contract.

In Witness Whereof, the parties have signed this _____ day

of _____ A.D. 19 66

WITNESSES:

Boston Professional Hockey Asn . Inc.

By _____

Parry Sound, Ontario, Canada

Home Address of Player

It is further mutually agreed that in the event that this contract is assigned, or the Player's services are loaned, to another Club, the Club shall, by notice in writing delivered personally to the Player or by mail to the address set out below his signature hereto advise the Player of the name and address of the Club to which he has been assigned or loaned, and specifying the time and place of reporting to such club. If the Player fails to report to such other Club he may be suspended by such other Club and no salary shall be payable to him during the period of such suspension.

The Club shall pay the actual moving expenses incurred by a player during the playing season when such move is directed by the Club and is not part of disciplinary action.

12.   If the Club shall default in the payments to the Player provided for in Section 1 hereof or shall fail to perform any other obligation agreed to be performed by the Club hereunder, the Player may, by notice in writing to the Club, specify the nature of the default, and if the Club shall fail to remedy the default within fifteen (15) days from receipt of such notice, this contract shall be terminated, and upon the date of such termination all obligations of both parties shall cease, except the obligation of the Club to pay the Player's compensation to that date.

13.   The Club may terminate this contract upon written notice to the Player (but only after obtaining waivers from all other League clubs) if the player shall at any time:

(a) fail, refuse or neglect to obey the Club's rules governing training and conduct of players,

(b) fail, refuse or neglect to render his services hereunder or in any other manner materially breach this contract,

(c) fail, in the opinion of the Club's management, to exhibit sufficient skill or competitive ability to warrant further employment as a member of the Club's team.

In the event of termination under sub-section (a) or (b) the Player shall only be entitled to compensation due to him to the date such notice is delivered to him or the date of the mailing of such notice to his address as set out below his signature hereto.

In the event of termination under sub-section (c) it shall take effect fourteen days from the date upon which such notice is delivered to the Player, and the Player shall only be entitled to the compensation herein provided to the end of such fourteen-day period.

In the event that this contract is terminated by the Club while the Player is "away" with the Club for the purpose of playing games the instalment then falling due shall be paid on the first week-day after the return "home" of the Club.

14.   The Player further agrees that the Club may carry out and put into effect any order or ruling of the League or its President for his suspension or expulsion and that in the event of suspension his salary shall cease for the duration thereof and that in the event of expulsion this contract, at the option of the Club, shall terminate forthwith.

15.   The Player further agrees that in the event of his suspension pursuant to any of the provisions of this contract, there shall be deducted from the salary stipulated in Section 1 hereof an amount equal to the exact proportion of such salary as the number of days' suspension bears to the total number of days of the League Championship Schedule of games.

16.   If because of any condition arising from a state of war or other cause beyond the control of the League or of the Club, it shall be deemed advisable by the League or the Club to suspend or cease or reduce operations, then:

(a) in the event of suspension of operations, the Player shall be entitled only to the proportion of salary due at the date of suspension,

(b) in the event of cessation of operations, the salary stipulated in Section 1 hereof shall be automatically cancelled on the date of cessation, and

(c) in the event of reduction of operations, the salary stipulated in Section 1 hereof shall be replaced by that mutually agreed upon between the Club and the Player.

17.   The Club agrees that it will on or before October 15th next following the season covered by this contract tender to the Player personally or by mail directed to the Player at his address set out below his signature hereto a contract upon the same terms as this contract save as to salary.

The Player hereby undertakes that he will at the request of the Club enter into a contract for the following playing season upon the same terms and conditions as this contract save as to salary which shall be determined by mutual agreement. In the event that the Player and the Club do not agree upon the salary to be paid the matter shall be referred to the President of the League, and both parties agree to accept his decision as final.

18.   The Club and the Player severally and mutually promise and agree to be legally bound by the Constitution and By-Laws of the League and by all the terms and provisions thereof, a copy of which is open and available for inspection by Club, its directors and officers, and the Player, at the main office of the League and at the main office of the Club.

The Club and the Player further agree that in case of dispute between them, the dispute shall be referred within one year from the date it arose to the President of the League as an arbitrator and his decision shall be accepted as final by both parties.

The Club and the Player further agree that all fines imposed upon the Player under the Playing Rules, or under the provisions of the League By-Laws, shall be deducted from the salary of the Player and be remitted by the Club to the N.H.L. Players' Emergency Fund.

19.   The Player agrees that the Club's right to reserve this contract as provided in Section 17 and the promise of the Player to play hockey only with the Club, or such other club as provided in Section 2 and Section 11, and the Club's right to take pictures of and to televise the Player as provided in Section 8 have all been taken into consideration in determining the salary payable to the Player under Section 1 hereof.

20.   The Player authorizes and directs the Club to deduct and pay, and the Club hereby agrees to deduct and pay, to the National Hockey League Pension Society, out of the salary stipulated in Section 1 hereof on behalf of the Player the sum of Fifteen Hundred Dollars ($1500.00) (Canadian Funds) or such lesser proportion thereof as the number of days' service of the Player with the Club under this contract bears to the number of days of the League Championship Schedule of games, and to obtain from the National Hockey League Pension Society a proper receipt for such sum in the name of the Player.

21.   It is severally and mutually agree that the only contracts recognized by the President of the League are the Standard Player's Contracts which have been duly executed and filed in the League's office and approved by him, and that this Agreement contains the entire agreement of the Parties and there are no oral or written inducements, promises or agreements except as contained herein.

In Witness Whereof, the parties have signed this _____ day

of _____ A.D. 19 66

WITNESSES:

Boston Professional Hockey Asn . Inc.
Club

By _____
Director

_____
Player

Parry Sound, Ontario, Canada

Home Address of Player

CAREER STATISTICS AND RECORDS

SEASON	TEAM	LEAGUE
1962–63	Oshawa Generals	Metro Jr. A
1963–64	Oshawa Generals	OHA
1964–65	Oshawa Generals	OHA
1965–66	Oshawa Generals	OHA
1966–67	Boston Bruins	NHL
1967–68	Boston Bruins	NHL
1968–69	Boston Bruins	NHL
1969–70	Boston Bruins	NHL
1970–71	Boston Bruins	NHL
1971–72	Boston Bruins	NHL
1972–73	Boston Bruins	NHL
1973–74	Boston Bruins	NHL
1974–75	Boston Bruins	NHL
1975–76	Boston Bruins	NHL
1976–77	Chicago Black Hawks	NHL
1978–79	Chicago Black Hawks	NHL
OHA totals		
NHL totals		

Regular season									Playoffs				
GP	G	A	PTS	PIM	+/-	PP	SH	GW	GP	G	A	PTS	PIM
34	6	15	21	45	—	—	—	—	—	—	—	—	—
56	29	43	72	142	—	—	—	—	6	0	7	7	21
56	34	59	93	112	—	—	—	—	6	0	6	6	10
47	38	56	94	92	—	—	—	—	17	9	19	28	14
61	13	28	41	102	—	3	1	0	—	—	—	—	—
46	11	20	31	63	+30	3	0	1	4	0	2	2	2
67	21	43	64	**133**	+65	4	0	2	10	1	7	8	10
76	33	87	120	125	+54	11	**4**	3	14	**9**	11	20	14
78	37	**102**	**139**	91	**+124**	5	3	**5**	7	5	7	12	10
76	37	80	117	106	+86	11	**4**	4	15	5	**19**	**24**	19
63	29	72	101	99	+56	7	1	3	5	1	1	2	7
74	32	90	122	82	+84	11	0	4	**16**	4	14	18	**28**
80	**46**	89	135	101	+80	**16**	2	4	3	1	5	6	2
10	5	13	18	22	+10	3	1	0	—	—	—	—	—
20	4	19	23	25	+6	2	0	0	—	—	—	—	—
6	2	2	4	4	+2	0	0	0	—	—	—	—	—
193	**107**	**173**	**280**	**391**					**29**	**9**	**32**	**41**	**45**
657	**270**	**645**	**915**	**953**	**+597**	**76**	**16**	**26**	**74**	**26**	**66**	**92**	**92**

Records

- Most points in one NHL season by a defenseman (139; 1970–71)
- Most assists in one NHL season by a defenseman (102; 1970–71)
- Highest plus/minus in one NHL season (+124; 1970–71)
- Tied for most assists in one NHL game by a defenseman (6; tied with Babe Pratt, Pat Stapleton, Ron Stackhouse, Paul Coffey, and Gary Suter)

Awards

- OHA First All-Star Team in 1964, 1965, and 1966
- Awarded the Calder Memorial Trophy (rookie of the year) in 1967, the youngest ever to win the award, and the youngest ever to win a major NHL award up to that time
- Named to the NHL Second All-Star Team in 1966–67 (as a rookie; his only full season when he did not make the First Team)
- Named to the NHL First All-Star Team eight times consecutively (from 1968 to 1975)
- Awarded the James Norris Trophy (for best defenseman) eight times (from 1968 to 1975, his last full season)
- Played in the NHL All-Star Game eight times (from 1968 to 1975)
- Won the Art Ross Trophy (awarded to league's top scorer) in 1969–70 and 1974–75
- NHL Plus/Minus leader in 1969, 1970, 1971, 1972, 1974, and 1975, the most in history

- Awarded the Hart Memorial Trophy (awarded for league's most valuable player) three times consecutively (from 1970 to 1972)
- Awarded the Conn Smythe Trophy (awarded to playoff MVP) in 1970 and 1972, the first two-time winner of the playoff MVP award
- Stanley Cup winner in 1970 and 1972
- Won Lou Marsh Trophy (Canadian athlete of the year) in 1970
- NHL All-Star Game MVP in 1972
- Received *Sports Illustrated* magazine's Sportsman of the Year award in 1970
- Voted the greatest athlete in Boston history in the *Boston Globe* newspaper's poll of New Englanders in 1975, beating out baseball and basketball stars such as Ted Williams, Bill Russell, Carl Yastrzemski, and Bob Cousy
- Awarded the Lester B. Pearson Award (league MVP as voted by players) in 1975
- Named the Canada Cup Tournament MVP in 1976
- Awarded the Lester Patrick Trophy (league MVP as voted by players) in 1979
- Inducted into the Hockey Hall of Fame in 1979, with the mandatory three-year waiting period waived, making him the youngest inductee at thirty-one years old
- Voted the second greatest hockey player of all time by an expert committee in 1997 by the *Hockey News*, behind only Wayne Gretzky and ahead of Gordie Howe, as well as being named the top defenseman of all time.

CAREER STATISTICS AND RECORDS

- Ranked 31 in ESPN's *SportsCentury: 50 Greatest Athletes of the 20th Century* in 1999
- Named the top defenseman of all time in 2010 by the *Hockey News*

AFTERWORD

If you are supposed to meet Bobby Orr at 6:30 A.M., make sure you're there for 6:15. You have to adjust your clock to "Orr time" if you don't want to be late. He's a morning person.

In spring 2010, I was waiting for Bobby on the practice green of a golf course in Florida. We were to tee off at 7 A.M., which meant that, according to Orr time, I should get there fifteen minutes early, half an hour if I wanted to get a coffee and take a few practice putts before we headed out at 6:45.

Right on time he rolled up at the end of the practice green, signaling from the golf cart that he was ready to play. We hit off the first tee and away we went, my head snapping back and forth every time the vehicle accelerated. That's just the way Bobby Orr drives a golf cart.

Things were going along swimmingly as we finished up at the

seventh green. If memory serves me correctly, I had just birdied the hole to Bob's par, which meant that I was now three up in our match. (Yes, that's my story and I'm sticking to it.) Anyway, I sat down in the passenger side of the cart and waited for Bobby to stomp on the gas pedal again.

I braced for the whiplash but nothing happened. "This is kind of weird," I thought. "We are out of rhythm here." When I glanced over to my left, Number 4 was leaning on the steering wheel looking at me. He was giving me an odd kind of contemplative stare. Then he smiled and said, "Okay ... let's do the book."

Over the next eleven holes that day, we mapped out in general terms what the objectives for the book would be as well as some of the potential chapter topics. I was using one of the pencils you get from the clubhouse to mark your score card and scribbling notes and reminders to myself on any scrap of paper I could find. If Bobby Orr wants to write a book, you don't want to miss a word. The first words of this book were recorded on a napkin in the Florida sunshine.

It was a special day for me because we had talked about this project many years before. Bobby and I have worked together on other projects, and I've worked on other books, so it seemed like a natural fit. But when I first broached the topic, his response was terse. "I'm not ever doing a book" was his first reaction, followed by "Who would want to read that book anyway?"

That's Bobby Orr right there. This is a guy who redefined the game of hockey. A player who did things on the ice that still give people chills thirty-five years later. A man whose life off the ice has become the stuff of legend. And he actually wonders whether his story is worth reading. It's not false modesty. He knows very well who he is and what he has done. He just doesn't assume that anything he has done automatically makes him deserving of anyone else's praise.

More than anything, perhaps, *that* is what is most impressive about Bobby Orr. He's a small-town guy who not only made it big but also became arguably the best to ever play the game—and it didn't change him one bit. He really doesn't think he is better than anyone else. I hope that is the way he comes across in these pages.

If there is one thing Bobby Orr doesn't want to talk about, it's himself. So writing a book was never going to be easy. Finding the right words for something he would have been happy to leave unsaid is a challenge we struggled with for a long time, and there is a whole category of stories that didn't make it into the book: anything that might seem like bragging. Goals he scored, fights he won, records he set, awards he took home. He is just not interested in seeing any of that in print.

That is another way he is unique—I know that whole generations of hockey fans *are* interested. I am glad Bobby asked me to help him get his words on paper because that gave me the opportunity to get him to talk about himself in a way he otherwise wouldn't. The words and thoughts in this book are all Bobby's, from start to finish, but I'd like to think that some of them would never have been written if he hadn't been pushed. Not that it was easy. If I tried to get one of his accomplishments into the book, he shut me down. If I suggested a phrase that didn't sound like him, he would shake his head and say, "Too much honey." No one is going to get Bobby Orr to do something he doesn't want to do, and no one is going to put words in his mouth. Luckily that was never my job. My job was to help put forward the real voice of Bobby Orr, because that is the way he wanted it to read.

Having been around Bobby over the years, I have a pretty good sense of how he speaks and how he delivers a thought. When he begins a sentence, I can usually tell you how he will finish it. I suppose that means that I have come to know the real Bobby Orr pretty well, and that is the person who needed to speak authentically in these pages.

Bobby Orr is held to a certain kind of mythical status by the general public, and often people who breathe that rarefied air aren't who they appear to be. But that's not the case here. Am I suggesting that he never has a bad day? No, you bet he does. Truth be told, there are some days when it is best that people just keep their distance. Will he occasionally get irritated when the 415th person in an autograph line that has gone on for three hours brings in several items to sign when a limit of one had been set? I've seen him cast the odd nasty glare on such occasions. But I can tell you that he has never forgotten where he comes from. Knowing the man, having helped with the research, and having spent some time helping put this book together, I've come to appreciate him even more for who he was, who he is, and what he stands for. Nothing is free in this world, and people such as Bobby Orr inevitably pay a price for their fame. In his case, I believe that he has handled his celebrity with a kind of dignity and grace far beyond what most of us should expect.

His parents did a great job. He's the real deal.

Vern Stenlund

ACKNOWLEDGMENTS

I wish to acknowledge several people for helping me achieve my objectives for this project. Without the integrity and hard work of Nick Garrison and his crew at Penguin Books in Canada, we never could have made it to the finish line. His tremendous support in making this book a reality cannot be underestimated. So thank you, Nick, and all the gang in Toronto. In addition, the people from Penguin in New York, headed by Neil Nyren, also stepped up and provided invaluable assistance as well with the U.S. launch. Many thanks.

Thank you to all those friends and family who helped in jogging my memory about details from the past while allowing me to confirm my own remembrances of specific events. You are too numerous to mention, but you know who you are and I am so very grateful to you for your help. Thank you.

ACKNOWLEDGMENTS

Finally, my special thanks go to my friend Vern Stenlund for helping me get all this down on paper. We've worked on a few projects over the years, but this one required special patience.

SOURCES

Some information contained throughout Chapters 1 and 2 was verified through the self-published book *Early Hockey Years in Parry Sound: The Orr/ Crisp Years*, Part 2, 1942–1973, by Rick Thomas.

Some information contained in Chapter 3 with respect to the Oshawa years was verified through the book *The Bird: The Life and Times of Hockey Legend Wren Blair*, by Wren Blair, with Ron Brown and Jill Blair, published by Quarry Heritage Books, Kingston, Ontario, 2003.

Some information contained in Chapter 9 with respect to Alan Eagleson was verified through the book *Game Misconduct: Alan Eagleson and the Corruption of Hockey*, revised edition, by Russ Conway, published by Macfarlane Walter & Ross, Toronto, 1997.

Some information contained in Chapter 11 under the heading "So You Want to Be a Professional Hockey Player …" is a modified version of information previously provided by Dale Dunbar for clients of Orr Hockey Group.

Some information in the appendix, "Career Statistics and Records," is reprinted from bobbyorr.com.

PHOTO CREDITS

INDEX

INDEX

INDEX